MUSLIM NAVAL ORGANISATION
IN THE EASTERN MEDITERRANEAN
From the Seventh to the Tenth Century A.D.

BY

ALY MOHAMED FAHMY

Doctor of Philosophy in History
University of London.
Associate, London Institute of Education.

National Publication & Printing House
Cairo, U.A.R.

MUSLIM NAVAL ORGANISATION
IN THE EASTERN MEDITERRANEAN
From the Seventh to the Tenth Century A.D.

By

ALY MOHAMED FAHMY

Doctor of Philosophy in History, University of London.
Associate, London Institute of Education.

« *Allah is He who made subservient to you the sea that the ships may run therein by his command, and that you may seek of His grace and that you may give thanks* ».
Qur'ân.

SECOND EDITION
1966

National Publication & Printing House
Cairo, U.A.R.

PREFACE

This book comprises studies in Muslim naval organisation in the Eastern Mediterranean from the 1st/7th to the 4th/10th century. No such work has as yet been written, either in Arabic or any other language, as far as I have been able to discover. In 1880 Wüstenfeld affirms in his report to the University of Göttingen that no coherent study of Muslim maritime activities has been made. In 1946 Gateau stresses this fact in the «Revue Africaine», pointing out that the lack of documents seems to tempt no one to this field of research. It is indeed remarkable that no serious and detailed study of the subject exists; this is due, in great measure, to the fact that the material for this particular aspect of Muslim domination is so widely scattered.

The subject, therefore, has been wrapped in profound obscurity and it is no exaggeration to say that the investigator risks losing his way in a gloomy labyrinth. Much interesting material lies buried in the Arabic texts of Muslim historians, geographers and travellers of the Middle Ages. Amongst the most valuable documents are the papyri which have made a great contribution to the knowledge of naval matters and have shed much light on the history of Egypt under Arab rule. These new documents and the evaluation of old ones have made a critical study possible.

I acknowledge with gratitude the great help I have received from Dr. Bernard Lewis, of the School of Oriental Studies, who gave me every encouragement during the preparation of this book. The kindly advice and assistance of Professor R.J.H. Jenkins, of King's College, were of inestimable value. I am indebted to Mr. T. Hill and Miss L.G. Thomas for translations from German works and to Mr. R.H. Dolley for translations from Greek texts. The Librarians of the

School of Oriental Studies, London, and of the British Museum greatly facilitated my studies by their unfailing courtesy and assistance. The treasures in their charge were essential to the writing of this book. It is impossible to name all, including scholars of many lands, who have readily answered my enquiries relative to subjects within their particular spheres. Finally, I owe much to my friend, miss Margaretta Kirby, for her careful reading of the manuscript.

A. M. Fahmy

London, November, 1948.

REVIEW OF THE BOOK

I

To many readers this book will reveal a new world :
«Together let us beat this ample field ;
Try what the open, what the covert yield.»

And what a treasury of information is contained in the covers of Dr. Aly Mohamed Fahmy's book !

....

Altogether Dr. Fahmy is to be heartily congratulated on filling such a void in nautical knowledge by writing his book, and on the industry in consulting over 300 authorities in the process.

Francis Cadogan

J.R.A.S., 1952, 80-81.

II

Dr. Fahmy has done a most useful of pioneer research on a subject about which very little is known. When a comprehensive study of Byzantino-Saracen naval history comes to be written, this book will be an indispensable source.

R.J.H. Jenkins.

B.S.O.A.S., XIV, I, 181.

CONTENTS

	Page
Preface	III
Review of the Book	V
Chronological Dates of Caliphs and Emperors	XI
Introduction	1

Survey of Sources. Papyri — Graeco-Roman Papyri — Arabic and Aphrodito Papyri — Value of Papyri. Historical — Geographical and Other Sources.

CHAPTER I.

Arsenals and Naval Centres in Egypt.

Arsenals at Clysma — Alexandria — Rosetta — Damietta — Tinnîs. First Muslim Arsenal at Babylon — Its Site and History under Tûlûnids and Ikhshîdids 23

CHAPTER II.

Arsenals and Naval Centres in Syria, Africa and Crete.

Arsenals and Naval Centres in Syria — First Muslim Arsenal at 'Akkâ — Transfer of Arsenal to Sûr — Reestablishment of Shipbuilding Yards at 'Akkâ and Ibn Tûlûn's Fortifications — Naval Centre at

	Page
Tarsus	51
Naval Centres in Africa — Barqa — First Muslim Arsenal in North Africa at Tûnis — Its Site	64
Naval Centre in Crete — Comparison with Cyprus	72

CHAPTER III.

Materials for Shipbuilding.

Timber — Different Kinds — Availability of Suitable Timber in Egypt and Syria	75
Metals — Iron Industry — Copper Chains	80
Cables — Anchors — Cushions — Pads — Sails	84

CHAPTER IV.

Naval Organisation.

Disposition of Fleets — Institution of « *Cursus* » — Raiding Fleets of Egypt, « *Oriens* » and Africa	87
Maintenance of Fleet — Naval Expenditure — Taxes for Fleet — Liturgy — Muslim Civil Service — Maritime Service — Recruitment of Sailors — Adaeratio — Security for Fulfilment of Service — Workmen — Supplies and Provisions — Wages and cost of Supplies	95
Fugitives and Passports	112

CHAPTER V.

Muslim Mediterranean Warships.

Characteristics of Mediterranean Warships	115

	Page
Types of Muslim Warships — *Ustûl* — *Qit'a* — *Harbî* — *Shalandî* — *Shînî* — *Ghurâb* — *Harrâqa* — *Tarrâda*	125
Staff of Mediterranean Warships — Responsibilities of Commander of Fleet	138

APPENDIX I.

Forests in Egypt 143

APPENDIX II.

Names of Ships of Tûlûnid Fleet 149

APPENDIX III.

Names of Ships mentioned by Muqaddasî 155

Bibliography 167

Abbreviations 197

Index 199

Maps and Illustrations

	Page
Early Egyptian Naval Centres as shown on the Maps of Jayhânî, Balkhî and Muqaddasî	33
Early Syrian Naval Centres as shown on the Maps of Jayhânî, Balkhî and Muqaddasî	57
Early African Naval Centres as shown on the Maps of Jayhânî, Balkhî and Istakhrî	67
Mediterranean Naval Centres as shown on the Map of Istakhrî	89
Early Mediterranean Naval Centres of Eastern Muslims	89
Mediterranean Naval Centres as shown on the Maps of Jayhânî, Balkhî and Muqaddasî	93
Greek War Galley — 4th. Century B.C.	117
Roman Merchant Ship — 2nd. Century A.D.	117
Fragment of Faience with Painted Underglaze Decoration showing a Boat with a Chequered Sail	121
Faience Dish with Metallic Reflections showing a Galley with Rigging, Oars and Oriflammes — 3rd./9th. Century.	121

Chronological Dates of Caliphs and Emperors

CALIPHS
ORTHODOX CALIPHS.

Abû Bakr	11/632
'Umar	13/634
'Uthmân	23/644
'Alî	35/656
	-40/-661

UMAYYAD CALIPHS.

Mu'âwiya I	41/661
Yazîd I	60/680
Mu'âwiya II	64/683
Marwân I	64/683
'Abd Al-Malik	65/685
Walîd I	86/705
Sulaymân	96/715
'Umar	99/717
Yazîd II	101/720
Hishâm	105/724
Walîd II	125/843
Yazîd III	126/744
Ibrâhîm	126/744
Marwân II	127/744
	-132/750

'ABBASID CALIPHS.

Saffâh	132/750
Mansûr	136/754
Mahdî	158/775
Hâdî	169/785
Rashîd	170/786

EMPERORS
HERACLIAN DYNASTY. 610/711

Heraclius	610-641
Constantine II	641
Heraclonas (Heracleon)	641
Constantine III (Constans II)	641-668
Constantine IV	668-685
Justinian II. (Rhinotmetus)	685-695
Leontius	695-698
Tiberius III. (Apsimares)	698-705
Justinian II. (Second Time)	705-711
Phillipicus (Bardanes)	711-713
Anastasius II. (Artemius)	713-715
Theodosius III	715-717

ISAURIAN DYNASTY.

Leo III	717-741
Constantine V. (Copronymus)	641-775
Leo IV. (The Khazar)	775-780
Constantine VI	780-797
Irene	797-802
Nicephorus I	802-811
Stauracius	811

XI

Amîn	193/809	Michael I. (Rangabe)	811-813
Ma'mûn	198/813	Leo V. (The Armenian)	813-820
Mu'tasim	218/833	**AMORIAN DYNASTY.**	820-867
Wâthiq	227/842	Michael II. (The Stammerer)	820-829
Mutawakkil	232/847		
Muntasir	247/861	Theophilus	829-842
Musta'în	248/862		
Mu'tazz	251/866	Michael III. (The Drunkard)	842-867
Muhtadî	255/869	**MACEDONIAN DYNASTY.**	
Mu'tamid	256/870		867-1056
Mu'tadid	279/892	Basil I	867-886
Muktafî	289/902	Leo VI. (The Philosopher)	886-912
Muqtadir	295/908	Alexander	912-913
Qâhir	320/932	Constantine VII (Porphyrogenitos)	913-959
Râdî	322/934	Romanus I. Lecapenus. (co-Emperor)	919-944
Muttaqî	329/940	Stephen & Constantine	
Mustakfî	333/944	(Sons of Romanus Lecapenus)	
Mutî'	334/946	Dec. 944 - Jan. 945.	
Tâ'i'	363/974	Romanus II	959-963
	-381/-991	Nicephorus II. (Phocas)	963-969

EGYPT AND SYRIA.

Tûlûnids.

Ahmad Ibn Tûlûn	254/868
Khumârawayh Ibn Ahmad	270/883
Abû'l-'Asâkir Jaysh Ibn Khmârawayh	282/895
Hârûn Ibn Khumârawayh	283/896
Shaybân Ibn Ahmad	292/904
	-292/-905

Ikhshîdids.

Muhammad Ibn Tughj Al-Ikhshîd	323/935
Abû'l-Qâsim Unûjûr Ibn Al-Ikhshîd	334/946
Abû'l-Hasan 'Alî Ibn Al-Ikhshîd	349/960
Abû'l-Misk Kâfûr	355/966
Abû'l-Fawâris Ahmad Ibn 'Alî	357/968
	-358/-969

N.B.

The chronology for the Caliphs is based on Lane-Poole, Mohammadan Dynasties, 9, 12, 68, 69; and that for the Emperors on Vasiliev, Byzantine Empire, II, 450 sq.

DATING.

A.H. and A.D. indicate years of the Muslim and Christian era respectively. Within the text proper double datings are expressed by the use of/between the year numbers. e.g., 868/1463 means A.H. 868 and A.D. 1463. In the identification of Hijra with Christian dates I have followed Haig, Comparative Tables.

TRANSLITERATION.

The fatha is always represented by a, the kasra by i, and the damma by u. Long vowels are indicated as follows: â, î, û. I have followed the written rather than the spoken usage. Thus I have written 'Abd Al-Rahmân, though the correct pronunciation is 'Abd Ar-Rahmân.

INTRODUCTION

SURVEY OF SOURCES.

An examination of the primary sources available is undoubtedly a fitting approach to this study. The fact that many have already been studied does not necessarily mean that they have been valued aright. A further investigation, aided by new data recently brought to light, some of which are here used for the first time, may result in a profitable reconsideration of their worth.

I. Papyri.

The first and most important source is the papyri. The technical term papyrology, signifying the science or study of these documents in all languages, is generally accepted in its narrower sense, namely the Greek papyri from the Graeco-Roman period of Egyptian history.

From the time of Alexander's conquest of Egypt in 332 B.C. till the Arab invasion in the middle of the seventh century A.D. the official language of the country was Greek. It was still the vehicle for government communications for nearly a century after the Arab conquest but its survival was threatened on the one hand by Coptic and on the other by Arabic, which gradually replaced it so that it eventually died out. It can be said that the use of Arabic started, if not with, then soon after, the conquest, that is about half a century before the general official change. In spite of this the papyrologist is primarily concerned with the decipherment of Greek rather than of Coptic or Arabic papyri, although he would not neglect evidence from contemporary documents in Coptic or Arabic which supply important data in some cases.

The banks of the Nile have usually been regarded as the habitat of the papyrus and consequently the centre of the manufacture of writing material from it, both in ancient and medieval times. Subsequent to the Islamic conquest of Egypt it was cultivated and manufactured until the widespread use of paper caused the industry to decline. With the conquest of Egypt papyrus became available in larger quantities, and the Caliphs used it as the medium for all official communications, the material being called by the Arabic name *qirtâs*. The Egyptian and Syrian Dîwâns followed the same practice, depending almost entirely upon it.(1) By the middle of the 2nd/8th century some countries could secure supplies of paper.(2) There was a period of transition until the close of the 4th/10th century when papyrus was used as well as paper. By this time, however, both quality and quantity were on a downward grade(3) except in Egypt which was the source of supplies as long as there was any demand for it.(4) Eventually the advantages of paper over papyrus were universally recognised and during the 4th/10th century the Egyptian manufacture of papyrus for writing material probably ceased, though papyrus was still used at irregular intervals.(5) Dated papyrus disappear entirely by 370/981,(6) whereas dated paper documents start in 300/912.

---

(1) Balâdhurî, Futûh, 465.

(2) Tha'âlibî, 97 (12); Margoliouth, Arabic Papyri, XI; Mez, 468, n. 9; Thompson, E.B., XVII, 229, 248.

(3) Grohmann, C.P.R., Bd. I, Teil I, 29-32; Karabacek, 14.

(4) v. Suyûtî, Husn, II, 238 (II).

(5) Maqrîzî, Khitat, I, 91; Karabacek, 10-15; Carter, 98.

(6) Margoliouth, ibid, No, 63, 181. Cf. Mez, 468.

A. — Graeco-Roman Rapyri.

It was not until the close of the ninteenth century that Egypt presented a unique hunting ground for the papyrologist and the « *age of papyrus* » really began with several Fayyûm discoveries. Under the supervision of Drs. Hogarth, Grenfell and Hunt, the work was carried out in the north of Fayyûm. The results inspired fresh undertakings which brought forth important finds at Bahnasâ (the ancient Oxyrhynchus).(1) No such valuable site has been found since.

The value of papyri having been generally recognised, they have been used as a basis for a study in the history of Graeco-Roman Egypt. In order to arrive at an adequate understanding of the naval organisation of the early Caliphate and the immense activity of the civil service, including the method adopted for the recruitment of sailors and workmen for naval undertakings, it is necessary to search far back in the Byzantine period, which in its turn was the heir of Ptolemaic and Roman times. Fortunately contemporary papyri(2) help to explain the liturgical system through which public service became more oppressive under the Byzantines. The succession of the son to the public office of the father was adhered to rigorously and could even be followed in the case of shippers, whose services were of vital importance for the transport of grain to Rome or Constantinople.

That the Arabs took over the Byzantine system almost entirely is the general verdict of historians and scholars dealing with Egypt under Arab rule. Like most generalised assertions, however, this statement needs to be modified in several important points. The position held by Byzantine sea power in the Mediterranean and its naval organisation before the rise of Islam show those Byzantine factors which the Arabs discarded, and those particularly Arab ones which they

---

(1) v. Infra, App. I, 144, n. 3.

(2) For documents relating to naval organisation of Graeco-Roman Egypt v. P. Amherst; P. Cairo, Maspero; P. Goodspeed; Nicole, P. Genève; Kenyon, P. Lond., I. II, III; P. Oxy.; Crum and Bell, Wadi Sarga; Hunt, P. Ryl.; Miligan, Greek Papyri. The literary texts relating to the period are in Oldfather, Greek Texts.

introduced into the naval organisation. It is in this double set of factors that Egypt under Arab rule is to be distinguished from the periods before and after.

B. — Arabic and Aphrodito Papyri.

The progress of Arabic papyrology followed that of papyrology in general. In 1825 interest was aroused by the appearance of two papyri which are known to be passport letters of A.H. 133 and which were published by Silvestre de Sacy in the «*Journal des Savans.*» In 1827 a similar letter came out, which with another communication, was also published by De Sacy, this time in the «*Journal Asiatique*».(1) Karabacek(2) was the first to make a study of Arabic papyrology but owing to lack of time did not work upon the collection which was passed on to John Rylands Library. Margoliouth verified this material in his «*Catalogue of Arabic Papyri*»(3) but it was worked upon with less reliability. Considering the amount of material collected by Grohmann these large supplies were amassed very quickly. He reveals the methods and problems of papyrology in three important articles.(4) The collection which gives the best idea of the nature of these documents is the «*Arabic Papyri in the Egyptian Library*». Each papyrus is described, translated and annotated, and has a facsimile photograph attached.(5) The very rich store in Vienna, which was known collectively as the «*Papyrus Erzherzog Rainer*», has been made the object of systematic publication by Grohmann,(6) the most eminent specialist. The less important collections have also

---

(1) Becker, P.S.R., 1-6, and Grohmann, C.P.R., Bd. I, Teil I, 1-17, have given a comprehensive survey of Arabic papyrology up to the years 1906 and 1924 respectively.

(2) For an estimate of Karabacek as a scholar v. Becker, Der Islam, X, 233-238.

(3) Preface, IX.

(4) Aperçu de Pap. Arabe, 23-95; Archiv Orientalni, V, 1933, 273; VI, 1933, 125; VI, 1934, 377; Museon, LII, 199, 325-336.

(5) A detailed summary of this work is to be found in Revue des Etudes Islamiques, 1940, A77-A79.

(6) C.P.R., Bd. I, Teil I.

been published.(1)   The works of De Sacy, Merx, Moritz(2) and Caetani are concerned with the palaeographic aspect. It is workers like Becker and Grohmann that Arabic papyri need — nay, challenge.

The discovery of the greatest importance was the famous Aphrodito papyri. About seven kilometres to the south-west of Timâ in Upper Egypt, lies the small town of Kûm Ashqûh, known in ancient times as Aphrodito, and established by the Ancient Egyptians under the protection of Hathor. The Greeks, having identified this goddess with Aphrodite, renamed the town after her. Under Arab rule it became important as the capital of an administrative area known as Kûra until the time of the Fâtimids who abolished these administrative units.(3)

In 1901, whilst digging a well, some workmen uncovered a large papyrus dump to which they paid little attention until the village chief's brother, realising its importance, carried off the greater part. Others followed suit, but once the authorities got wind of the discovery, police took charge. It was too late however — the papyri had vanished. It seems that some were burnt and others hidden temporarily until dealers came to secure all they could lay their hands on.(4) Most of the pieces came to the British Museum, many went to Heidelberg, Strassburg and Russia, and a considerable portion of the collection remained in Cairo.

An account of the find was first given by Guibell in 1902. The *Arabic Palaeography* of Moritz(5) appeared in 1905, giving facsimiles of three Arabic letters from the governor Qurra ibn Sharîk to Bâsilyûs Sâhib Ashqûh. The first valuable publication of a part of the collection appeared as the *Papyri Schott Reinhardt I*, by Becker in which the Heidelberg and Strassburg Arabic letters from Qurra and five Arabic-Greek letters addressed to various places in the district of Ashqûh, were included. Other important publications

---

(1) Grohmann, Der Islam, XXII, 1 sq.; Archiv Orientalni, X, 1938, 149-162.
(2) Moritz, Ar. Pal.; in spite of its title « *Arabic Palaeography* », it is only a collection of specimens of writing.
(3) Toussoun, Géographie de l'Egypte, I, XIV.
(4) v. Abbott, 7 sq.
(5) Z.A., XX, 94-102.

followed in quick succession. Some of the Arabic papyri held by the British Museum were published by Becker(1) in 1907. The following year Bell(2) contributed an article entitled « *The Aphrodio Papyri* » and in 1910 he included a complete study oof the whole collection in the Museum with the exception of the Arabic documents.(3) A year later Becker(4) published Arabic pieces from the Egyptian Library in Cairo and the Ottoman Museum in Constantinople, and Bell(5) produced the first two instalments of his translation of the British Museum Greek Aphrodito Papyri. Unfortunately the first Great War intervened and caused a lull in scientific research, but in 1926 Bell's «*Two Official Letters of the Arab Period*» appeared.(6) He also continued the translation of the Aphrodito papyri.(7) A year latter, his article on «*the Administration of Egypt under the Umayyad Khaliphs*» was published,(8) this being a paper read at the Congress of Orientalists at Oxford. In this article Bell attempted to sketch the general scheme of administration of Egypt under the early Caliphate, to indicate how much the Arabs took over from the Byzantines and what changes they introduced, in order to estimate their success in the main task of government.

The Aphrodito papyri consist of two main divisicns, letters and accounts. The letters, all of which are from the governor, fall into two classes, some being addressed to the people but the greater number being sent to Bâsilyûs, the pagarch of Aphrodito. Qurra ibn Sharîk(9) was governor

---

(1) P.A.F., Z.A., XX, 68-104 sq.
(2) J.H.S., XXVIII, 97-120.
(3) P. Lond., IV.
(4) Der Islam, II, 245-268. v. Der Islam, II, 359-371; Z.A., XXII, 137-154.
(5) Der Islam, II, 269-283, 372-384; III, 132-140, 369-373; IV, 87-96.
(6) J.E.A.., XII, 265-281.
(7) Der Islam, XVII, 4-8.
(8) Byz. Zeit., XXVIII, 278-286.
(9) Qurra was governor of Egypt from Rabî' I 90 — Rabî' I 96/January 709 — December 714. The literary tradition of Muslim historians pictures him as an unrelenting oppressor whose tyranny became proverbial for harshness and inhumanity. The Aphrodito papyri show him to be an efficient statesman of the practical Umayyad régime. For his historical account v. Ibn 'Abd Al-Hakam, 238 sq.; Kindî, Governors, 63-66; Abbott, 57-59; Lammens, Gouverneur Omaiyade.

most of the time so that all the dated letters may be from him. Those published by Bell are all in Greek which distinguishes them from similar letters in Arabic published by Becker.(1) This would suggest that the same letters were sent in two languages and those with the beginning intact show not only the address, but the date of receipt, the name of the courier and the matter dealt with, duly noted by the clerk at Aphrodito. In some cases there are notes in Greek and occasionally in Arabic, made by the clerk at head-quarters.(2)

Value of Papyri

Karabacek's studies aimed at finding an historical interpretation of the documents, while the combined efforts of Becker and Bell have revealed much valuable information relating to the history of Egypt under Muslim rule, the former through his study of the Arabic and the latter through the Greek texts of the Aphrodito papyri.

The thoroughness of the civil service as part of the remarkable centralisation of government under the Muslims in Egypt is clear from the correspondence sent to Bâsilyûs, the pagarch of the village of Ashqûh. The contents of the letters often concern taxation. In tracing the taxes of the 1st/7th century in Egypt, it was necessary to go back to the ancient institutions of the Roman Empire. Now the numerous papyri give a fair idea of the situation in the period before and after the Muslim conquest.

More important for this study than these items are the constant references in both letters and accounts which give details of vital importance in the organisation of the navy under the early Caliphate. Mention is made of the first arsenals in Egypt, the cleaning and refitting of ships and their repair or construction. Numerous references are made to materials for shipbuilding such as timber, iron for nails,

---

(1) Cf. Becker, P.A.F., Z.A., XX, No. IX, 88, with Bell, Der Islam, III, No. 1408, 132.
(2) Bell, J.H.S., XXVIII, 99 sq.

cables, pads and cushions. One of the papyri letters throws light on the iron industry at that period. Plans were drawn up for the disposition of the fleet, its headquarters and the raids to be carried out on the coasts of the Byzantine Empire. Mention is made also of special government taxes for the maintenance of the fleet and of public service. They show that the principle of conscription and hereditary service was applied to the navy as well as to other offices. The methods adopted for the recruitment of sailors, their wages and security measures for the carrying out of their duties are clear. In addition to sailors, the allowances for fighting men as distinct from the rowers and helmsmen, wages for workmen such as carpenters, caulkers, blacksmiths and unskilled labourers are mentioned. Arrangements had to be made for supplies, including bread, butter, salt, oil and wine, for the ships and the raiding fleet. The papyri also refer to the flight of fugitives, which would be of still greater interest if there were an explanation of their escape. A system of passports was adhered to and papyri dealing with permission to stay in the country or travel abroad have been published.

All these facts mentioned in the papyri were expressly drawn up in answer to the urgent demands of daily life which make them differ from other official documents. They are first of all records, authentic memorials supplying impartial objective documentary evidence, admirably suited for research in scientific truths which history claims to have as its aim. They also differ from literary sources in that they give no grounds for uncertainty. Their value for the historian is inestimable and of an unusual interest. He seizes upon them for reference as the basis of his work, for they are undoubtedly a prime source of information. As Kenyon (1) says: « *In both departments, of philology and history proper, the value of the papyri consists, not so much in the revelation of new facts of first rate importance, as in the accumulation of small details, in themselves not striking, but collectively forming a foundation on which the constructive historian may base his inferences* ».

---

(1) Quoted by Oldfather, Preface, V.

The documents are undoubtedly unique in Medieval Islamic history in that never has so great a number, relating to a comparatively short period, been found in one spot. Their value for Muslim sea power cannot be estimated. An example of their importance is letter No. 1393 (1) which was published by Bell among the incomplete and undated correspondence of Qurra ibn Sharîk. It lacked the beginning and the right side, but the part published showed that it related to the recruitment of sailors and skilled workers, and the supplies for them and for the raiding fleet, but details were not clear because of the missing fragments. Information sometimes comes to hand in the most unexpected way. A part of the missing portions was found among a collection of papyri purchased by the British Museum in 1924, and in the following year's assignment, another fragment turned up and this practically completed the letter. Bell fitted the pieces together and, though the beginning is still missing, it is now possible to read from an almost unbroken text. He published it and though it adds little that is new to the information relative to the Muslim administration to be found in the other texts, its great value lies in the details it gives for the recruitment of men and supplies for the annual raiding expeditions despatched under the Umayyad Caliphate against the Byzantine Empire and its dependencies.

II. Historical, Geographical and Other Sources

The Muslims produced no account of their seafaring activities. The great historical works of Arab writers (2) contain references to sailing and wider treatises even give brief sketches. Geographers and travellers (3) supplement, to a considerable extent, the gaps left by the historians and

---

(1) Bell, P. Lond.. IV, 65-66; J.E.A., XII, 279. v. Infra, 99 sq.

(2) For Muslim historiography v. Margoliouth, Arabic Historians; Gibb, E.I., Supp., 233-245.

(3) The best survey of geographical literature is that of Kramers, E. I., Supp., 61-73. v. also Legacy of Islam, 79-108 ; Bartold, Preface to Amîr Abû'l-Hârith, 3-44 ; Mieli, 79 sq.; Sauvaget, Introduction, 42 sq.

often provide information about naval matters. Some were at the same time historians whilst many historical works contain a certain amount of geographical knowledge. The difficulty of this study lies in the fact that so many of these writers have to be consulted. Most of them are given in the bibliography but the survey is confined to the most important. It has seemed best to divide them into two groups: those who are chiefly concerned with naval matters in Egypt, Syria and North Africa, and those helpful for the study of types of Muslim Mediterranean warships, their staffs and the responsibilities attached to the various naval ranks. There is, however, sporadic mention of names of ships in the writing of some authors of the first group which helps to complete the information supplied by those of the second, thereby making a comprehensive study possible.

First Group

A prime source for the maritime history of Egypt is the account of the Patriarchs of the Egyptian church, based on Greek and Coptic documents for the earlier portion (1) and written by the celebrated historian Severus, bishop of Ushmûnayn (d. end 4th/10th century).(2) The greater part is edited by Evetts; that produced by 'Abd-Al-Masîh and Burmester is taken from a manuscript in the Library of the Coptic Museum, Cairo.(3) It gives important information about the Egyptian arsenals, naval expenditure, maritime naval service and passports, which supplement the material supplied by the papyri.

The earliest extant account from Arab sources of the Muslim conquest of Egypt and the west is that of Ibn 'Abd Al-Hakam(4) (d. 257/871), an Egyptian by birth and

---

(1) v. Intro. to Abû Sâlih, XVI.
(2) Butcher, II, 13.
(3) v. 'Abd Al-Masîh, Preface to Severus.
(4) v. Brockelmann, I, 148. In giving dates of deaths of authors I have followard where possible, Sauvaget, Introduction and Historiens Arabes.

residence. The parts dealing with the Muslim conquest under 'Amr ibn Al-'As, the early settlements of the Muslims in Fustât and Jîza, together with the organisation under 'Amr and Ibn Abî al-Sarh, help in fixing the site of the first arsenal in Egypt. A very rich and relatively reliable source, in spite of its date, is «*Subh Al-A'shâ*» of Qalqashandî (d. 821/1418), which is the broadest and most complete work of its kind.(1) In his simple and clear style he gives much knowledge concerning the island of Rawda and the details about the maritime administration of his time help us in understanding Muslim practice in general.

Most important are the works of the brilliant Egyptian school of historians which emerged during the last centuries of the Mameluke period. Of these mention must be made of the topography of Ibn Duqmâq (2) (d. 809/1406), of which two volumes are extant, the «*Khitat*» of Maqrîzî (3) (d. 845/1442), and the works of Suyûtî (d. 911/1505). The first place must be given to Maqrîzî to whom we owe a comprehensive chapter, not found in the earlier chronicles, devoted to the arsenals. Some of the information is derived from Ibn Duqmâq who seems to have used better sources. A native of Cairo, Maqrîzî devoted himself to Egyptian history and antiquities and spared no effort in collecting contemporary evidence, some of which, but for him, might have been lost. He utilised the works of Ibn 'Abd Al-Hakam, Kindî and Qudâ'î (d. 454/1062), for the early period. To him we owe the best extant topography of Cairo in Arabic which contains an inexhaustible fund of information relative to Muslim sea power. Suyûtî gives a chapter on the island of Rawda in «*Husn Al-Muhâdara*» which he bases largely on Maqrîzî, quoting entire passages from him. Another of his works must be noted here, the «*Kawkab Al-Rawda*» in which he traces the history of the island from the time of the Muslim conquest. It is still in manuscript but has been consulted for this purpose.

---

(1) For analysis of this work v. Sauvaget, Introduction, 73-74.

(2) v. Brockelmann, II, 50 ; Wüstenfeld, Gesh. der Arab., No. 547.

(3) Maqrîzî's works are enumerated by Suyûtî, Husn, I, 321. v. Brockelmann, II,38 ; Guest, J.R.A.S., 1902, 103 sq.; Wiet, B.I.F.A.O., XII, 1916.

A serious study of the Tûlûnid and Ikshîdid navies cannot be made as there is not sufficient material. Ibn Al-Dâya (1) (d. about 330/941), who seems to have possessed the culture deemed essential for the *«honnête homme»* of that time, is the chief source for the Tûlûnid navy. Unfortunately his biographies of the Tûlûnid princes, Khumârawayh and Hârûn, which formed the greater part of his work, are lost. The biography of Ibn Tûlûn is reproduced by the later Maghrib historian Ibn Sa'd(2) (d. 673/1275), as an introduction to his work. Vollers published it under the title *«Fragmenta aus dem Mughrib»*. Ibn Al-Dâya was an eye witness for some years of the reign of Ahmad ibn Tûlûn and his account can be regarded as trustworthy. He not only gives the name of the director of the arsenal and Ibn Tûlûn's instructions to him concerning shipbuilding but furnishes information about the passport system under the Tûlûnids.

Another authority utilised for this study is Madaynî (d. after 330/941), who wrote *«Sîrat Ahmad ibn Tûlûn»*, in the preface of which he states that he had been asked to write a biography which would be more comprehensive than that of Ibn Al-Dâya. It is not certain when he wrote this book, but, according to the editor Kurd 'Alî(3) it might have been more than sixty Hijra years after the death of Ibn Tûlûn. Thus much correspondence and numerous records which were not available to Ibn Al-Dâya seem to have been at his disposal; furthermore, he had the evidence of previous writers. Madaynî copied from Ibn Al-Dâya and gives a similar narrative concerning the instruction to the director of the arnesal, adding names of ships of Ibn Tûlûn's fleet as well as the number of vessels at the time of his death. Five centuries later Maqrîzî used Madaynî's statements to a great extent.

The *«Kitâb Al-Wulâh»* of Kindî (d. 350/961), gives, in addition to material about the first arsenal in Egypt, some details relative to its site in the time of the Tûlûnids, the

---

(1) Yâqût, Irshâd, II, 157 sq.; Zakî Mubârak, 242 sq.; Huart, 187.

(2) Suyûtî, Husn, I, 320, places his death in 685/1286.

(3) Preface to Madaynî.

naval precautions taken by Ibn Tûlûn for the defence of his capital and accounts of the attempts of the Fâtimid caliph to conquer Egypt. The date when Kindî wrote and the fact that he was an Egyptian, give his narrative an inestimable value. Ibn Sa'îd, already mentioned, wrote a continuation of Kindî's work from the death of the Ikhshîd to the arrival of Al-Mu'izz in Egypt. In his «Kitâb Al-Mughrib fî Hulâ Al-Maghrib» he quotes a part of the work of Ibn Zûlâq (1) (d. 387/997), entitled (Al-'Uyûn Al-Du'j fî Hulâ Dawlat Banî Tughj», a biography of the Ikhshîd written in 350/961, at the command of Abû'l-Hasan 'Alî ibn Al-Ikhshîd. This work is of great value for the study of the arsenals in the time of the Ikhshîd, especially as Ibn Zûlâq, a native of Egypt and eminent for his knowledge of history, was a recognised authority. Yahyâ ibn Sa'îd (2) (d. 458/1066), relates a narrative in connection with the arsenal after Al-Ikhshîd's death, in his «Continuation of the History of Eutychius» which covers the years 326-417/938-1026. The fact that this writer was probably born in Egypt where he spent the first forty years of his life, helps to make his account reliable as regards time and place.

For the availability of timber for shipbuilding in Egypt the chief authorities are Abû Sâlih the Armenian (d. beginning 7th/13th century), Ibn Mamâtî (d. 606/1209), and 'Abd Al-Latîf Al-Baghdâdî (d. 629/1232). Abû Sâlih's familiarity with the history of Egypt was due to the fact that he was born and bred there, (3) and though his work is entitled «The Churches and Monasteries of Egypt» he supplies information of all sorts about the country and the neighbouring lands. Ibn Mamâtî acted as minister under the Ayyûbid dynasty (4) and therefore his «Kitâb Qawânîn Al-Dawâwîn», which gives interesting details about forests in Egypt under Muslim domination, can be regarded as an official document. His list of ships of the Ayyûbid fleet, though later in time, is invaluable because of the description of the various types.

---

(1) For Ibn Zûlâq's works v. Yâqût, Irshâd, III, 7.

(2) v. Antâkî, in E.I., I, 539; Brockelmann, I, 148.

(3) Intro. to Abû Sâlih, X.

(4) Suryâl, Preface to Ibn Mamâtî.

The account of Egypt by 'Abd Al-Latîf Al-Baghdâdî, which De Sacy calls «Relation de l'Egypte», is very important. He was in service of Al-'Adil (596-615/1199-1218), in Syria or in Egypt (1) and made advanced studies in different subjects. The various kinds of timber mentioned by him as being in both these countries help to prove the availability of this material. His great book on the wonders of Egypt is unfortunately lost.

The chief work for the study of Syrian naval centres is «Futûh Al-Buldân» of Balâdhurî (2) (d. about 272/885), which, in Mas'ûdî's (3) opinion, is the best book on the history of the Arab conquests. On the whole he is an accurate recorder; if he has two conflicting accounts, he gives both. He visited many cities of Syria and recorded the traditions he collected from persons who had committed them to memory, such as Hishâm ibn Al-Layth, Abû'l Yasa' and Muhammad ibn Sahm Al-Antâkî, all natives of Syria, a fact which gives their traditions some colour of truth, thus making the information about sea-coast towns and arsenals of that country valuable material. Wâqidî (4) (d. 207/823), is by far the most important of Balâdhurî's sources, and, like Tabarî, was an authority on history, acquiring great fame. Most of his works are lost but some information has come down to us through the quotations of Balâdhurî who also relates traditions of one of his teachers, Muhammad ibn Sa'd, Wâqidî's secretary.

The Muslim conquest of Palestine did not put an end to the pilgrimages to Jerusalem (5) Three accounts of Christian pilgrims are important for the description of Syrian seaports and contribute to the knowledge of Islamic countries. The first pilgrimage is that of the bishop Arculf (6) (d. A.D. 680),

---

(1) Cahen, La Syrie, 61.

(2) v. Ibn Al-Nadîm, I, 113; Brockelmann, I, 141; Becker, E.I., I, 611-612.

(3) Murûj, I. 14.

(4) v. Ibn Al-Nadîm, I, 98-99; Ibn Khallikân, I, 506-507; Kremer, Eng. Tr., Bukhsh, Studies, 151, n. 1.

(5) v. Bernard the Wise, P.P.T.S., III, 11 ; Kramers, Legacy of Islam, 81. Cf. Jenkins, C., 66.

(6) v. Preface to Arculf's Narrative, P.P.T.S., III, XI sq., 51-52.

a native of Gaul who set out about A.D. 670, and, having visited Jerusalem, Tyre and Damascus, eventually sailed to Alexandria. The second pilgrimage is that of Saint Willibard (1) (d. A.D. 785), the first English pilgrim to go to the Holy Land. Having entered Islamic territory on his way to Emessa (Hims), and Damascus, he was able to give first-hand knowledge of the passports required. Similar information is also found in the short account of Bernard the Wise,(2) (d. after A.D. 870), a French monk who set out from Rome.

The geographical works written in the third and fourth centuries A.H., which have been edited by De Coeje under the general title «*Bibliotheca Geographorum Arabicorum*», are important for material relative to naval matters both in Egypt and Syria and contribute to the knowledge of Muslim countries as a whole. The information provided by most of them is mainly based on government documents which, in many cases, replace missing archives. (3) The oldest of them is that of Ibn Khurdâdhbih (4) (d. 272/885), who held the office of Chief of the Post in the province of Jibâl (ancient Media). According to De Goeje (5) the book was written in 232/846 and completely revised in 272/885; this version is only an abridged form of the original. Though Muqaddasî (6) regards it as too brief to be of much use, nevertheless Ibn Khurdâdhbih may be considered one of the best of the earlier geographers. As his book is an official itinerary, giving precise information, his statement regarding the expense of a maritime expedition can be looked upon as trustworthy. His statements concerning the Egyptian and Syrian seaports, the arsenal at Tyre and the activities of Jewish merchants are valuable, not only for the date when they were written but also for the great care with which the author collected his

---

(1) v. Intro. to St. Willibard, P.P.T.S., III, VII sq.

(2) v. P.P.T.S., III; Beazley, Dawn of Modern Geog., I, 166-174.

(3) Sauvaget, Introduction, 42-43.

(4) v. Ibn Al-Nadîm, I, 149; Brockelmann, I, 225 ; Defrémery, J. As., VII, 1866, 239-277.

(5) B.G.A., VI, XV-XX.

(6) B.G.A., III, 4.

material for the work. (1) Later writers, such as Ya'qûbî, Ibn Al-Faqîh and Ibn Rusta, copied from his book.

Next in point of time is Ya'qûbî (2) (d. 284/897), who wrote his geographical work in 278/891, many years later than his history. Unfortunately the existing text is incomplete. As he was born in Egypt and spent his later years there his description of the country has a particular value. He, too, seems to have taken part in government administration. His account of the Syrian coast and the arsenal at Tyre are especially interesting for he appears to have gathered detailed knowledge regarding the countries and towns he visited. He (3) asserts having checked it by interviewing reliable witnesses and there is no doubt that his work is based, to a great extent, on his observations and experiences. To Ibn Rusta (4) (d. after 291/903), Ibn Al-Faqîh (5) (d. after 291/903), and Istakhrî (d. 339/951), we are indebted for descriptions of naval centres in Egypt and Syria, the last two writers also giving information concerning timber.

Istakhrî's work is really an elaboration of that of Balkhî (d. 322/934), written, according to De Goeje,(6) about 308-9/934. Muqaddasî (7) says it consisted chiefly of geographical maps. His book was in its turn revised by Ibn Hawqal (d. 366/977). The original manuscripts of all these works included coloured maps of Maghrib, Egypt, Syria, the Mediterranean and other parts of the Islamic world; they have been reproduced by Miller (8) and some are utilised for this study to show the naval centres. Their value lies in the period when they were drawn. Ibn Hawqal's geography,

---

(1) v. Mas'ûdî, Murûj. I, 12-13.

(2) v. Yâqût, Irshâd, II, 156 sq.; Brockelmann, I, 226; Reinaud, Géog. d'Aboul Féda, I, LXI.

(3) B.G.A., VII, 232-233.

(4) v. Brockelmann, I, 227 ; De Goeje, Preface, B.G.A., VII, V-VII.

(5) v. Brockelmann, I, 227 ; De Goeje, Preface, B.G.A., V.

(6) Z.D.M.G., XXV, 49.

(7) B.G.A., III, 4.

(8) v. Also Kamal Youssouf, Monumenta Geographica.

based on that of Istakhrî, supplies much the same information about Syria and Egypt and is characterised by identity of expressions; nevertheless his work is more developed. He (1) maintains that he collected all the knowledge to make geography interesting for people of all classes. The new edition of his work by Kramers comprises materially all that is actually known from Ibn Hawqal and includes his maps.

Muqaddasî (2) (d. 378/988), a native of Jerusalem, was able to give an eye witness's description of Syria. His graphic account of the construction of the massive stone embankments surrounding the harbour of 'Akkâ in the time of Ibn Tûlûn can be regarded as trustworthy, especially as the author's grandfather was the architect, and forms a valuable contribution to this study. Muqaddasî visited Egypt and his observations on that country, in particular the ships at Fustât, are of unusual interest. In his preface he (3) states that his book consisted of three parts: the first, what he has seen; the second, what he has heard from reliable people; and the third, what he has gathered from books. There is a certain amount of conceit in his self-praise but it is not an empty boast, for he developed original and valuable ideas. In his systematic account he includes naval facts as well as a list of ships' names (4) used in various countries, as he believed that a knowledge of them would doubtless be serviceable to people visiting those places.

Among the works of later geographers and travellers is «Safar Nâma» by the Persian, Nâsirî Khusrû (5) (d. 481/1088), whose description of the Muslim seaports, including the harbour of 'Akkâ and its chain shows him to have been a keen observer. The «Nuzhat Al-Mushtâq» of Idrîsî (6) (d. 561/1166), an elaborate description of the medieval world

---

(1) B.G.A., II, 4 sq.; Kramers Edition, 2 sq.
(2) v. Brockelmann, I, 230; De Goeje, Preface, B.G.A., III.
(3) B.G.A., III, 43. v. also 2-6, 8.
(4) v. Infra, App. III, 155 sq.
(5) v. Khashshâb, Preface to Nâsirî Khusrû.
(6) v. Brockelmann, I, 477; Reinaud, Géog. d'Aboul Féda, I. cxiii-cxxii.

known to the author at that time, is mainly based on earlier geographers, especially Ibn Hawqal. The record of the journeys of the Jewish traveller, Benjamin of Tudela (d. end 6th/12th century), which Adler (1) suggests must be reckoned between 562/1166 and 567/1171, is the earliest important work of its kind in Hebrew literature. He visited the important cities along the Mediterranean coast and gives accurate first-hand information. The Spanish traveller Ibn Jubayr (2) (d. 614/1217), whose journey lasted from 579/1183 to 581/1185, wrote a full account of it which is interesting from many points of view as it contains nautical terms and geographical observations. «Mu'jam Al-Buldân», the geographical dictionary by Yâqût (3) (d. 626/1229), was based on the writing of earlier geographers but supplemented by experiences gained from his travels which included Egypt and Syria. Yâqût used a scientific approach and endeavoured to make his work as complete as possible; it is a storehouse of information, both for geography and history. He refers to some sources now missing and enumerates most of the towns and naval bases. His book is indispensable for the study of Muslim sea power.

Among other geographers consulted two must be mentioned. The first is Qazwînî (4) (d. 682/1283), who wrote a cosmography, «'Ajâ'ib Al-Makhlûqât», and a geography, «'Ajâ'ib Al-Buldân», known as «Athâr Al-Bilâd», which contains many curious and fabulous details. He uses Yâqût's work but in several passages he gives information not found in the «Mu'jam.» The second is Abû'l-Fidâ (5) (d. 732/1331), who was nominated governor of Hamâ in 710/1310. His great scientific work «Taqwîm Al-Buldân», an achievement no less remarkable than that of Yâqût, contains a description of his native country, Syria and Palestine, which is the result of his own observations.

---

(1) Preface to Benjamin, I.

(2) v. Brockelmann, I, 478.

(3) v. Brockelmann, I, 479-481 ; Cahen, La Syrie, 91.

(4) v. Brockelmann, I, 481 ; Browne, Lit. Hist. of Persia, II, 482 sq.

(5) v. Reinaud, Géog. d'Aboul-Féda, I.

For the study of the first arsenal in Africa the works of Ibn Qutayba (1) (d. 276/889), Bakrî (2) (d. 487/1094), Ibn 'Idhârî (d. 7th/13th century), and Ibn Khaldûn (3) (d. 808/1406), are of value. The «*Kitâb Al-Imâma Wa Al-Siyâsa*», attributed to Ibn Qutayba, includes a part dealing with the conquest of Africa and Spain in which is an account of the establishment of the first arsenal in North Africa at Tûnis, but the writer rarely mentions any authorities for his statements. Full details of the raid led by 'Ata' ibn Râfi' are given and these are partly confirmed by a papyrus letter. Of Bakrî's main work only the portion dealing with northern Africa and Egypt is extant and full of interest. It contains a description of Tûnis, including the establishment of the arsenal, for which he quotes Abû Muhâjir. Although Bakrî made use of information given by previous authors, the fact that he lived in the west makes his narrative more convincing. He mentions the sea route from Mahdiyya to Alexandria and Antioch, giving a full list of the harbours in North Africa. «*Al-Bayân Al-Mughrib*», written by Ibn 'Idhârî at the end of the 7th/13th century, contains several references to the North African fleet, the arsenal at Tûnis and a description of the ancient city of Carthage.

The universal history of Ibn Khaldûn, who spent the greater part of his life in Africa, is only an outline of events but is, nevertheless, of unique value for North African affairs and the activities of the African fleet. The historico-philosophical views expressed in his famous preface, «*the beautiful façade to a commonplace edifice,*» are of considerable significance. For the first time in Muslim chronicles there is a chapter devoted to the commander of the fleet and another to the art of carpentry as related to shipbuilding. Ibn Khaldûn also gives a most graphic account of Muslim navigation, containing more than one fact, confirmed by papyri, about naval organisation.

---

(1) v. Brockelmann, I, 102-123.

(2) v. Brockelmann, I, 476; De Slane, Intro, to Bakrî, 7-20.

(3) v. Schmidt, Ibn Khaldoûn, New York, 1930.

Second Group

The first authority to be mentioned in the second group is Tabarî, (1) (d. 310/923), one of the greatest of Muslim historians whose compilation is a prime source of information. He aimed at assimilating all the historical knowledge of the Arabs and, as De Goeje (2) observes, his work is distinguished by completeness of detail, accuracy and the truly stupendous learning of its author. Mas'ûdî (3) declares that no other book can be compared with Tabarî's, which supplements all other works. Among his references to the sea and ships he mentions the type of warship employed by the Byzantines in the sack of Damietta and, in relating the wars against the Turks and Zinj, speaks of many types of ships together with their staffs. This information partly explains Muqaddasî's list of ships and his annals sometimes throw light upon Muslim naval centres, as in the case of Tarsus.

Tabarî's chronicles end in A.H. 302 and are continued till A.H. 320 by 'Arîb ibn Sa'd of Cordova (4) (d. 370/980), who sometimes gives ships' names corresponding with those of Tabarî. Ibn Al-Athîr (5) (d. 630/1233), based the first three centuries of Islam on Tabarî and not only gives the same names of ships but, in his accounts of the later period, brought down to A.H. 628, mentions those used in the Mediterranean, thus supplementing Tabarî to a considerable extent. The question of relationship between the two writers has been investigated by Brockelmann (6) who concludes that Ibn Al-Athîr's work holds an outstanding place amongst original sources. Ibn Khallikân (7) praises it highly as one of the best productions of its kind. It gives a fair conception of the types of ships employed at different periods, for the author,

---

(1) v. Brockelmann, I, 142.
(2) Quoted by Nicholson, 351.
(3) Murûj, I, 16.
(4) v. Brockelmann, I, 236 ; Dozy, Intro. to Ibn 'Idhârî, 43-63
(5) v. Brockelmann, I, 345 sq.
(6) Quoted by Bartold, Turkestan, 2, n. 6.
(7) De Slane Tr., II, 289.

in addition to pointing out their chief characteristics, gives an idea of crews and equipment. This helps to determine the types of vessels comprising the fleet.

Among other compilations giving similar information are «*Nishwâr Al-Muhâdara*» of Tanûkhî (1) (d. 384/994), a storehouse of anecdotes; «*Tajârib Al-Umam*» of Ibn Miskawayh (2) (d. 421/1030), which covers a later period than Tabarî's, ending in 369/980; «*Nihâyat Al-Arab*» of Nuwayrî (3) (d. 732/1332), written in 714/1314. The last named work is an encyclopaedia of immense value, partly published by the Royal Library, Cairo. It contains a section in which the author quotes earlier writers who describe the sea, ships and naval battles. He reproduces the poem of Buhturî (d. 284/897), about a sea fight not found in Muslim chronicles, and prose passages of Abû 'Amr Al-Qurtubî and Ibn Al-'Amîd, portraying ships.

A most important authority among the early writers for this subject is Mas'ûdî (4) (d. 345/956), who spent most of his life in travelling (5) and saw regions which no contemporary Muslim writer has described. He is apparently a faithful recorder of the events of his time. The fact that he visited and settled in Egypt makes his information about the site of the first Muslim arsenal at Babylon particularly valuable. Unfortunately the greater part of his works, entitled «*Akhbâr Al-Zamân*» is lost but references are made to them in his other books. In «*Tanbîh*» Mas'ûdî describes the seas, rivers and islands and definitely gives the derivation and meaning of the Arabic word for fleet. His «*Murûj*», an historico-geographical encyclopaedia containing first-hand knowledge, enlightens us upon the career of Leo of Tripolis which has been ignored or confused by other Muslim chronicles. The never-failing interest of this writer in seafarers and his

---

(1) v. Yâqût, Irshâd, VI, 251-267 ; Ibn Khallikân, I, 563-565.
(2) v. Yâqût, ibid, II, 88 ; Brockelmann, I, 342.
(3) v. Brockelmann, II, 139 ; Cahen, La Syrie, 81-82.
(4) v. Ibn Khaldûn, Muqaddima, I, 3, 157, 196 ; Brockelmann, I. 143-145
(5) v. Mas'ûdî, Murûj, I, 5; Reinaud, Géog. d'Aboul Féda, I, LXV.

acquaintance with captains and sailors of warships and trading vessels (1) make his remarks on Mediterranean and Indian Ocean ships usually convincing.

The existence of nautical literature dealing with maritime geography of the Mediterranean can hardly be proved from Muslim sources. That for the Indian Ocean has an ancient tradition of its own which links it to the early narratives of seafarers, (2) as found in the adventures of the merchant Sulaymân, (written in 237/851), and the information given in «Silsilat Al-Tawârikh» of Abû Zayd Al-Sirafî (first half 4th/10th century). Buzurg ibn Shahriyâr, a Persian sailor, also edited a collection of sailors' tales entitled «Kitâb 'Ajâ'ib Al-Hind», after 343/954. A series of such stories crystalised round the name of Sindbad the Sailor. A maritime geography, «Usûl 'Ilm Al-Bahr» was produced by Ibn Mâjid (d. after 906/1500). This type of literature, however, only affects the present study indirectly, but it has been consulted for nautical terms in the Indian Ocean, helpful for comparison with those used in the Mediterranean.

Finally, Mas'ûdî's information about staff of ships is supplemented by the official instructions issued to the commander of sea forces during the lifetime of Qudâma (d. after 320/932), (3) which are preserved in the copy of his «Kitâb Al-Kharâj», in the Kuprili Library, Istanbul. It was first recognised by De Slane, and Hamîdullâh selected some extracts for his book. These instructions indicate the duties attached to this high office and are of great historical significance as Qudâma was an accountant in the Revenue Department at Baghdad.

---

(1) v. Mas'ûdî, Murûj, I, 281-282.

(2) v. Reinaud, Relation; Géog. d'Aboul-Féda, Ferrand, Voyage du Marchand Arabe Sulaymân; Brockelmann, I, 523 ; Beazley, E.B., 143-144 ; E.I., I, 809.

(3) Hamîdullâh, 303, gives the year of his death 310/922. Sauvaget, Introduction, 80, gives a date after 320/932, and in Historiens Arabes, 51, says it was after 317/929.

CHAPTER I.

ARSENALS AND NAVAL CENTRES IN EGYPT

Dâr al-sinâ'a is the Arabic word for dockyard (1) but as the literal meaning is «*house of work*», the term can be used in a very wide sense. It may signify any workshop, (2) but the most common interpretation is **dâr sinâ'at al-bahr** which, as in the case of numerous other Arabic nautical terms, has passed into the Romance languages. Its Italian forms are **darsena** and **arsenale;** in Spanish it is **arsenal** and as such has passed into almost all European languages. (3)

The Byzantine Empire had maintained dockyards at Alexandria and Clysma. From the papyri, it seems that the Muslims utilised both of these and began to build their own fleet with the help of Greek and Coptic shipwrights.

I. Arsenal at Clysma

The importance of Clysma must not be overlooked for it was a link between the Mediterranean and Eastern seas, as ships could pass through by way of the Khalîj Amîr Al-

---

(1) Idrîsî, Nuzhat Al-Mushtâq, [93]; Ibn Battûta, Voyage, IV, 356, 357, 359; Ibn Duqmâq, IV, 35(25), 82(20); V, 38(3), sometimes calls it sinâ'at al-'imâra; Ibn Khaldûn, Muqaddima, II, 34; Maqrîzî, Khitat, II, 107; Lammens, Mots Français, 28, 95; Defrémery, J. As., April 1867, 416; June 1869, 537, n. 1; Casanova, **Noms Coptes**, B.I.F.A.O., I, 159.

(2) Dozy, Supplément, I, 848; Becker, E.I., I, 918; Casanova, ibid, I, 159; Foustât, M.I.F.A.O., XXXV, XXXVI.

(3) Dozy et Engelmann, 205 sq.; Becker, E.I., I, 918.

Mu'minîn canal. According to Maqrîzî (1) the ancient town was a harbour of Egypt. The surrounding country was inhabited by Muslims at an early date. Numerous references to the arsenal at Clysma are to be found in the papyri. Letter No. 1336, dated 91/709, is an order from the governor Qurra to the pagarch Bâsilyûs for a carpenter to be sent to serve in person in the building of ships for transporting either workmen or goods to Clysma, possibly by way of the Khalîj Amîr Al-Mu'minîn canal. He was to work under the supervision of the controller of the dockyards, Muhammad ibn Abî Habîba : *«In the name of God. Qurra ibn Sharîk, Governor, to Bâsîl, administrator of the village of Aphrodito. We have apportioned to your administrative district 1 carpenter for 4 months for work at the* **barges** *(2) which convey to Clysma in the present 8th indiction, having fixed his wages and supplies at 2/3 solidus per month excluding..., to be paid from the Treasury, and having made out the demand note for him we have sent it to you. Send him, therefore, with his tools in accordance with the powers given by the demand note [immediately(?)], (3) and hand him over to Muhammad ibn Abî Habîba, who is in charge of the work».* (4)

In letter No. 1346, dated 92/710, Bâsilyûs was reproved for failing to despatch articles and supplies for ships at Clysma, thereby incurring the liability for freightage. There is a reference to the canal of Trajan which left the Nile at Babylon and went by way of Bubastis to Clysma. The Muslims found it silted up, and although 'Amr had it cleared and reopened under the name of Khalîj Amîr Al-Mu'minîn, (5) it was apparently only available during flood periods. After the customary formal opening the letter continues : *«We have assessed on your administrative district various articles for the cleaning and fitting up of the ships at Clysma, and also*

---

(1) Khitat, I, 213 ; I.F., I, 58-59.
(2) The word **barges** here denotes some kind of vessel perhaps used on the canal from Babylon to Clysma.
(3) Explanatory phrases are given in round brackets.
(4) Bell, Der Islam, II, No. 1336, 271.
(5) v. Ibn 'Ab Al-Hakam, 136, 165 ; Ya'qûbî, Hist., II, 177 ; Tabarî, I. 2577 ; Mas'ûdî, Murûj, IV, 97-98 ; Abû Sâlih, 88 ; Yâqût, Mu'jam, II, 466 ; Ibn Duqmâq, 120 ; Maqrîzî, Khitat, I, 71.

supplies for the sailors of the ships which are at the same Clysma, and we sent you also the demand notes for these many days ago, and wrote you to send them off quickly before the waters of (the canal of) Trajan subside, and till this day you have not sent any of them at all worth mentioning. On receiving the present letter, therefore, immediately and at the very instant send whatever there is of them in your district, not delaying anything at all, nor yet requiring another letter from us about this if at least you have any understanding and are in your right mind. For you will know that (if) you delay anything whatsoever of the said articles and supplies and the waters subside, you will have to convey them speedily (by land) to the said Clysma, paying for their carriage out of your own property... Brought by Sa'îd». (1)

Letter No. 1387 is an order from Qurra to Bâsilyûs, dated between 91-6/709-14, for money in payment of the freightage of certain articles intended for Clysma: «In the name of God. Qurra, etc... We have apportioned to your administrative district for the freight of the ships which conveyed the requisitions for the **carabi** and Clysma and the r[aid?...Solidi?] in the present... indiction, and having made out the demand notes for these to the people of the separate places we have sent them to you. On receiving the present letter, therefore, in accordance with the powers given by the demand notes despatch the said money by your man with instructions to pay it over. [? and see to it that you do not pay anything] by a requisition on the separate places for [? freight except for the frieght of the] wheat and barley [which is paid] to the granaries of Babylon ».(2)

Letter No. 1386, dated 90-1/708-9, is apparently a requisition for the cost of articles intended for the refitting of ships at Clysma and provisions for the sailors. The money is to be given to Sa'îd who is probably the person mentioned at the end of the letter No. 1346. Qurra threatened Bâsilyûs with loss of life and estate if, upon inquiry, he was found to have disobeyed previous instruction: (3) «Articles for the

---

(1) Bell, Der Islam, II, No. 1346, 277; P. Lond., IV, 19.
(2) Bell, ibid, II, No. 1387, 381; P. Lond., IV, 60.
(3) This imperious tone must not be taken seriously as the pagarch continued in office, in spite of renewed threats.

cleaning and fitting up of the... (ships) at Clysma, and also for sailors... and others for the Government service in the 7th indiction and we have apportioned to your administrative district... nominal solidi, and having made out the demand notes for them we have sent them to you. Immediately on the receipt of the present letter, therefore, in accordance with the powers given by the demand notes collect the said money and send it by your man with instructions to pay it over to Sa'îd our servant. And see to it that you do not pay anything at all for freight except that of the [wheat ?] of the embola which is paid to the granaries of Babylon; for I intend to make inquiries and find out the truth about this, and if I find that you have paid anything at all for freight except for the said embola for the granaries I will requite you with a retribution which will threaten your life and estate.» (1)

One of the best preserved accounts of the Aphrodito collection is No. 1433, dated 88-9/706-7, which related to miscelaneous taxes for the village of Aphrodito and contains registers for requisitions, money, sailors and workmen for the **carabi** at Clysma. Particular names are mentioned in connection with various details, as for example, register of wages and provisions for Ezekiel, son of Psempnuthius; the hiring of a sailor by David, son of Andrew, to serve in person; the cost of articles carried by Peter the priest and Abû Yazîd.(2) Further interesting items concerning the arsenal at Clysma are given in Nos. 1414, 1434 and 1449:(3) mention of two caulkers and one carpenter for the **barges;** cost of oil and salt for the maintenance of a skilled workman; conveyance of wheat and other articles; anchors, acacia wood, cables of palm fibre and pads for building and fitting up the ships. Account No. 1434 specifies the date and mentions, in many cases, the messenger who brought it. Bell (4) suggests that it was written at various times as the ink is of a different colour in some portions. The Coptic papyrus No. 1515 (5) relates also to provisions for the fleet at Clysma.

---

(1) Bell, Der Islam, II, No. 1386, 380-381; P. Lond. IV, 59-60.
(2) Bell, Ibid, III, No. 1433, 369, 381, 372.
(3) Bell. ibid, III, No. 1414, 137 ; IV, No. 1434, 89, 93 ; XVII, No. 1449, 4, 6, 7.
(4) P. Lond., IV, 308.
(5) Crum, P. Lond., IV, No. 1515 (8-11), 449.

From these numerous references to the requisitions for, and the building and repair of ships, it is evident that Clysma was an important naval centre under an Arab official named Muhammad ibn Abî Habîba.(1) The town owed its importance to the Khalîj Amîr Al-Mu'minîn, through which the corn ships of Fustât passed on their way to Al-Jâr and Jidda. Muqaddasî (2) counted no less than three thousand camel loads exported every week. Ibn Khurdâdhbih (3) says that the Jewish merchants, known as Al-Râdhâniyya, (4) came from the south of France to Al-Faramâ; (5) thence they carried their goods on camels to Al-Qulzum, where they were loaded on ships bound for India and China. The same geographer (6) also states that Al-Qulzum, with Al-Tûr and Ayla, formed a district of Egypt. Later on, it seems to have become a desolate site without water and vegetation. Muqaddasî (7) already mentions Al-Suways (Suez), which gradually took the place of Al-Qulzum, a mile away.

II. Arsenal at Alexandria

Alexandria was the largest market and busiest port of the Mediterranean during the Byzantine period. Whatever be the poverty of information about the fleet in Egypt at that time its importance is obvious from the constant traffic which centred there. (8) Of all the industrial arts carried on, shipbuilding was probably the most important, and continued to

---

(1) He is mentioned as superintendent at Clysma in Bell, Der Islam, II, No. 1336, 271 ; IV, No. 1434, 89, 90, and in the Coptic papyrus, P. Lond., IV, No. 1507, 444.
(2) B.G.A., III, 195.
(3) B.G.A., VI, 153 ; reproduced by Maqrîzî, Khitat, I, 213.
(4) Simonsen, Revue des Etudes Juives, 1907, 141, suggests that they got their name from the river Rhone, Rhodanus, which seems likely ; but this is not approved by De Goeje, quoted by Mez, 471, For their commercial activities v. also Ibn Al-Faqih, B.G.A., V, 270; Pirenne, Economic and Social History, II, 113 ; Mediaeval Cities, 31-32 ; Lopez, Speculum, January 1945, 25-26 ; Adler, 2 ; Heyd, I, 40-41.
(5) The classical Pelusium lay near the north-eastern frontier of Egypt. v. Yâqût, Mu'jam, III, 883 ; Butler, Notes to Abû Sâlih, 61, n. 2.
(6) Ibn Khurdâdhbih, B.G.A., VI, 81 ; Maqrîzî, Khitat, I, 213.
(7) B.G.A., III, 196. Maspero et Wiet, Matériaux, 107, gives the distance as one mile. v. Muqaddasî, Bib. Ind., 320-321 ; Yâqût, Mu'jam, IV, 158 ; Butler, ibid 61, n. 1.
(8) v. Rouillard, 136 sq., 141 sq.; Wiet, Précis de l'Histoire d'Egypte, II, 76.

flourish during the 1st/7th century under Muslim rule. Undoubtedly the city was of vital importance as a naval centre to the Arabs for it particularly provided ships and sailors for the fleet. Mu'âwiya ordered a number of warships to be built there. (1) The capture of Alexandria was therefore, an important factor in the development of Muslim sea power.

From the papyrus letter No. 1392, dated 92-3/710-1, of the governor Qurra to the pagarch, it is evident that Alexandria was an important starting place for raids. The subject in question was butter for the maintenance of the fighting men of the raiding fleet of Egypt. It was to be sent direct to the Augustal Theodore (2) who administered Alexandria and seems to have been a Christian. The fleet was probably on the point of departure from the port: «*In the name of God. Qurra, etc... For the maintenance of the Corsairs who go out to the raids in the (present ?) 9th indiction we have requisitioned from your administrative district 9 measures of butter at 1 1/6 solidus each, and having made out the demand notes for them to the people of the separate places we have sent them to you. On receiving the present letter, therefore, [requisition?] the [said 9 measures] from the people of each place,... send to Alexandria in full the 9 measures apportioned to your district by your faithful men with instructions to pay the said butter to Theodore the Augustal... and to receive the receipt for it; and order them (the taxpayers) to give good butter and [such as will please us ?], because this is a matter of special concern to [the Amîr Al-Mu'minîn ?]. Therefore, without delay send off the said butter as aforesaid in full, not sending a money composition but the article itself*».(3)

Another letter of the same nature, No. 1353, dated 92/710, is an urgent demand for sailors, skilled workmen and supplies, both for them and the raiding fleet of Egypt, to be sent via

---

(1) According to Sebeos, quoted by Butler, 113, n. 1, the ships were of two classes ; probably battleships and cruisers.

(2) Bell, P. Lond., IV, XXXIII, n. 4, says it has been assumed that persons bearing Greek or Coptic names in the papyri were Christians and those described as Mawâlî (Non-Arab Muslims), invariably had Arabic names. He refers to Becker's remark that the conversion to Islam always seems to have been followed by a change of name.

(3) Bell, Der Islam, II, No. 1392, 381-382 ; P. Lond. IV, 64.

the canal of Alexandria (1) whilst the water was still high. It was accompanied by a threat from Qurra, that Bâsilyûs would be liable for the freightage, should he neglect to carry out these instructions. The supplies were to be sent direct to the dockyards at Alexandria: «*In the name of God. Qurra etc... The demand notes for the requisition of sailors and skilled workmen and their supplies and those of the fighting men of the raiding fleet of Egypt for the 9th indiction came to you (or were returned to you ?)... On receiving the present letter, therefore, send off immediately with all speed the supplies requisitioned from your administrative district before the water in the canal of Alexandria goes down; otherwise you will be compelled to pay the carriage of the said supplies (by land) to Alexandria. And (take care) that the sailors are good and experienced men; for we have instructed the present messenger not to give you a discharge until you have despatched in full all that is required from your district*».(2)

In No. 1412 there is reference to a State Treasury in Alexandria together with the name of the treasurer Al-Hârith ibn 'Abs, an Arab. On one occasion, in 83-4/702-3, the whole treasury payment was sent there. (3) These facts confirm the importance of the city at that time.

The port of Alexandria was famous for its lighthouse about which Arab writers have given many particulars and told marvellous stories, most of which are reproduced by Maqrîzî.(4) Though Mas'ûdî (5) relates that the Byzantines succeeded in destroying half of the tower and the mirror by trickery during the Caliphate of Al-Walîd I it seems that it was used as a guide for mariners for some time after the Arab conquest. Arculf (6) says it was seen by voyagers at

---

(1) What is meant is probably the new Mahmûdiyya canal. It was called the canal of Alexandria. v. Bell, P. Lond., IV, XXXIII, n. 5, No. 1353, 28(11).
(2) Bell, Der Islam, II, No. 1353, 280-281.
(3) Bell, P. Lond., IV, XXXIII; No. 1412, 96(279), 100 (456, 457).
(4) Khitat, I, 251 sq. v. Ibn Khurdâdhbih, B.G.A., VI, 115; Ibn Al-Faqîh, B.G.A., V, 71; Mas'ûdî, Murûj, II, 439-440, 445; Kindî, Fadâ'il Misr, 26; Qazwînî, Athâr Al-Bilâd, 96-98.
(5) Murûj, II, 444-445.
(6) P.P.T.S., III, 50.

a great distance and that men were employed to light torches to serve as a guide to the land and show the narrow entrance to the straits. Ya'qûbî (1) speaks of fires that were lit in the torches when the watchers saw ships at a great distance. Nâsirî Khusrû states that he saw the lighthouse and Benjamin (2) affirms that to his day it was a landmark to all seafarers who came to Alexandria, for one could see it at a distance of a hundred miles day by day; at night the keeper lighted a torch which mariners could see from a distance and thus sail towards it.

III. Naval Centres at Rosetta, Damietta and Tinnîs

In the early period of the Caliphate Rosetta and Damietta were naval centres, each administered by a Christian official, (3) as was Alexandria. Register No. 1149 mentions supplies for the Muhâjirûn of the «*castellated ships*» to be sent to Rosetta and account No. 1414 contains an item concerning the cost of articles to be delivered to its administrator, Paphnuthius. (4) The town commanded the entrance to the western branch of the Nile. (5) Ya'qûbî (6) states that it was a populous city with a harbour through which the Nile flowed into the sea and by way of which ships from the Mediterranean reached the Nile.

Register No. 1449 (7) also refers to supplies, including wheaten flour, loaves, pulse, oil, vinegar and salt for twenty sailors and the Muhâjirûn of the raiding fleet of the Orient, to be delivered at Damietta. The interesting letter No. 1354, dated 92/710, contains instructions relating to supplies for the raiding fleet. Bâsilyûs was emphatically told to make no further demands upon the taxpayers until after the harvest

---

(1) B.G.A., VII, 338-339. v. Istakhrî, B.G.A., I, 51 ; Ibn Hawqal, Ed. Kramers, 151 ; Amîr Abû'l-Hârith, 151 ; Muqaddasî, B.G.A., III,211.
(2) Nâsirî Khusrû, Ed. Khashshâb, 43 ; Benjamin, 75.
(3) Bell, P. Lond., IV, XXXIV.
(4) Bell, Der Islam, III, No. 1414, 140 ; XVII, No. 1449, 8.
(5) v. Ibn Hawqal, B.G.A., II 90; Ibn Duqmâq, V, 113-114 ; Yâqût, Mu'jam, II, 781.
(6) B.G.A., VII, 338.
(7) Bell, Der Islam, XVII, No. 1449, 8.

when arrears were to be sent at once to Damietta. He was ordered to send the « *people of the district* » at once « *the wheat and bread requisitioned... for supplies for the raiding fleet as aforesaid... what you have (already) loaded on to the boats cause to be returned [to the tax-payers ?], and if it appears that any of the people of your administrative district have given to any of your officials any money composition whatsoever for the said supplies contrary to the rate of prices which we laid down in our demand notes, return this to them in full, and do not make any demands on the people of the places for wheat and bread from now till the time of harvest by God's command; but when they begin the harvest demand from them in full all that is in arrear of the said wheat and bread, and send it to Damietta, not delaying one single artaba of it. And follow our command in all these matters exactly, not bearing hardly on [shifting the responsibility on to ?] any one but performing the duty yourself. For behold ! we have written to the messenger who was sent from us to you for the said supplies to bring us a register containing the amount you have embarked and sent off by each supercargo (?) of the supplies and the money compositions for them. Therefore let it not come to our knowledge that there has been collected from the people of your district any money composition at all for the supplies below the aforesaid valuation which we included in our demand notes; but the pulse and vinegar-oil send out immediately to Damietta not waiting for a single moment; do not neglect this...* ». (1)

Maqrîzî (2) records a number of Byzantine raids against Damietta. Tabarî's (3) account concerning the sack of the city in 238/853 shows that the Byzantines found a supply of arms destined for the ruler of Crete and that they burnt a storehouse for sails of ships. Kindî (4) relates that as a result of this expedition the construction of the fortress at Damietta began by order of the Caliph Mutawakkil on 3 Ramadân 239/8 February 854. The Byzantine descent on the

---

(1) Bell, Der Islam, II, 1354, 281; P. Lond., IV, 29.
(2) Khitat, I, 214.
(3) III, 1417, 1418.
(4) Governors, 202. v. Ibn Duqmâq, V, 80-81.

city, probably in 245/859, (1) caused the governor of Egypt, Yazîd ibn 'Abdallah, to fortify the coastal cities, including Damietta and Rosetta. According to Balâdhurî (2) the Caliph Mutawakkil ordered ships and garrisons to be stationed along the sea-coast.

Muqaddasî (3) describes Damietta as having a stone fortress and many gates and as being within ear-shot of the Mediterranean where the Nile flows into it. Yâqût (4) explains that there were two towers at this place, one on each side of the river, between which was a chain, guarded so that no ship could leave or enter the sea without permission. Qazwînî gives the same narrative and Ibn Iyâs adds that the chain is said to have existed before the Muslim conquest. (5) Ibn Battûta (6) says that the ancient city was destroyed during the reign of Al-Malik Al-Sâlih and that the new one had been built recently. The old Damietta was closer to the sea than the later town which the Mameluke Sultan Baybars founded in the 7th/13th century. (7) It was situated on the eastern arm of the Nile delta, about seven miles from its mouth and less than one mile to the west of Lake Manzala ; to the north lay a narrow belt of sand dividing it from the Mediterranean and forming a corridor to the sea.

Ya'qûbî (8) says the Nile divided into two at Damietta, one branch going to Lake Tinnîs in which ships and large boats sailed and the other running into the Mediterranean. He adds that Tinnîs, encircled by the sea, was an ancient city with a harbour for ships coming from Syria and Maghrib. Muqaddasî (9) speaks of it as situated on an island with a

---

(1) The date in Maqrîzî, Khitat, I, 214, is not clear. Wiet, in his edition of Maqrîzî, I.F., IV, 41, emending the text, suggests the year 239/853-4. Maqrîzî may mean the expedition in 245/859 mentioned by Kindî, Governors, 203, and Ibn Taghrî Birdî, II, 308,309 v. also Severus, Ed, 'Abd Al-Masîh, II, Pt. I, 10.
(2) 163.
(3) B.G.A., III, 202.
(4) Mu'jam, II, 602.
(5) Qazwînî, Athâr Al-Bilâd, 129; Ibn Iyâs, I, 87 (10).
(6) I, 61.
(7) Quatremère, Mamlouks, Ia, 15; Amélineau, 117; Maspero et Wiet, 93; Becker, E.i., I, 911; Vasiliev, Byzance, I, n. I ; Bury, Eastern, 292.
(8) B.G.A., VII, 337-338.
(9) B.G.A., III, 201.

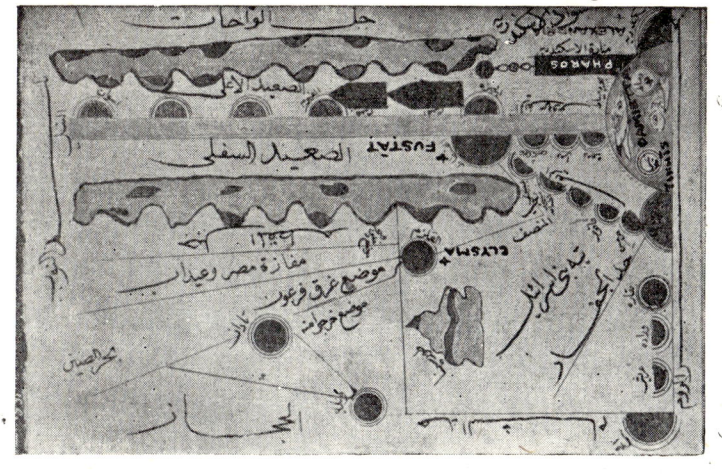

Early Egyptian Naval Centres as shown on Muqaddasi's map. Facsimile Miller, II Bd. Beiheft, Tafel 8.

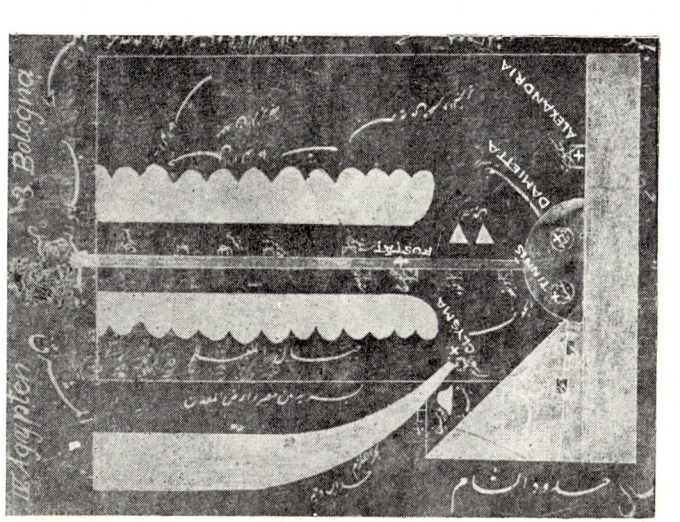

Early Egyptian Naval Centres as shown on Balkhi's map. Facsimile Miller. II Bd. Beiheft, Tafel 8.

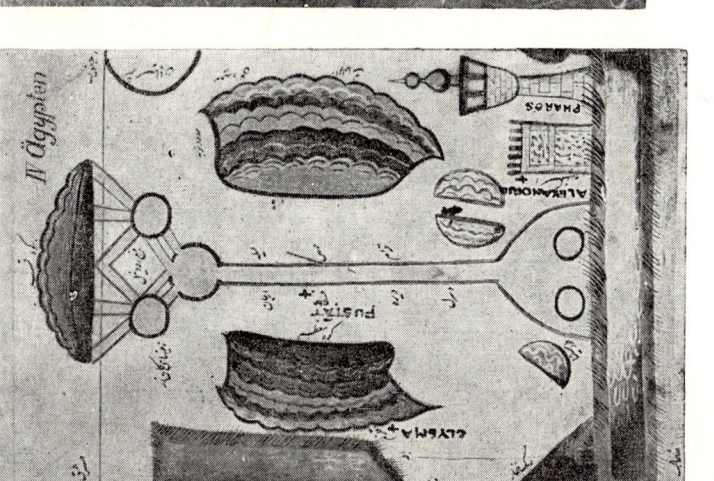

Early Egyptian Naval Centres as shown on Jayhānī's map. Facsimile Miller. V Bd. Beiheft, Tafel 8.

delightful seashore and Nâsirî Khusrû (1) states that a thousand vessels were moored there. Ibn Hawqal (2) says that it was among the important island which relied entirely upon ships for communications and he was impressed by the seamanship he saw there in spite of his remark that the lake was not deep. Its shallowness can be gathered from Tabarî's (3) narrative which says that after the Byzantines sacked Damietta in 238/853 their ships were unable to sail because they feared they would stick in the mud; they therefore went to its Ushtûm, a harbour about four parasangs (4) from Tinnîs, with a wall and iron gate built by the Caliph Mu'tasim. From the same historian's acount it is clear that they found catapults and balistae there which they burnt. According to Ibn Iyâs (5) the town was populous till 573/1177 and was finally destroyed in 624/1226.

IV. Arsenal on Island of Babylon

In 53/672-3, while Maslama ibn Mukhallad was governor in Egypt, the Byzantine fleet raided the town of Barallus, inflicting great losses on the Muslims. (6) As a result of this effective attack the first arsenal was established by the Muslims in Egypt in the following year on the island of Rawda. (7) Wiet (8) suggests that the project does not seem to have been completed because the Byzantines had made a descent on Tinnîs in 101/720 (9) and succeeded in their attack on Damietta in 238/853 which was, according to Muslim

---

(1) Ed. Schefer, 113; Ed. Khashshâb, 39.
(2) B.G.A., II, 102-103; Ed. Kramers, 156. For other descriptions v. Istakharî, B.G.A., I, 52; Amîr Abû'l-Hârith, 55; Yâqût, Mu'jam, I, 882 sq.; Qazwînî, Athâr Al-Bilâd, 117-118; Abû Sâlih, fol. 7 b 16; Amélineau, 507-508.
(3) III, 1418.
(4) Yâqût, Mu'jam, I, 276, gives six parasangs.
(5) I, 50.
(6) Ibn 'Abd Al-Hakam, 124 ; Kindî, Governors, 38 ; Maqrîzî, I.F., V, 80; Ibn Taghrî Birdî, I, 133 ; Caetani, Chronog., 588.
(7) Kindî, quoted by Qalqashandî, III, 339 ; Maqrîzî, Khitat, II, 178; 196; Suyûtî, Husn, II, 264; Casanova, Description de l'Egypte, III, 121, n. I; Caetani, Chronog., 600; Becker, E.I., I, 820.
(8) Corpus, II, 167.
(9) v. Kindî, ibid, 70; Maqrîzî, I.F., V, 87-88; Ibn Taghrî Birdî, I 244.

chroniclers, an incentive for building the first fleet in Egypt and fortifying the ports on the Mediterranean coast by the governor 'Anbasa ibn Ishâq.

The successful Byzantine attack in 238/853 was undoubtedly a lesson which was not lost upon the Muslims of Egypt. It forced them to contemplate seriously the building of a fleet and they set to work with zeal. Severus (1) records this fact and states that 'Anbasa «*ordered the construction of ships in all coastal towns because the Greeks came to Damietta at that time... Consequently many ships were built and every year they repaired those which were damaged and built new ones in place of those which were wrecked. They sailed in them to the land of the Greeks and made war on them*». Maqrîzî (2) relates that as a consequence of this attack the first fleet was built and that from this time it became a matter of prime importance in Egypt.

Wiet (3) tries to reconcile this with the foundation of the arsenal in 54/674 by suggesting that these historians mean that 'Anbasa was particularly concerned with building ships of war and that the arsenal founded in 54/674 had only constructed ships destined for the navigation of the Nile. Severus, (4) however, says that when Marwân II reached Egypt during his struggle with the 'Abbâsids he burnt the city of Fustât and when he knew his enemies had arrived at Al-Faramâ «*he sent troops in boats to the north to every district, that they might burn all the boats that they found on the river; and this purpose they carried out*». His object was to prevent his enemy from finding in the land «*anything to repay their trouble, nor boats by which they might cross over to him, and so that they would not remain there, but would turn upon their heels*». It would seem therefore, that the fleet built as the result of the sack of Damietta in 238/853 was the first after the destruction of ships by Marwân II.

The papyri show that warships were built at the arsenal

---

(1) Ed. 'Abd Al-Masîh, II, Pt. I, 9; Eng. Tr., 13.
(2) Khitat, II, 191.
(3) Corpus, II, 168.
(4) Pat. Or., V, fasc. I, 167 [421], 168 [422], 169 [423]. Kindî, Governors 95 (12) mentions that Marwân II burnt the two bridges.

of Babylon as the word **dromonaria** (1) is mentioned among the names of vessels built there, and that the arsenal was the chief dockyard as well as a naval base. In letter No. 1410, dated 91/709, the governor orders the people of Aphrodito to furnish four skilled workmen, three carpenters and one caulker, for the repair of ships at the arsenal of Babylon. «*In the name of God. Qurra ibn Sharîk, Governor, to you, the people of the village of Aphrodito. Furnish for the cleaning of the* **carabi** *and* **acatenaria** *and* **dromonaria**, *which are in the island of Babylon under the superintendence of ʽAbd Al-Aʽlâ ibn Abî Hakîm the superintendent in the present 8th indiction and the raid of the 9th indiction 4 = four skilled workmen with supplies for 3 months, viz. 2 = ship's carpenters at 2 S. per month, 1 = one carpenter at 1 1/3 S. per month, 1 = one caulker at 1 1/2 S. per month, and if you compound in money, pay for their wages and supplies as above specified only...*» (2)

Letter No. 1371 is an order for the refitting of ships in the island of Babylon and No. 1408 for the making of nails.(3) Accounts Nos. 1433 and 1434 (4) give details about sailors and skilled workmen including caulkers, carpenters, iron workers, blacksmiths and other labourers for the rapair, building and cleaning of ships. No. 1414 (5) mentions supplies of oil and salt «*for the maintenance of skilled workmen employed on the* **carabi** *at Babylon*». Nos. 1433 and 1434 (6) refer to fig and palm wood, copper chains, ropes, pads, piles and yarn as necessary supplies for the ships. In the last account, which Bell dates between 96-8/714-6, Al-Aʽlâ ibn Abî Hakîm seems to have been succeeded as superintendent of the arsenal by Al-Qâsim ibn Kaʽb who is mentioned as such in «*the present 14th indiction and for the raid of the 15th indiction*». (7)

---

(1) It is mentioned in letter No. 1410, and also in Bell, Der Islam IV, No. 1434, 92. For the meaning of the word, v. Infra, 125 sq.
(2) Bell, ibid, III, No. 1410, 132-133; P. Lond., IV, 79.
(3) No. 1371, quoted Infra, 77 sq.
No. 1408, quoted Infra, 81.
(4) Bell, Der Islam, III, No. 1433, 370-371, 373; IV, No. 1434, 92, 93.
(5) Bell, ibid, III, No. 1414, 137; P. Lond. IV, 124 sq.
(6) Bell, ibid, III, No. 1433, 369-370; IV, No. 1434, 89, 90, 91, 93.
(7) Bell, ibid, IV, No. 1434, 89, 90, 91.

The many references to the construction and repair of ships show that, in addition to the docks, there were extensive shipbuilding yards. The fact that sailors were mentioned as stationed at Babylon, suggests naval barracks connected with the arsenal (1) which is referred to in the papyri as the island of Babylon. By Babylon was meant the ancient town and fortifications of the Greeks, situated on the border of Upper and Lower Egypt and commanding the interior. Even to the present day portions of the ancient fortifications have survived in Qasr Al-Sham'. (2) The papyri collection seems to identify it with Fustât, (3) the new capital of Egypt. The difference was probably that Fustât was the name given more especially to the new official quarter as the seat of government, whereas Babylon, properly speaking, the name of the old fortress with its storehouses and arsenal, was applied loosely to the whole city as a place of residence. This may be borne out by the fact that the Muhâjirûn or Arab settlers, were always alluded to as of Fustât and never of Babylon. The term is said to have been practically on the site of old Memphis (4) which was still mentioned in the papyri, (5) in spite of its having fallen into decay since the foundation of Alexandria. Ya'qûbî (6) says that the city of Memphis was in ruins. Its remains are recorded by Ibn Al-Faqîh (7) who relates that he heard from an old man of a great palace which was in one block of stones and remarks that « *Memphis, the city of Pharaoh, has seventy gates and walls of iron and copper*». It seems that vast ruins and remains still marked the position of the ancient city at the time.

---

(1) Bell, P. Lond., IV, XXXIII.

(2) Becker, E.I., I, 550.

(3) Bell, ibid, IV, XVIII: Becker, E.I., I, 550. Cf. Bell, Der Islam, II, No. 1378, 377; P. Lond., IV, 51, with Bell, Der Islam, III, No. 1433, 370 sq.; P. Lond., IV, 282 sq.

(4) Lane-Poole, Hist. of Egypt,3. The town round Qasr Al-Sham' was called Misr, but Misr and Menf sometimes seem to have been interchanged. Thus 'Abd Al-Latîf, 65, says : « *Then there are the monuments which are in Misr Al-Qadîma and this city is by Al-Jîza beyond Fustât, and it is the city which the Pharoahs dwelt in, which was the seat of the kingly, government* ».

(5) Bell, P. Lond. IV, No. 1433 (180 sq.), 292; XVIII, n. 5.

(6) B.G.A., VII, 331.

(7) B.G.A., V, 58, 73.

Site of Arsenal

In the time of Ibn 'Abd Al-Hakam the arsenal was called **Jazîrat Al-Sinâ'a** (1) and the island **Jazîrat Misr,** or simply **Al Jazîra.** (2) The original distinction between Fustât and Babylon was naturally soon lost and the latter name fell into disuse except with the Copts. (3) When the Muslims conquered Egypt there was but one island in the Nile in this neighbourhood (4) which later formed the nucleus of the modern island of **Rawda.** This last name was not known to Istakhrî, Ibn Hawqal, Muqaddasî and Yâqût; (5) it is first found in the work of Ibn Duqmâq (6) (d. 809/1406). Qalqashandî (7) says the island of **Al-Sinâ'a** was commonly known as **Al-Rawda** (the Park), on account of its excellent site, palaces, gardens and beautiful surroundings. The name is said to have been in use since the time of the Fâtimid Minister Al-Afdal ibn Badr Al-Jamâlî (d. 515/1121), down to the present day. (8) In the time of Al-Idrîsî (d. 561/1166), it was also called **Dâr Al-Miqyâs** (9) (the place of the Nilometer), which Usâma ibn Zayd Al-Tanûkhî set up (10) at the southern end of the island, during the Caliphate of

---

(1) Ibn 'Abd Al-Hakam, 90, 127; Mas'ûdî, Murûj, II, 366; Kindî, Governors, 78 (4), 287 (7); Qalqashandî, III, Germ. Tr., 59; Maqrîzî, Khitat, II, 178; Wiet, Corpus, II, 167. Maspero et Wiet, Matériaux, 68, say that the arsenal was called **Jazîrat Al-Sinâ'a** in the time of Kindî (d. 350/961). Ibn 'Abd Al-Hakam mentions the name earlier.

(2) Ibn 'Abd Al-Hakam, 16, 64; Istakhrî, B.G.A., I, 49; Ibn Hawqal, B.G.A., II, 96; Muqaddasî, B.G.A., III, 198; Abû Sâlih, fol. 33b, 112, calls it the island of Misr; Maqrîzî, Khitat, II, 177-178; Suyûtî, Husn, II, 263-268, repeats the narrative of Maqrîzî; 'Alî Mubârak, XVIII, 7.

(3) Becker, E.I., 550.

(4) Qalqashandî, III, 339; Maqrîzi, Khitat, II, 177-178; Suyûtî, Husn, II, 263.

(5) Istakhrî, B.G.A., I. 49; Ibn Hawqal, B.G.A., II, 96; Muqaddasî, B.G.A., II, 197-200; Yâqût, Mu'jam, II, 80 sq.; Mushtarak, 103; Marâsid, I, 255.

(6) IV, 109.

(7) III, 339; Germ. Tr., 59. Ibn Al-Mutawwaj, quoted by Suyûtî, Husn, II, 263, says that it was called **Rawda** because it was unique among the islands in Egypt as it was encircled by the Nile.

(8) Ibn Muyassar, quoted by Suyûtî, Husn, II, 2 65, says that Al-Afdal built **Al-Rawda.**

(9) Idrîsî, Nuzhat Al-Mushtâq, [112].

(10) Ibn 'Abd Al-Hakam, 16; Ibn Duqmâq, IV, 64; Maqrîzî, I.F., I, 247, 249. Ibn 'Abd Al-Hakam, 99, and Ibn Taghrî Birdî, I, 71, 231, state that Usâma was the manager of finance in Egypt.

Al-Walîd ibn 'Abd Al-Malik to replace the earlier one inside the fortress of Babylon. (1)

With Babylon the island formed a single strong fortress guarding the passage of the Nile. Ibn Duqmâq (2) says that the Muslims attacked the island during the siege of Babylon and that when the Byzantines withdrew 'Amr demolished part of its walls and towers which remained in a dismantled state until they were rebuilt by Ibn Tûlûn in 263/876. Maqrîzî describes the fort as overlooking the Nile, up which boats came to the Iron Gate on the western side. He further adds that the river had taken a more westward course since that time, and that the entire district east of the fortress was an open cultivated plain. Gardens and vineyards spread to the north, while churches and convents dotted the landscape between them and the mountains as far as the mosque of Ibn Tûlûn. A few of them exist today within and without the walls of Cairo, though many were destroyed in the 8th/14th century by Al-Malik Al-Nâsir ibn Qalâwûn. (3)

Opposite the fortress, situated on the Nile bank, lay the island of Rawda which was connected with Babylon (4) on the east bank and Jîza (5) on the west bank by means of two bridges (6) of boats fastened together with planks. Istakhrî mentions both of them and Ibn Hawqal adds that each was made of thirty boats. (7) Idrîsî (8) states that one

---

(1) Maqrîzî, translated by Butler, App. to Abû Sâlih, 325, says : «Here (in Qasr Al-Sham'), before Islam, was the Nilometer of which there are traces to this day». The Nilometer of Usâma was destroyed by the water according to Al-Qudâ'î, quoted by Maqrîzî, I.F., I, 253.
(2) IV, 109, Qalqashandî, III ,339; Suyûtî, Husn, II, 263-264, and 'Alî Mubârak, XVIII, 7, say that the island was there from early times and that in the Byzantine period there was a fortress with walls. For the origin of the fortress v. Butler, 243 sq.
(3) Maqrîzî, Khitat, I, 286. Abû Sâlih, 133, mentions many churches in this region which long survived the conquest.
(4) Butler, 245, says that the name Babylon lingers on today, not as the name of the fortress which is called Qasr Al-Sham', but in connection with a little convent a short distance to the south.
(5) Al-Jîza is the name of the town on the west bank of the Nile, opposite Cairo, and it gives its name to the province.
(6) Ibn 'Abd Al-Hakam, 132, and Kindî, Governors, 78 (4), 95 (12, 16), 218 (4), mention that Jazîrat Al-Fustât lay between the two bridges.
(7) Istakhrî, B.G.A., I, 49; Ibn Hawqal, B.G.A., II, 96.
(8) Nuzhat Al-Mushtâq [112]. v. also Maqrîzî, II, 170; I.F., I, 265; Suyûtî, Husn, II, 267-268.

consisted of that number whilst the other, which was connected with Al-Jîza, was of nearly double that number. Butler, (1) following Hamaker, says that the two bridges existed before the conquest, as part of the contract made on the surrender of Babylon was that the Copts should keep them in repair. In the time of the 'Abbâsid Caliph Al-Ma'mûn there was one known as the old bridge extending across the whole width of the Nile. (2) Qalqashandî (3) says that the bridge of boats which joined the island with Fustât remained until the Caliph Al-Ma'mûn went to Egypt and had a new wooden bridge built. He adds that both were destroyed by a gale after his departure; the new bridge was then replaced and the old one completely done away with. (4) The old bridge may probably date back to the beginnings of Muslim rule when it was replaced by a new one.

The above details aid in deciding the important question of the site of the arsenal. Mas'ûdî, (5) trying to fix its position, says: «*The island of Al-Sinâ'a is situated between Al-Fustât and Al-Jîza. It is necessary to cross one bridge to get to Fustât on the east side and another to get to Al-Jîza on the west side.*» Ibn Hawqal(6) adds: «*Fustât is situated on the eastern bank of the Nile ... It is a magnificent city at which the Nile is divided into two parts ... The first part contains magnificent buildings and beautiful houses and is called Al-Jazîra* (the island)*, to which they pass from Fustât by a bridge made of thirty boats; from Al-Jazîra there is another bridge to the other part which is called Al-Jîza*». According to some statements, (7) the island was at first practically in the centre

---

(1) 129, n. 19. Becker, E.I., I, 820, says that there is apparently no definite information regarding the existence of both bridges at the time of the conquest. They may have existed and may have suffered damage when Fustât was burnt in 132/749. v. Supra, 36, n. 4.
(2) Kindî, Governors, 192. Ibn 'Abd Al-Hakam, 136 (20), mentions the old bridge.
(3) III, 339.
(4) Qudâ'î quoted by Maqrîzî, Khitat, II, 170, remarks that it still existed in his life time (at the time of the Fâtimids). Muqaddasî, B.G.A., III, 200, says that the bridge which joined Jîza with the island was destroyed when the Fâtimids arrived.
(5) Murûj, II, 366.
(6) B.G.A., II, 96.
(7) Ibn Duqmâq, IV, 109; Maqrîzî, Khitat, II, 170; Suyûtî, Husn, II, 263; 'Alî Mubârak, XVIII, 7.

of the river. The arm which separated it from Babylon, however, became silted up. The arsenal also seems to have been closely connected with the fortress.

The Arsenal in the time of the Tûlûnids

From the time Babylon fell into Muslim hands, no further information is given about the island fortress. Ibn Tûlûn, feeling his power threatened, was the first (1) to restore it to its former position in 263/876. Al-Muwaffaq, jealous of his independent attitude, sent Mûsâ ibn Bughâ at the head of an army to subdue him. (2) Hearing of his approach, Ibn Tûlûn set about fortifying his capital and prepared for a vigorous defence. The Iraqi troops halted at Raqqa where they revolted because of the lack of provisions and arrears in pay. Mûsâ having estimated the enemy forces, decided to abandon his rebellious army and returned to Iraq. Thus the Caliph's expedition against Egypt failed (3) and the energetic military preparations of Ibn Tûlûn were begun. He had taken the precaution of constructing a fortress (4) on the island of Rawda as a refuge for his family and a storehouse for his wealth and treasures in time of need. Madaynî (5) estimates that each stone cost one dirhem and that the total expense of its construction was two hundred thousand dinars.

Ibn Tûlûn also provided himself with a fleet of a hundred warships for the defence of his capital. (6) Realising the necessity of a well equipped naval base, he enlarged the arsenal

---

(1) Ibn Duqmâq, IV, 109, says that the walls and towers of the island remained in a dismantled state till Ibn Tûlûn rebuilt them in 263/876.
(2) The Caliph wanted to replace Ibn Tûlûn by Mâjûr who was governor of Damascus. For this expedition v. Madaynî, 86; Kindî, Governors, 218; Zakî Hassan, 58-63.
(3) Becker, Beiträge, II, 149; Zakî Hassan, 62.
(4) Kindî, ibid, 218, says that the fortress of Al-Jazîra was between the two bridges. v. Madaynî, 86; Qalqashandî, III, 339; Ibn Duqmâq, IV, 109; Maqrîzî, Khitât, II, 180; Suyûyî, Husn, II, 264; 'Alî Mubârak, XVIII, 7; Wiet, Corpus, II, 168.
(5) 87, 351. Ibn Taghrî Birdî, III, 12, gives 80,000 dinars for the expenses of fortress.
(6) Madaynî, 87; Kindî, ibid, 218, 219; Ibn Khaldûn, 'Ibar, IV, 300; Maqrîzî, Khitat, II, 180; Suyûtî, Husn, II, 264; 'Alî Mubârak, XVIII, 7-8; Becker, Beiträge, II, 167. For names of ships of Ibn Tûlûn's fleet v. Infra, App, II, 149 sq.

at Al-Jazîra, retaining the site (1) where it was established in 54/674. It is impossible to make a serious study of the Tûlûnid fleet owing to the scarcity of texts but it seems that it did not play an important part during the Tûlûnid dynasty. Madaynî (2) has preserved a text relating to Abû Kâmil Shujâ' ibn Aslam, the director of the arsenal, who was ordered by Ibn Tûlûn to spare no expense for good, solid shipbuilding: «*I am highly esteemed by all my people — the sea alone has no respect for me. Therefore be extravagant in one thing only — the building of ships. By showing great skill and care in this you will, with God's help, be preserved from all its dangers.*» This director seems to have been imprisoned (3) by Ibn Tûlûn for some unknown reason. It may have been merely because he was a relative of Ahmad ibn Al-Qâsim ibn Aslam who had taken part in the revolt of Ibn Tûlûn's son, Al-'Abbâs. (4) Whatever the cause may have been, the imprisonment must have been prior to the appointment to this high office.

Ibn Tûlûn's military preparations probably ceased after Mûsâ's retreat. Al-Muwaffaq, whose resources were exhausted by the war against the Zinj, was forced to neglect Egypt and to conclude terms of peace with Ibn Tûlûn. (5) Madaynî (6) says that ibn Tûlûn stopped his military preparations as soon as he heard of the death of Mûsâ and gave money as charity for the poor and the workmen who were employed. The poet Muhammad ibn Dâ'ûd, who was well known for his satirical writings against the Tûlûnids, made the most of the cessation of ibn Tûlûn's military activities. He wrote verses to ridicule him which Muslim historians have preserved. (7) The following translation gives the sense but none of its original charm:

---

(1) Kindî, Governors, 218; Maqrîzî, Khitat, II, 196-197; Suyûtî, Husn, II, 265; 'Alî Mubârak, XVIII, 7; Wiet, Corpus, II, 168.
(2) 208; reproduced by Ibn Sa'îd, Ed. Vollers, 28.
(3) Madaynî, 208; Ibn Sa'îd, Ed. Vollers, 28.
(4) Kindî, ibid, 220. For the revolt of Al-'Abbâs v. Zakî Hassan, 64 sq.
(5) Zakî Hassan, 63; Muir, Caliphate, 545, 550.
(6) 88. v. Ibn Duqmâq, IV, 109.
(7) Kindî, ibid, 218; Maqrîzî, Khitat, II, 180; Suyûtî, Husn, II, 264-265.

« When Ibn Bughâ was resting at Raqqa,
Ibn Tûlûn soiled his legs, ankles and heels.

He built a fortress on the island of Rawda,
A sure retreat in which to lie hid.

The workmen, overwhelmed with fatigue,
He roughly and violenty treated.

He dug trenches all round Al-Jîza,
Nearly dying of fear and alarm.

His galleys lay still in the river,
Only wood and tar could be seen.

When launched, they were covered with shame,
Not once were triumphant with glory.

Not fitted to fight the Byzantines
But to flee in time of disaster.»

Maqrîzî (1) quotes some other lines of the poet Sa'îd ibn Al-Qâdî in praise of the Tûlûnids and the fortress of Rawda. The following gives the literal meaning but again the translation lacks the Arabic charm:

« When you come to the top of the bridge, gaze on the fortress with wonder, or cross over and approach it.

There you will see a monument the like of which no one could build, neither among the Bedouin nor among the settled people.

Such memorials never perish, though their builders pass away, but have an unfading glory which is an inspiration to those who come after them.»

---

(1) Khitat, II, 181. For other verses in praise of Ibn Tûlûn v. Kindî, Governors, 227-233.

The founder of the Tûlûnid dynasty was able to maintain his hold over Syria (1) and, according to Madaynî, (2) left two hundred large warships complete with equipment when he died. His successor Khumârawayh concluded peace with the ʿAbbâsid Caliph who assigned him the government of Egypt, Syria and Upper Mesopotamia for thirty years. (3)

The Arsenal in the time of the Ikhshîdids

Kindî mentions three attacks by the Fâtimid Caliph of North Africa during the governorship of Tikkîn. (4) The first attack (5) was in 302/914 when a fleet, under the leadership of Habâsa ibn Yûsuf, set sail for Alexandria and seized it without opposition. More than a hundred thousand men then marched towards Fustât but were beaten back by the governor's forces. Five years later a second attempt was made (6) and then in 308/921 the son of the Fâtimid Caliph ʿAbd Al-Rahmân was in charge of the fleet which reached Alexandria. He then captured Fayyûm and finding himself opposed by the combined forces of the ʿAbbâsid Caliph and Tikkîn he withdrew and returned home. (7)

Though these attempts of the Fâtimid Caliph were checked, they led Muhammad ibn Tughj to take precautions against any further attack. Kindî (8) relates that when the ʿAbbâsid Caliph Al-Râdî appointed Ibn Tughj governor of

---

(1) Zakî Hassan, 64 sq.; Muir, Caliphate, 549; Lane-Poole, Hist. of Egypt, 61 sq.
(2) 340, 349. Ibn Iyâs, I, 40, says one thousand ships. Lane-Poole, ibid, 71, gives one hundred warships.
(3) Kindî, Governors, 238, 240; Gibb, E.I., IV, 834.
(4) Tikkîn was govrenor of Egypt three times: the first from 297-302/910-5, the second from 307-9/920-1 and the third from 311-21/924-33. v. Kindî, ibid, 267, 273, 276, 278, 280-281; Maqrîzî I.F., V, 200-205; Suyûtî, Husn, II, 13; Ibn Iyâs, I, 42.
(5) Kindî, ibid, 269. Accounts of these attacks are given according to Kindî. For this expedition v. Tabarî, II, 2291, 2292-2293; Eutychius, Corp. Script. Christ., VII, 80, 110; Ibn Miskawayh, Margoliouth Edition, I, 36; Ibn Khallikân. II, 35; Ibn ʿIdhârî, I. 170; Maqrîzî, Ittiʿâz, 42; Suyûtî, Khulafâ, 153; Eng. Tr., 398.
(6) v. Infra, 63.
(7) Kindî, ibid, 277-278. v. Madaynî, 102; Ibn Al-Athîr, VIII, 98; Ibn Khaldûn, ʿIbar, IV, 39; Maqrîzî, ibid., 45.
(8) Governors, 286-287.

Egypt for the second time in 323/935, Habashî ibn Ahmad Al-Salamî (nickname Abû Mâlik), advanced with his North African troops (Maghâriba), and seized Fayyûm. He captured Ibn Tughj's fleet as it lay at anchor there and killed the admiral Sâ'id ibn Kalamlam and some of his men. The invaders returned to Alexandria and thence to Barqa, but on their way they stopped at the arsenal of Al-Rawda which they set on fire while Ibn Tughj and his forces watched the proceedings.(1) Ibn Sa'îd (2) adds that the governor was at the house of Khadîja bint Al-Fath, a widow of Ahmad Ibn Tûlûn, and, finding himself powerless to oppose the enemy, said: «*The arsenal there* (at Jazîra), *is a mistake. Build the arsenal here,* (Dâr bint Al-Fath).» Ibn Zûlâq records the following narrative of Al-Ikhshîd about the foundation of the new arsenal : «*I remember once, while I was taking a meal with Abû Mansûr Tikkîn, the governor of Egypt, the conversation turned upon the arsenal. He said that an arsenal separated from the governor by water was hardly worthty of the name. Those present agreed to its transfer, but when he raised the question of the position of the new site I decided not to say anything for the moment, although I would like to have proposed Dâr bint Al-Fath. I kept the idea to myself until such time as I should be governor. Now, by the will of God, I have fulfilled my aim.*» Ibn Sa'îd (3) gives another interesting tradition: «*When the new arsenal was still under construction and ships were being built, Al-Ikhshîd happened to ride past. An unknown woman called out to him in a loud voice, and was consequently brought before him that evening. She asked for help so that she might bring him money and treasures. He accordingly ordered some of his men to accompany her to the house of Bint Al-Fath and they returned laden with money, jewels, clothes and various other treasures such as had never seen before. The governor then commanded his officers to bring the woman before him that he might reward her, but unfortunately she had disappeared.*» The tradition further

---

(1) For this narrative v. Ibn Sa'îd, Ed. Tallqvist, 12-13; Ibn Duqmâq, IV, 12; Maqrîzî, Khitat, II, 181; Suyûtî, Kawkab, 15 (a).
(2) Ibid, 13-14. Also mentioned briefly by Ibn Duqmâq, IV, 12; Maqrîzî, Khitat, II, 181; Suyûtî, Kawkab, 15 (a).
(3) Ibid, 13-14, on the authority of Al-Husayn ibn Ahmad ibn Arîkha. v. Maqrîzî, Khitat, II, 181.

adds that this was the first money Al-Akhshîd received in Egypt and that he sent for the so called Sâlih ibn Nâfi' and said: «*It was my intention that when I became governor to build the arsenal at Dâr bint Al-Fath and turn the site of the old arsenal into a garden to be named Al-Mukhtâr* (the chosen). *Set to work immediately and plan a house and garden there for me and give me an estimate for the work.*» Accordingly Sâlih and some others drew up a plan for the garden and the palace, including accommodation for slaves and storerooms for clothes and provisions. Al-Ikhshîd was pleased with the proposed design but not with the cost of thirty thousand dinars which he said must be reduced. He accepted a second estimate of five thousand dinars (1) as being reasonable but finally said the work must be done at their own expense! Sâlih therefore raised subscriptions for it, contributing three hundred dinars himself and receiving five hundred dinars each from Abû 'Alî Khayr, Abû Bakr ibn Kalâ and Abû'l-ja'far ibn Al-Munfiq. Eventually six thousand dinars were collected. Zuqâq and Abû'l-Raddâd supervised the building operations. The magnificent garden was laid out for the exclusive use of Al-Ikhshîd who used to boast of it to the people of Iraq. (2)

Al-Ikhshîd died leaving one hundred warships, each being valued at three thousand dinars, and a number of pleasure boats known as '**ushâriyyât.** (3) Yahyâ ibn Sa'îd (4) says that ships were launched from the new arsenal after Ikhshîd's death and describes an accident which happened there on 9 Safar 349/April 960: «*The Muslims were making hasty preparations for a war with the Byzantines. Kâfûr Al-Ikhshîd had gone to the arsenal where he was waiting to launch a large warship. On another vessel, lying at anchor near the river bank, many people had crowded together, sitting on one side of the boat to watch the proceedings. Unfortunately the packed boat overtuned and all lost their lives. Nearby were*

---

(1) Ibn Sa'îd, Ed. Tallqvist, 13-14; Maqrîzî, Khitat, II, 181, and Suyûtî, Kawkab, 16 (b); Husn, II, 265, say that the expenses of building the garden were about 5000 dinars. 'Alî Mubârak, XVIII, 8, gives 500,000.

(2) Ibn Sa'îd, ibid, 14. v. Maqrîzî, Khitat, II, 181; Suyûtî, Husn, II, 265.

(3) Ibn Sa'îd, ibid, 44. For '**ushâriyyât** v. Infra, App. II, 150 sq.

(4) Pat. Or., XVIII, 780 [82].

several other boats, alongside each other, also filled with sightseers. These too, sank and all on board perished, the total loss of life being about five hundred persons. There was no street that did not mourn for the lost ones.» A passage in Kindî (1) indicates that Fustât was an important centre for ships : «*All the cities of Egypt were reached by vessels which carried food, property and implements to Fustât, each one conveying a cargo of five hundred camel loads.»* Muqaddasî (2) also gives an interesting account of the ships there: «*I was walking along the bank of the river one day, wondering at the great number of ships at anchor or under way, when a man accosted me, saying: 'What is your country?' I said I came from the Holy City, to which he replied: 'It is a large city, but I tell you, my friend (May God preserve your honour), that the vessels along this shore and those that have left it for different towns and villages, are so numerous that were they to go to your native town they would be able to carry away all the inhabitants and the stones and wood so that people would say: 'There was a city here.'»*

Site of New Arsenal

Ibn Tûlûm was the first to convert the island of Rawda into a regular fortress. But the Nile was more powerful than his will, for the fortifications were partly destroyed by its waters; (3) they were finally demolished by Al-Ikhshîd in 323/935. Two years later, in Sha'bân 325/June 937, this governor set up a new arsenal (4) north of Fustât on the ruins of the house belonging to the widow of Ibn Tûlûn, and the island of Rawda became more of a royal country residence where he erected a palace and laid out a garden called Al-**Mukhtâr.**

After the transfer of the arsenal to the borders of Fustât, historians give no information about that of Rawda, until they mention the new organisation of the Fâtimid minister Al-Ma'mûm Al-Batâ'ihî in 516/1122. No author consulted mentions the date when the naval constructions were

---

(1) Fadâ'il Misr, 25, 32.
(2) B.G.A., III, 198.
(3) Qalqashandî, III, 339; Suyûtî, Husn, II, 265; Kawkab, 15 (b); Becker, E.I., I, 820.
(4) v. Supra. 45 sq.

abandoned at Fustât (Misr), to be transferred again to Rawda. (1) It is supposed that the latter arsenal was used by the Ikhshîdids and Fâtimids and that both dockyards functioned at the same time. (2) Wiet (3) suggests that perhaps a new arsenal was built by Al-Afdal ibn Badr Al-Jamâlî to whom the island owes its name. However, when the arsenal of Rawda was finally given up, that of Misr continued to be used until about 700/1300. (4) Ibn Al-Ma'mûn (5) says: *«When Wazîr Ma'mûn was in power, all the fleet, without exception, docked at the arsenal of Rawda. He disapproved of this procedure and decided that* **shawâni** *(6) and ships of the State fleet used for navigation on the Nile should be built at the arsenal of Misr which he had enlarged by the addition of Dâr Al-Zibîb* (Hotel of Dried Grapes). *He erected the pavilion there, on which his name can be seen to this day, and to which the Caliph used to go to see the fleet launched. The Wazîr agreed that the* **shalandiyyât** *and* **harbiyyât** *(7) (warships), should be built at the arsenal of Rawda».* Some lines before this passage Maqrîzî gives the following details: *«Near one of the pavilions of the Caliphs there was an arsenal on the old bank of the river* (Nile) *at Misr. The Caliph and his suite used to go there to get the* **'ushâriyyât** (pleasure boats) *which were brought for his use. Thence he would go to the Nilometer at the time of high floods to take part in the ceremony connected with it. (8) This arsenal was the headquarters of maritime construction,* **Dîwân Al-'Amâ'ir.** *(9)* Both it and the pavilion

---

(1) v. Maqrîzî, Khitat, II, 181; Suyûtî, Husn, II, 265; 'Alî Mubârak, XVIII, 8.
(2) Casanova, Noms Coptes, B.I.F.A.O., I, 160.
(3) Corpus, II, 168-169.
(4) Maqrîzî, Khitât, II, 197, gives this year and says that Ibn Al-Mutawwaj (d. 730/1330), saw the gate of the arsenal in Ibn Kaysân's garden. 'Alî Mubârak, I, 16, follows Maqrîzî.
(5) Quoted by Maqrîzî, Khitat, I, 482, reproduced, II, 197; Ibn Muyassar, quoted by Suyûtî, Husn, II, 265; Kawkab, 15 (a) ; 'Alî Mubârak, I, 16; XVIII, 8.
(6) Maqrîzî, Khitat, I, 482, mentions **shawânî**. Suyûtî, Kawkab, 15 (a), mentions **sarâyir** which ought to be emended. For **shawâni** v. Infra, 131 sq.
(7) For these two types of ships v. Infra, 129 sq.
(8) v. Qalqashandî, III, 516-518; Germ. Tr., 209-210; Quatremère, Mamlouks, IIa, 24.
(9) The Ministry of the Holy War was called «Dîwân Al-Jihâd» of which «Dîwân Al-'Amâ'ir» was a part. v. Qalqashandî, X, 366, 413, 445; Maqrîzî, Khitat, II, 197.

were used until the fall of the Fâtimids when they were replaced by a garden called Bustân ibn Kaysân, known to-day as Bustân Al-Tawâshî, situated at the entrance to Al-Marâgha, opposite to Bustân Al-Jurf, and on the left hand side when leaving Al-Marâgha to go to Al-Kayyâra and the gate (bâb) of Misr. »

The directions given at the end of the last text help to determine approximately the site of Al-Ikhshîd's arsenal. The following conclusions can now be drawn: Bustân Al-Tawâshî, previously known as Bustân ibn Kaysân, was the site of the arsenal and pavilion which Al-Ma'mûn Al-Bata'ihî built on the site of Al-Ikhshîd's arsenal.(1) It lay between Mashhad Zîn Al-'Abdîn and Qantarat Al-Sad.(2) To the west, facing Ibn Kaysân's garden, and divided from it by the Khatt Al-Marâgha road, was another garden called Bustân Al-Jurf.(3) The arsenal lay towards to the north, near the convent of St. Mennas which can still be seen north of Misr Al-'Atîqa (Old Cairo), near the Christian cemetery.(4) Casanova(5) seems less inspired when he says that the arsenal may have corresponded to that which Ibn Duqmâq (6) calls **sinâ'at al-'askar,** which is, to be exact, in the district belonging to Al-'Askar rather than to Misr. But it is not certain that **sinâ'at al-'askar,** was an arsenal; (7) on the other hand, Ibn Duqmâq (8) knew the arsenal of Misr well and this seems to dispel any doubt.

---

(1) Maqrîzî, Khitat, I, 482; II, 117, 197; Suyûti, Husn, II, 265; Kawkab, 15 (a); 'Alî Mubârak, I, 16; XVIII, 8; Wiet, Corpus, II, 168.

(2) The garden, according to various passages in Maqrîzî, Khitat, I, 286 (34), 345 (29), 482 (31); II, 133 (5), 143 (14), 197 (22 sq.), was next to Al-Khalîj. Casanova, Noms Coptes, B.I.F.A.O., I, 160, says that Maqrîzî was probably somewhat confused as that district was some distance from the Nile.

(3) v. Maqrîzî, Khitat, I, 482; 'Alî Mubârak, I, 16; Guest and Richmond, J.R.A.S., 1903, 799.

(4) Wiet, Corpus, II, 167, v. Casanova, Foustât, M.I.F.A.O., XXXV, pl. III, 6.

(5) Noms Coptes, B.I.F.A.O., XXXV, 224.

(6) IV, 29 (7), 34 (19).

(7) Casanova, Foustât, M.I.F.A.O., XXXV, 224.

(8) Ibn Duqmâq, IV. 12, says that **al-sinâ'a** was at first on the **Jazîra** (island).

CHAPTER II

ARSENALS AND NAVAL CENTRES IN SYRIA, AFRICA AND CRETE

I. Arsenals and Naval Centres in Syria

The Muslim adminstration soon began to regard the navy as one of its chief preoccupations. It was Mu'âwiya who first encouraged the Muslims to undertake maritime activities and is said to have asked 'Umar's permission to lead a naval expedition. (1) The latter obstinately refused and would go no further than order the fortification and garrisoning of the coastal towns. (2) Mu'âwiya, however, insisted so much that 'Uthmân is said to have allowed him to carry out a naval enterprise, instructing him to keep reinforcements in readiness in coastal areas. (3) By this time Syria had come entirely under Mu'âwiya and the revenue, soldiers and ships of that powerful kingdom were dedicated to increasing the empire of the Caliphs. He actively began the construction of new vessels in his Phoenician ports (4) and the Syrian and Egyptian squadrons worked in the greatest harmony. Maritime operations, whether from Egypt under Ibn Abî Al-Sarh or from Syria under Mu'âwiya, were

---

(1) Tabarî, I, 2820-2821; Ibn Khaldûn, Muqaddima, II, 33; Maqrîzî, Khitat. II. 190.

(2) Balâdhurî, 128. v. Caetani, Chronog., 218, 239.

(3) Balâdhurî, 128; Ibn Khaldûn, ibid, II, 33.

(4) Vasiliev, Byz. Empire, I, 259; Kindermann, E.I., Supp., 194.

directed against the Byzantines. Wâqidî (1) relates that the Egyptian and Syrian fleets combined for the first expedition against Cyprus. Both he and the Tyrian Hishâm ibn Al-Layth (2) state that Mu'âwiya made repairs in 'Akkâ (Acre) and Sûr (Tyre), at the time of his expedition against Cyprus. According to Theophanes and Michael the Syrian (3) he prepared a fleet at Tripolis in 35/655 with a view to attacking Constantinople.

The Umayyads paid greater attention to nautical activities. The Caliph Mu'âwiya realised the importance of seacoast cities. A tradition related by Balâdhurî (4) says : «*He transferred a number of Persians in 42/662 from Ba'labak, Hims and Antioch to towns on the sea-coast, of the district of Al-Urdun, namely, Tyre, Acre and elsewhere.*» Ya'qûbî (5) says that the district was entirely peopled by Persians, brought there by the Caliph Mu'âwiya. He also established a considerable number of Jews at Tripolis in order to increase the population. (6)

In 49/669 the Byzantine fleet raided the Syrian coast towns after which Mu'âwiya built dockyards at 'Akkâ for the district of Al-Urdun and arranged for artisans to settle along the coast. (7) Balâdhurî, (8) quoting a tradition of Muhammad ibn Sahm Al-Antâkî, says that **al-sinâ'a** at that time (49/669), was confined to Egypt. Becker, (9) following Balâdhurî, concludes that there appears to have been a **dâr-sinâ'a** only in Egypt. From the early naval activities of Mu'âwiya it seems that the Muslims utilised the Byzantine

---

(1) Quoted by Tabarî, I, 2826. v. Balâdhurî, 154; Tabarî, I, 2820, 2824; Maqrîzî, Khitat, II, 190; Wellhausen, N.G.W. Gött, 1901, 418.
(2) Balâdhurî, 117 (11); Yâqût, Mu'jam, III, 708.
(3) Theophanes, quoted by Bury, Later, II, 290, and Finlay, I, 377; Michael, Ed. Chabot, II, fasc. V, 445; Ed. Langlois, 239. v. Brooks, C.M.H., II, 393.
(4) 117.
(5) B.G.A., VII, 327.
(6) Balâdhurî, 127.
(7) Balâdhurî, 117. Agapius, Pat. Or., VIII, 492 [232], merely says that in the fourteenth year of Mu'âwiya, the Byzantine fleet raided the Syrian coast towns (Tyre and Sidon).
(8) 117 (18).
(9) E.I., I, 918. Honigmann, E.I., IV, 557, and Buhl, E.I., I, 241, merely say that Mu'âwiya caused dockyards to be built at 'Akkâ after the Byzantine raid.

dockyards in Syria and, according to the papyri, in Egypt also. Moreover, as the date of the first Muslim arsenal in Egypt was 54/674,(1) that in Syria at 'Akkâ was five years earlier.

'Abd Al-Malik ibn Marwân restored Sûr, Caesarea and the suburbs of 'Akkâ which had fallen into ruins.(2) The papyri show that Laodicea, on the Syrian coast, was one of the principal naval centres. Account No. 1434 contains items dated 96/714 which refer to certain sailors setting out from there. In it there is mention of four sailors from Aphrodito sent to the Orient «*for the* **acatia** *and* **dromonaria** *for the raid of the 12th indiction, who set out from Laodicea and returned in the present 13th indiction.*»(3) According to Wâqidî(4) Sûr replaced 'Akkâ as a naval station under the Marwânids and remained as such till Mutawakkil's reign. A tradition quoted by Balâdhurî(5) gives the reason for the transfer of the arsenal to Sûr. When the Caliph Hishâm wished to purchase mills and storehouses from one of the descendants of Abû Mu'ayt, and the latter refused to sell them, he had the arsenal removed to Sûr where he built magazines and docks.

Muslim geographers describe Sûr as a strongly fortified city on the Syrian coast, thickly populated and surrounded by fertile country. Ya'qûbî(6) describes it thus : «*Tyre is the chief of the coastal cities and contains the arsenal* (**dâr al-sinâ'a**). *From here sail the Caliph's ships on expeditions against the Greeks. In spite of its fortifications it is a beautiful place.*» Qudâma(7) also states that «*the seacoast cities of Al-Urdun are Sûr, and 'Akkâ; the former contains the shipbuilding yards.*» (8) Muqaddasî (9) writes : «*Tyre is a fortified city on the sea and one enters the town*

---

(1) v. Supra, 35.
(2) Balâdhurî, 117, 143.
(3) Bell, P. Lond., IV, No. 1434 (241-242); Der Islam, IV, 91-2. For similar information v. Bell, P. Lond., IV, No. 1435 (64-65), 327; Der Islam, IV, 94.
(4) Quoted by Balâdhurî, 118.
(5) 117. v. Yâqût, Mu'jam, III, 708.
(6) B.G.A., VII, 327.
(7) B.G.A., VI, 255.
(8) The arsenal of Tyre is mentioned by Ya'qûbî and Qudâma. Later geographers and travellers do not mention it.
(9) B.G.A., III, 163-4.

through one gate only, over a bridge, and the sea lies all round. The harbour is an area enclosed by triple walls with no earth appearing. The ships enter every night and then a chain (1) *is drawn across which is mentioned by Muhammad ibn Al-Hasan Al-Shaybânî in his work entitled Al-Ikrâh... Tyre is a beautiful and magnificent city. Many artificers dwell here and ply their special trades. Between Tyre and Acre lies a bay and thus it is said that 'Acre is opposite Tyre but getting to it you will tire,' that is, when travelling all along the seashore.* » (2)

The 'Abbâsid Caliphs apprehended the danger of Byzantine raids and maintained the shipbuilding yards established by the Umayyads at Sûr, but the Caliph Mutawakkil transferred them to 'Akkâ in 247/861. (3)

To maintain his hold on Syria, Ibn Tûlûn developed the naval base at 'Akkâ, surrounding the harbour by a massive stone embankment. There is a most interesting description of its construction in the account of Muqaddasî (4) whose grandfather was the architect; « *'Akkâ* », he says, « *was a fortified city on the sea-coast... the defences of which were greatly strengthened after Ibn Tûlûn visited it. He had already seen the fortifications of Tyre where the harbour was protected by an encircling wall, and he wanted to fortify 'Akkâ on similar lines. Artificers were brought from all over the province, but when the scheme was laid before them, everyone averred that no man was able to lay foundations under the water. Then someone mentioned my grandfather, Abû Bakr the architect, and said that if it were possible to do such a thing he was the only man who could undertake it. Ibn Tûlûn thereupon ordered his representative in Jerusalem to send my grandfather to him. On his arrival they asked*

---

(1) The chain was to prevent the Byzantines from molesting the city. v. B.G.A., III, 164, n. b. Ibn Battûta, Voyage, I, 131, mentions this chain across the mouth of the port. For Al-Shaybânî v. Hajjî Khalîfa, V, No. 9882, 48.

(2) For other descriptions of Tyre v. Arculf, P.P.T.S., III, 47; St. Willibard, P.P.T.S., III, 26; Ibn Al-Faqîh, B.G.A., V, 105, 123; Istakhrî, B.G.A., I, 59; Ibn Hawkal, B.G.A., II, 114; Nâsirî Khusrû, Ed. Schefer, 46-50; Ed. Khashshâb, 15; Benjamin, 18 sq.; Ibn Jubayr, 304-305; Yâqût, Mu'jam, III, 433. For a plan of Tyre v. Conder and Kitchener, III, App. 434 sq., and for the general account, I, 72.

(3) Balâdhurî, 118.

(4) B.G.A., III, 162-163.

his opinion. 'The matter is easy,' he replied 'Let them bring big strong sycamore beams.' When they were bound together, he caused them to be floated on the surface of the water, as for a land fort, with an opening on the west side for a mighty gateway. He then raised a structure of stone and cement upon them, strengthening it by inserting great columns after every few courses, until the beams began to sink under the enormous pressure. As soon as they rested on the sand, he ceased building for a year so that the structure might settle. He finally connected these defences with the ancient walls of the city and built a bridge across the gate of the port. When the ships entered the harbour at night a chain was drawn across as at Tyre. Before this measure was taken the enemy used to do serious damage to the vessels collected there. My grandfather is said to have received one thousand dinars besides robes of honour, horses and other gifts as his reward, and his name was inscribed over his work.» This account is quoted verbatim by Yâqût and Qazwînî(1) who add that the name of Abû Bakr was still there. The method of building described was frequently used by architects during the period of the Crusades. The remains of the double mole which formed the inner harbour of 'Akkâ still exist, though for the most part they lie under water.(2) The Persian traveller, Nâsirî Khusrû(3) mentions the harbour chain of 'Akkâ and describes how it was slackened until it was deep enough in the water to allow ships to pass safely into the harbour. It was then tightened to prevent any enemy vessel getting in to destroy them.

The Caliph Mutawakkil distributed the fleet and naval forces among the Syrian coast towns.(4) Speaking of the watch stations there when Byzantine ships brought Muslim captives for ransom, Muqaddasî(5) says: «Whenever a Greek vessel appears the Muslims sound the horns; at night they light a beacon on the tower and in the daytime they make a

(1) Yâqût, Mu'jam, III, 707-708; Qazwînî, Athâr Al-Bilâd, 148.
(2) v. Le Strange, P.P.T.S., III, 30, 31, n. I; Palestine, 328; Conder and Kitchener, I, 160 sq.
(3) Ed. Schefer, 50; Ed. Khashshâb, 15-16. For other descriptions of 'Akkâ v. Idrîsî, Nuzhat Al-Mushtâq, [133]; Benjamin, 19; Ibn Jubayr, 303, 305.
(4) Balâdhurî, 118.
(5) B.G.A., III, 177.

great smoke. Between the watch stations along the coast are high towers guarded by a company of men who light the beacon as soon as a Greek ship arrives and so pass on the signal from one tower to another. Before an hour has elapsed trumpets sound in the city and drums beat in the tower calling those responsible to their watch station; they hurry out in force with their arms.» Among these cities he mentions Gaza, Ascalon, Jaffa and Arsuf and states that, whereas Ascalon's harbour was poor that of Jaffa was excellent.(1) Arab geographers describe the latter town as the emporium of Palestine and the port of Al-Ramla.(2) Beirut was the harbour of Damascus and, like Sûr, had a chain which could be fixed across the entrance to prevent ships entering or leaving.(3) Yâqût(4) calls it a famous city. According to Ya'qûbî(5) Tripolis possessed a very fine harbour affording anchorage for a thousand vessels. Ibn Hawqal(6) says it was here that the Damascenes and other men of the provinces were garrisoned and that it was an assembly point for military expeditions. An excellent description of the city is given by Nâsirî Khusrû(7) who states that the town was so situated that three sides were on the sea whilst on the eastern side was a battlemented fortress of hewn stone, on the top of which ballistae were fixed as a means of defence, for the inhabitants feared the Greeks would attack in their ships.

Naval Centre at Tarsus

An important naval centre was Tarsus, pronounced Tarasûs or Tursûs in Arabic.(8) According to Wâqidî,(9) Al-Hasan ibn Qahtaba Al-Tâ'î raided Byzantine territories in 162/779; he then set out beyond Tarsus and told the Caliph Al-Mahdî of the advantages of building up, fortifying and garrisoning the city to increase the power of Islam in order

---

(1) Muqaddasî, B.G.A., III, 174.
(2) Ya'qûbî, B.G.A., VII, 329; Muqaddasî, B.G.A., III, 174.
(3) Ibn Hawqal, B.G.A., II, 242; Muqaddasî, B.G.A., III, 24, 65.
(4) Mu'jam, I, 785.
(5) B.G.A., VII, 327.
(6) B.G.A., II, 116.
(7) Ed. Khashshâb, 13.
(8) v. Bakrî, Mu'jam, II, 453; Yâqût, Mu'jam, III, 526.
(9) Quoted by Balâdhurî, 169 and Ibn Al-Faqîh, B.G.A., V, 113.

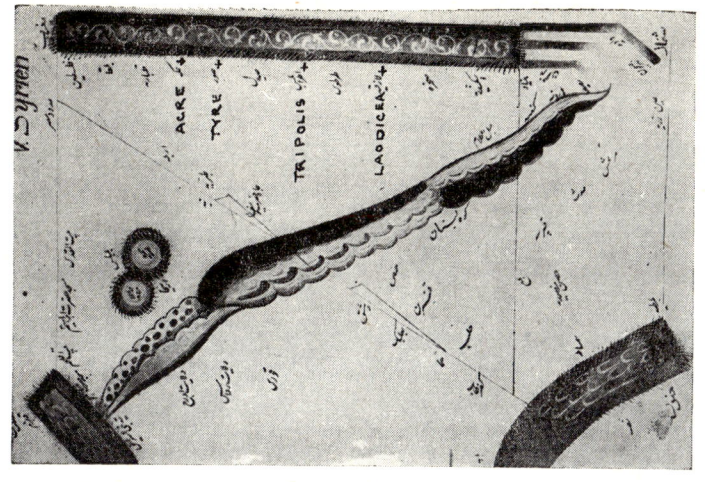

Early Syrian Naval Centres as shown on Jayhânî's map. Facsimile Miller. V. Bd. Beiheft, Tafel, 67.

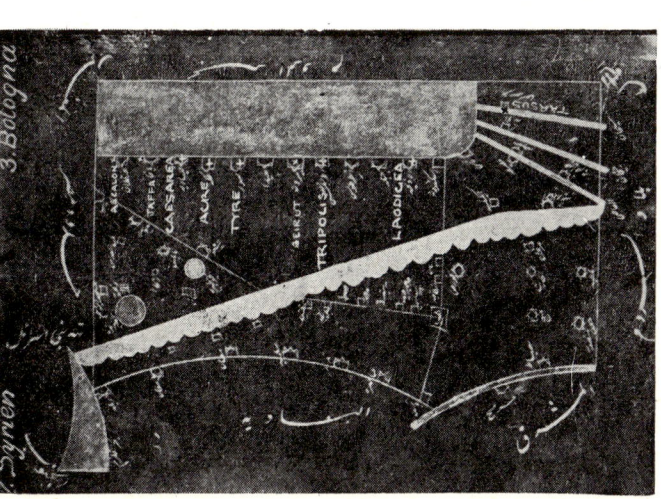

Early Syrian Naval Centres as shown on Balkhî's map. Facsimile Miller. III Bd. Beiheft, Tafel 11.

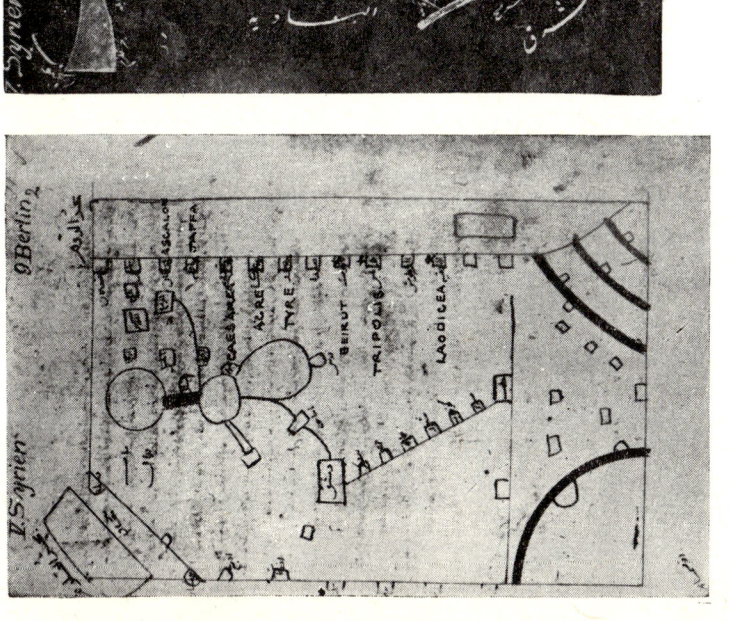

Early Syrian Naval Centres as shown on Muqaddasî's map. Facsimile Miller. III Bd. Beiheft, Tafel II.

to overcome the enemy. Another tradition(1) states that Ibn Qahtaba brought Al-Mahdî a description of the ruined Tarsus which, in his estimation, held one hundred thousand inhabitants; he finally persuaded the Caliph to rebuild it. At a later date, in 171/787, when the Caliph Al-Rashîd learned that the Byzantines intended to restore and fortify the town, he ordered Harthama ibn A'yan to anticipate them and entrusted Faraj ibn Sulaym with its reconstruction. Thus, in 172/788, it was rebuilt, populated by Muslims and given a mosque.(2)

The city, situated between Asia Minor and Syria, separated, according to Muqaddasî,(3) the Muslim and Christian worlds. Arab geographers(4) speak of it as belonging to the Syrian thughûr or frontier fortresses. Ibn Al-Faqîh and Abû'l-Fidâ(5) mention it as on the Syrian coast. Mas'ûdî(6) clearly fixes its site by explaining that the Baradân, the river of Tarsus, divided the city and flowed into the sea six miles away, a distance also given by Yâqût.(7) Istakhrî(8) relates that «*when you leave Awlâs you come to mountains called Qalamya which extend to the Mediterranean. Qalamya is also the name of a city which was at one time in the hands of the Greeks... It is neither on the sea nor on its shore. If you go about one march from the city you come to Al-Lâmis, a village on the sea-coast where the ransoming of Byzantine and Muslim captives took place, the former being on the ships at sea and the latter on land.*»(9). Ibn Khurdâbhbih(10) gives the distance between Qalamya

---

(1) Quoted by Balâdhurî, 169.
(2) Balâdhurî, 169-170; Ibn Al-Faqîh, B.G.A., V, 113; Mas'ûdî, B.A.G., VIII, 189; Murûj, VIII, 294-295. Ibn Hawqal, Kramers Edition, 183, says that the Caliph Ma'mûn rebuilt the city.
(3) B.G.A., III, 14-15.
(4) Ibn Rusta, B.G.A., VII, 97; Qudâma, B.G.A., VI, 253; Istakhrî, B.G.A., I, 55; Mas'ûdî, B.G.A., VIII, 44; Ibn Hawqal, Kramers Edition, 168; Yâqût, Mu'jam, I, 927; III, 625; Marâsid, I, 200.
(5) Ibn Al-Faqîh, B.G.A., V, 7; Abû'l-Fidâ, 248-249.
(6) B.G.A., VIII, 58.
(7) Mu'jam, I, 553; Marâsid, I, 140.
(8) B.G.A., I, 69.
(9) The same description is given by Ibn Hawqal, B.G.A., II, 134; Kramers Edition, 201.
(10) B.G.A., VI, 117.

and Tarsus as sixteen miles whilst Mas'ûdî(1) says there were thirty five miles between Al-Lâmis on the sea-coast and Tarsus. Istakhrî and Ibn Hawqal(2) both place Awlâs on the Mediterranean coast at a distance of two days' march from Tarsus.

The city became prosperous and its population was continually increased by immigrants from adjoining lands who were burning with enthusiasm to take part in the holy war for Islam until they met their death. Istakhrî, Mas'ûdî and Ibn Hawqal(3) give some particulars of the town in the 4th/10th century. Ibn Hawqal repeats Istakhrî's description, adding further details. He says it was a very great and celebrated city, surrounded by a double stone wall and that «*he who attacked from it was always victorious either by sea or land and seized much booty, as was evident from the news heard and the traces left behind.*»(4) From Sijistân to Maghrib «*there was no city of importance but had in Tarsus a house (dâr) for its citizens where its warriors lived. Once they arrived they settled down in garrison. They received rich and plentiful alms from the funds sent to them by the Sultans and wealthy men who gave voluntary aid. There was hardly a chief or a distinguished man of the countries mentioned but endowed for them farms or inns.*»(5) Muqaddasî(6) refused to describe Tarsus as it was in Byzantine hands.

Tabarî,(7) after relating how Mu'tadid overcame the revolt of Wasîf Al-Khâdim in 287/900, says that «*the Caliph ordered all the ships in which the Muslims used to wage war, together with the implements, to be burnt. It is said that Damyâna Ghulâm Yazmân, because of some personal grudge against the inhabitants of the city,(8) advised him to adopt*

---

(1) B.G.A., VIII, 189.
(2) Istakhrî, B.G.A., I, 68; Ibn Hawqal, B.G.A., II, 127; Kramers Edition, 188.
(3) Istakhrî, B.G.A., I, 64; Mas'ûdî; B.G.A., VIII, 351; Murûj, VII, 1-2, 101; Ibn Hawqal, B.G.A., II, 122-123; Kramers Edition, 183-184.
(4) Ibn Hawqal, Kramers Edition, 183.
(5) Ibn Hawqal, B.G.A., II, 123.
(6) B.G.A., III, 152.
(7) III, 2200; reproduced by Ibn Al-Athîr, VII, 344.
(8) Damyâna may have remembered his experience in 284/897 when Râghib, who seemed to have been able to gain the sympathy of the people, sent him bound to the Caliph. v. Tabarî, III, 2160-2161; Ibn Al-Athîr, VII, 335; Zakî Hassan, 112.

this measure. About fifty old ships, on which large sums of money had been spent and which could never be replaced at that time, were among those destroyed. The loss endangered the Muslims, lessened their power and increased that of the Greeks who were thus safeguarded from an attack by sea.» Whatever may have been the reason for burning the ships, this passage indicates that Tarsus was an important naval centre in the continual struggle against the Byzantines. The 'Abbâsids used to supplement land operations from this base by naval action.(1) Qudâma(2) includes it among the frontier towns of Syria from which the holy war was carried on by sea and land. Mas'ûdi(3) mentions Yazmân Al-Khâdim as Amîr of Tarsus and as «*being highly skilled in both sea and land expeditions. Under his orders he had mariners of incomparable bravery, the like of which had not been seen before. He inflicted severe losses upon the enemy who dreaded him exceedingly and trembled behind the walls of their fortresses.*» His death is recorded in 278/891 as the result of a wound received during a raid against the Byzantines.(4)

In spite of the effect of the loss of ships mentioned by Tabarî, the Syrian fleet based at Tarsus had become the terror of the Aegean by the end of the 3rd/beginning of the 10th century.(5) The same historian speaks of a letter written by Abû Ma'dân on 10 Ramadân 291/26 July 904 informing the minister that news had been received from Tarsus to the effect that «*God bestowed victory on the so called Ghulâm Zurâfa in one of the raids against the Byzantines at that time, in a city called Antâliya, on the seacoast and said to be equal to Constantinople. He took it by force killing about five thousand men, taking an equal number captive and setting free four thousand Muslims. In addition he secured sixty Byzantine ships which he loaded with booty, including gold, silver, goods and slaves. Every Muslim who took part in this raid received about a thousand dinars. Thus the Muslims rejoiced at the news.*»(6)

(1) v. Qudâma, B.G.A., VI, 259; Runciman, Romanus, 123.
(2) B.G.A., VI, 253.
(3) Murûj, VIII, 72.
(4) Tabarî, III, 2130; Mas'ûdî, Murûj, VIII, 72; Ibn Al-Athîr, VII, 313; Ibn Taghrî Birdî, III, 78.
(5) Brooks, Byz. Zeit., 1913, 384.
(6) Tabarî, III, 2250. Reproduced by 'Arîb, 6.

Practically the same account is given by Ibn Al-Athîr and Ibn Khaldûn(1) who definitely state that Ghulâm Zurâfa set out from Tarsus. It seems likely that this admiral was no other than Leo of Tripolis (mentioned by Cameniates), who sacked Thessalonica with a fleet of fifty four huge galleys manned by ten thousand men.(2) The Antâliya(3) mentioned in editions of Muslim chronicles may have been Thessalonica, for no other city in the whole empire was equal to Constantinople.(4) Furthermore, the date given by Arab writers for the sack of the city is nearly the same as that mentioned by Byzantine authors.(5) A passage in Mas'ûdî(6) supports the suggestion that Leo of Tripolis, whom he calls Lâwî(7) of Tripolis, surnamed Abû'l-Hârith, was Ghulâm Zurâfa, who was entrusted with the management of warships in the Mediterranean. The sack of Thessalonica was undoubtedly a proof of Muslim supremacy in this sea at this time.

Madaynî(8) says that one of Ibn Tûlûn's incentives for strengthening his fleet was his fear of ships coming from Tarsus. Maqrîzî(9) goes so far as to say it was as if Ibn Tûlûn foresaw future events. It was the fleet from Tarsus, commanded by Damyâna, which accompanied the expedition of Muhammad ibn Sulaymân and destroyed the Tûlûnid fleet at Tinnîs and then at Damietta, in 291/904, capturing the Tûlûnid ships with all they contained.(10) Kindî(11) makes it

---

(1) Ibn Al-Athîr, VII, 368-369; Ibn Khaldûn, 'Ibar, III, 357.
(2) Cameniates, Ed. Bonn, 512, 579, quoted by Jenkins, Speculum, April 1948, 228. Cameniates' narrative is paraphrased by Finlay, II, 267 sq.
(3) In Ibn Khaldûn, 'Ibar, III, 357, it is given as Antâkia. V. Tabarî, III, 2250, n. f.; 'Arîb, 6, n. f.
(4) v. Finlay II, 267, n. I; Schlumberger, 27; Runciman, Romanus, 24.
(5) Jenkins, Speculum, April 1948, 230, 235, quotes Cameniates for the date of 31 July 904 = 15 Ramadân 291. v. Finlay, II, 271, 272.
(6) Murûj,I, 282.
(7) Lâwî is apparently an Arabic corruption of Leo. Most of the names of leaders connected with Tarsus indicate that they may have been Greeks who became Muslims after being captured.
(8) 87.
(9) Khitat, II, 180.
(10) Kindî, Governors, 245-246. v. Tabarî, III, 2251-2252; 'Arîb, 7; Ibn Miskawayh, V. 42; Ibn Al-Athîr, VII, 370; Ibn Khaldûn, 'Ibar, IV, 310; Maqrîzî, Khitat, I, 322; Ibn Taghrî Birdî, III, 136; Gibb, E.I.,
(11) Governors, 245(2).

clear that Rashîq Al-Wardâmi, known as Ghulâm Zurâfa (Leo of Tripolis), accompanied Damyâna on this expedition. According to the same author(1) the latter went a second time from Tarsus to Egypt to help the Caliph in 293/905 to subdue the rebellious Muhammad ibn Al-Khalîj. Damyâna is also mentioned by Mas'ûdî(2) in 297/909-10 as the commander of the fleet operating in the Mediterranean, who seized Cyprus and «*held it for four months, burning, plundering, taking captives and seizing many places which he fortified.*»

When the Fâtimid Caliph sent Sulaymân Al-Khâdim in 307-920 to invade Egypt it was the fleet from Tarsus, led by the 'Abbâsid admiral Thamil Al-Khâdim which burnt the North African ships with naphtha in the waters of Rosetta, killed the crews and soldiers or took them prisoners to Fustât.(3) Eutychius(4) speaks of his fleet as consisting of eighty warships and Ibn Al-Athîr(5) mentions him as commander of the Mediterranean fleet. Mas'ûdî(6) says he was known as Al-Zulfî and refers to him as governor of the frontiers when an expedition under his leadership set out from Tarsus in 312/924-5. He further adds that it was on the ships of Tarsus that some Bulgarians embarked and accompanied the inhabitants to their city.

The various accounts given above show that Tarsus was undoubtedly a naval centre of considerable importance. It remained in Muslim hands until, as Yâqût(7) says Nicephorus conquered it in 354/965, «*destroyed its mosques and carried off a great quantity of arms from the stores.*»(8)

---

(1) Kindî, Governors, 260(16), 262(1), 263(2). v. Maqrîzî, Khitat, I, 327; Ibn Taghrî Birdî, III, 154(11).

(2) Murûj, VIII. 282.

(3) Eutychius, Corp. Script. Christ., VII, 80, 81; Kindî, ibid, 276; Ibn Al-Athîr, VIII, 89; Ibn 'Idhârî, I, 185; Ibn Khaldûn, 'Ibar, III, 371; IV, 312; Maqrîzî, Itti'âz, 43.

(4) Ibid, VII, 80. Ibn Khaldûn and Maqrîzî say twenty five.

(5) VIII, 89, 118(15).

(6) Murûj, II, 16-17.

(7) Mu'jam, III, 526-527. v. Mez, 4; Vasiliev, C.M.H., IV, 145.

(8) Le Strange, Palestine, 377; Eastern Caliphate, 133, translates this sentence to mean that Nicephorus «*took all the arms away from the arsenals.*» Yâqût, however, does not mention arsenals in this connection.

II. Naval Centre and Arsenal in Africa

In trying to fix the naval centre from which the first Muslim raiding fleet to Sicily in 44/664 set out, Becker(1) says it is quite certain that this expedition did not start from Syria but from Pentapolis (Barqa), which is shown by the papyri to have been an important naval base in the seventh century A.D.; it was here that the fleet operating in the west received recruits from the fleets coming from Egypt. Though he does not give a reference it seems that he is referring to the Berlin Qurra Papyrus, a bilingual (Arabic and Greek), which he published in 1908.(2) Bell,(3) in his article «*The Aphrodito Papyri*,» published in the same year, says that the papyri make no mention of the headquarters of the African fleet, and in«*Greek Papyri in the British Museum*,»(4) published in 1910, he states that there is no reference in the papyri to any arsenal in this province. Having visited Berlin and examined the Qurra Papyrus he published a translation of the Greek portion of the document in 1913.(5) In spite of the letter being dark and the ink in several cases very faint, some places being quite illegible, he believes he successfully deciphered it. It is dated 95/713 and is from the governor Qurra to the inhabitants of the village of Bubaliton concerning the supply of two and a half sailors together with provisions for their journey from Antinoopolis to Pentapolis. The village, in addition to paying the wages of the sailors during the term of service, was to provide their maintenance during the journey to headquarters; that for the expedition would be provided for separately: «*In the name of God, Qurra ibn Sharîk, Governor to you, the inhabitants of the village of Bubaliton in the district ... of the city of Antinoe.*(6) *Furnish for a relay of sailors intended for the* **carabi** *and* **acatia** *of the Amîr Al-Mu'minîn in (the province of) Africa with 'Abd-Allâh ibn Mûsâ ibn Nusayr in the present 12th indiction and the raid of the 13th indiction 2 1/2 = two and*

---

(1) C.M.H., II, 380.
(2) Z.A., XXII, 150.
(3) J.H.S., XXVIII, 115.
(4) P. Lond., IV, XXXIII.
(5) Archiv für Papyrusforschung, V, 189 sq.
(6) v. Infra, 76, n. 3.

a half sailors to serve in person,(1) *paying for each person for wages 1 1/6 nominal solidi, and for their maintenance on the journey as far as Pentapolis 11 1/6 = eleven and a sixth nominal solidi, which are to be paid to them out of the state treasury. Written Athyr 26th, twelfth indiction by Ambas son of Coumnas(?) ... 2 1/2 sailors.*» By Pentapolis is meant Cyrenaica whence presumably the fleet was to start. From this letter it can be concluded that Pentapolis was a naval centre of some importance during the early years of the Caliphate.

Muslim geographers(2) say that Barqa was the name of a town and district between Alexandria and Africa(3) and that in ancient times it was called Antâbulus, meaning «*the Five Cities.*» Yâqût(4) says it was one month's march from Alexandria and two hundred and twenty parasangs from Fustât. According to Istakhrî(5) its governors used to come from Egypt until Al-Mahdî took the city and removed them. Ya'qûbî, Qudâma and Bakrî(6) describe the sea route from Fustât to Barqa, the first giving details about the district and its harbours. He says that the city had a wall built by the Caliph Mutawakkil and was six miles from the Mediterranean. He mentions five harbours(7) of which Barnîq on the coast, two marches from Barqa, was extremely good; Ajdâbiya, the harbour of which was six miles from the town, was two marches from Barnîq; the other three, Ajiya, Tulmaytha and Surt were on the coast, the last being five marches from Ajdâbiya and on the boundary line.

There is another interesting papyrus letter, dated 92/710, from the governor Qurra to the pagarch.(8) It concerns the

---

(1) For requisition of a fraction of a sailor v. Infra, 101.
(2) Ibn Khurdâdhbih, B.G.A., VI, 91; Ya'qûbî, B.G.A., VII, 346; Istakhrî, B.G.A., I, 36-37; Muqaddasî, B.G.A., III, 216; Yâqût, Mu'jam, I, 381, 573; Abû'l-Fidâ, 127.
(3) Africa was the name for Muslim conquests stretching westward from Egypt to the Atlantic. More strictly Ifrîqiyya denotes the Roman province of Africa or Tûnis. v. Muir, Caliphate, 355, n. 2.
(4) Mu'jam, I, 574.
(5) B.G.A., I, 38.
(6) Ya'qûbî, B.G.A., VII, 342-343; Qudâma, B.G.A., VI, 220-221; Bakrî, 4-6.
(7) Ya'qûbî, B.G.A., VII, 343-344. v. also Ibn Hawqal, Kramers Edition, 63, 67, 68; Bakrî, 5, 6; Abû'l-Fidâ, 128, 148-149.
(8) Bell, P. Lond., IV, No. 1350, 24 sq.; Der Islam, II, 279.

expedition of 84/703, led by 'Atâ' ibn Râfi' who, after taking much booty, was wrecked on his return voyage off the African coast and perished with the greater part of his fleet. The letter is a request for information concerning the sailors who went out to the raiding fleet of Africa with 'Atâ' ibn Râfi' and who were sent back by Mûsâ ibn Nusayr. Qurra wanted to know the number of those who returned to Aphrodito, of those who remained in Africa, with their reasons for doing so, and of those who died, whether in Africa or after their return : «*In the name of God. Qurra, etc. We give thanks to God, and next : We do not know the number of the sailors who returned home to your administrative district of those who went out to the raiding fleet of Africa with 'Atâ' ibn Râfi', whom Mûsâ ibn Nusayr despatched (?), and of those who remained in Africa. Therefore, on receiving the present letter, write to us the number of the sailors who returned to your district as aforesaid, enquiring and asking of them concerning those who remained in the said Africa and for what reason they remained there, and so too the number of those who died there as aforesaid and on the journey after their discharge; and in fact, noting completely all they knew and can communicate, sent it to us with all speed after reading the present letter.*»

The letter does not mention whether the raid was against Sardinia or Sicily but Ibn 'Abd Al-Hakam (1) states that the expedition of 'Atâ' was against Sardinia. The fullest account is given in Kitâb Al-Imâma (2) in which the author says that 'Atâ' was despatched by 'Abd Al-'Azîz ibn Marwân, governor of Egypt, against Sardinia. Having put in at an African port he was forbidden by Mûsâ ibn Nusayr to proceed, on the grounds that the season was too late for safety, but he disobeyed the command, with disastrous results. The papyrus conifrms the fact that at least part of 'Atâ's fleet came from Egypt and seems to show that the despatch of the expedition was due to Mûsâ ibn Nusayr. The light thrown on the latter's part in the affair depends upon whether the sailors whom he sent back went to Egypt after the expedition or were despatched to Sardinia. The inquiry as to the sailors

---

(1) 209-210.

(2) Attributed to Ibn Quatayba, II, 110-111 = B.A.S., 163-164. For the expedition v. Amari, Storia, New Edition, I, 292, sq.

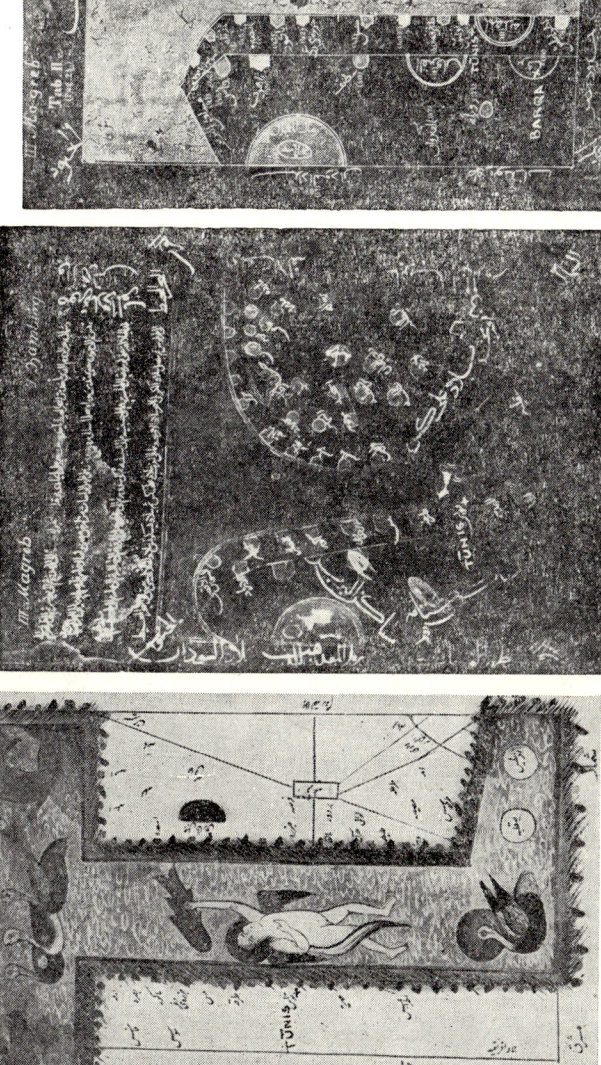

Early African naval centres as shown on Jayhānī's map. Facsimile Miller. V Bd. Beiheft, Tafel 67.

Early African naval centres as shown on Balkhī's map. Original in Hamburg. Stadtbibliothek. Facsimile Miller. I Bd. Heft, Tafel, 5.

Early African naval centres as shown on Istakhrī's map. Original in Gotha. Cd. 1521. Facsimile Miller. I Bd. Heft, Tafel 5.

who had remained in Africa suggests that some may have settled there. The author of Kitâb Al-Imâma(1) says that when the fleet of 'Atâ' was wrecked in 84/703 Mûsâ allowed the surviving sailors and ships to enter the arsenal at Tûnis. This was the first arsenal established by the Muslims in North Africa and the Caliph 'Abd Al-Malik ibn Marwân ordered warships to be built there.

Muslim historians disagree as to which governor was responsible for its construction. The author of Kitâb Al-Imâma(2) attributes it to Mûsâ ibn Nusayr and gives the following details: «*During his stay at Qayrawân for the months of Ramadân and Shawwâl (84/703), Mûsâ gave orders for the building of an arsenal* (**dâr sinâ'a**), *which was to be connected with the sea. The people generally did not approve of his project, but a Berber, who was a fervent convert to Islam, approached him saying: 'O Governor, I have lived a hundred and twenty years and I remember my father telling me that, when the governor of Carthage wished to cut a canal, the people protested, but one man advised him to complete the work, as kings were all-powerful and could do as they pleased. Therefore carry out your plan, O Governor, and God will help you to fulfuil your aim and will reward you for your work.' Acting upon this good advice Mûsâ built the dockyard and connected it with the sea twelve miles away. He then had a hundred warships constructed there and from that time the arsenal provided ships with a refuge from the wind and storms of winter.*»

According to Bakrî,(3) Hassân ibn Al-Nu'mân was entrusted with the building of the arsenal. He quotes the following tradition from Abû Muhâjir: «*When the Greeks sent a naval expedition against the defenceless Muslims stationed at Tûnis, many were killed or taken captive. Hassân therefore sent forty leading Arabs to the Caliph and wrote him a letter describing the calamities which had befallen the Muslims. He, meanwhile, waited at Tûnis for an answer. Two followers of the Prophet, Anas ibn Mâlik and Zayd ibn*

---

(1) II, 111.
(2) II, 110. Ibn Shibbât, B.A.S., 211, and Ibn Abî Dînâr, 33; B.A.S., 526, also refer to him.
(3) 38.

Thâbit, who were at the court, informed the Muslims that those stationed at Râdis (Tûnis), *for one day would surely enter heaven. They advised the Caliph to send help to the luckless city in case of any further attack, and assured him that God would reward him for his action, as Tûnis was considered a holy city whose people were blessed. It was in fact a garrison town for the protection of Qayrawân against any assault from Macedonia. The Caliph immediately sent to his brother 'Abd Al-'Azîz ibn Marwân, governor of Egypt, requesting him to despatch a thousand Copts* (Coptic shipwrights), *with their families, and to provide for them until they reached Tûnis.(1) He also wrote to Hassân authorising him to build an arsenal as an aid to the firm establishment of Muslim power. Berbers in the locality were to be employed for the transport of the timber required for building ships for raiding the Greek coasts. Thus the safety of Qayrawân would be assured. These orders were carried out; the arsenal was completed and connected with the sea in the harbour of Râdis.»* Bakrî gives no date otherwise than the Caliphate of 'Abd Al-Malik but according to Amari(2) this occurred between 79/698 and 84/703.

It is also related that 'Ubaydallah ibn Al-Habhâb, governor of Africa, (116-23/734-40), constructed the arsenal.(3) Bakrî's version sounds the most convincing, however, and is supported by Ibn Khaldûn and Maqrîzî.(4) It is probable, therefore, that Hassân built the arsenal which was later restored and further fortified by 'Ubaydallah ibn Al-Habhâb. Tûnis thus became an important naval centre from which

---

(1) For the Coptic mission to teach African Muslims the art of shipbuilding v. Ibn Khaldûn, Muqaddima, II, 34; Fr. Tr., II, 40; Amari, I Diplomi Arabi, X; Wiet, Précis de l'Hist. d'Egypte, II, 148; Les Communications en Egypte, 243, Gateau, Rev. Afr., 1946, 144; Vonderheyden, 274.

(2) Storia, New Edition, I, 292. Becker, C.M.H., II, 369, and Amari, Ibid, I, 290, fix the date 78/697 for Hassân's conquest of Africa.

(3) Bakrî, 37, 39; Ibn 'Idhârî, I, 38. Ibn Al-Shammâ', quoted by Ibn Abî Dînar, 7, gives the year 114/732. v. Yâqût, Mu'jam, 1, 899.

(4) Ibn Khaldûn, Muqaddima, II, 34; Maqrîzî, Khitat, II, 190. v. also Riyâd Al-Nufûs, B.A.S., 176; Ibn Abî Dînar, 11-12; Lane-Poole, Barbary Corsairs, 7; Nadvi, Is. Cult., XVI, January 1942. 72. Bury, Centinario, II, 26, following Amari, Ibid, New Edition, I, 290 sq.; Old Edition, I, 167, states that Mûsâ ibn Nusayr established the arsenal.

raids were carried out against the Byzantines.(1) When the Aghlabid dynasty was founded in North Africa and the lordship of the 'Abbâsid Caliph became merely nominal(2) the situation was changed. From their capital Al-Qayrawân, they dominated the mid-Mediterranean and naval supremacy passed into their hands.

Site of Arsenal

Tûnis, which ibn Hawqal (3) identifies with the ancient Tarshîsh, was founded, according to Ibn Al-Shammâ' (4), after 80/699. It replaced the old naval base of Carthage which ceased to be used for that purpose after the Muslim conquest.(5) Yu'qûbî (6) describes Tûnis as on the sea-coast and containing the arsenal. In his description of Tûnis, Bakrî says it was situated on high ground surrounded by a fortified wall with five gates giving access to the city. The high ground was known as the mountain of Umm 'Amr and the south gate which led to Al-Qayrawân as Al-Jazîra (from Jazîrat Sharîk). Opposite was the barren rock called Al-Tawba standing like a great building overlooking the sea ; west of this was the hill of Al-Sayyâda which sheltered a number of villages where olives, fruits and other produce were cultivated.(7) He also speaks of a lake, twenty four miles long, east of Tûnis, in the centre of which was an island, two miles in length, on which stood the ruins of a castle. Here the arsenal was built and connected with the harbour by means of the lake. A strong wall protected the harbour, to the south of which was a massive stone castle, known as the «*Castle of the Chain.*» Ships entering the harbour passed

---

(1) Bakrî, 39; Ibn Khaldûn, Muqaddima, II, 34-35; Ibn Abî Dînâr, 12. For raids on Sicily and Sardinia v. Amari, Storia, New Edition I, 290-304; Vasiliev, Byzance, I, 63 sq.
(2) Ibn Al-Athîr, VI, 106-108; Ibn 'Idhârî, I, 83.
(3) Ed. Kramers, 73; Bakrî, 37; Ibn Abî Dînâr, 6.
(4) Quoted by Ibn Abî Dînâr, 6.
(5) Ibn 'Idhârî, I, 19; Diehl, L'Afrique Byzantine, quoted by East, Historical Geog., 200; Bury. Later, II, 353.
(6) B.G.A., VII, 348.
(7) Bakrî, 39.

between the two stone walls but could be prevented by an iron chain stretched across.

III. Naval Centre in Crete

The island of Crete was strategically and commercially important. Arab historians (1) say that it was conquered in the Caliphate of Al-Ma'mûn by Muslim emigrants from Spain, who had first sought shelter in Alexandria and then crossed over to Crete. Abû Hafs, their leader, founded a new city which he surrounded by a deep moat called **Khandaq** in Arabic, from which the new name of **Chandax** or **Candia** originated. (2) Crete in the possession of the Muslims became a menace to the Empire and, according to Genesius, (3) when the strategos of the Cybyrrhaeot theme was sent against the invaders, his force was annihilated. Ooryphas then collected a naval force and expelled the marauders from other islands which they were ravaging. The Continuator (4) adds that the Byzantine fleet was entirely destroyed by the Muslims off Thasos in October 829. After this the islands lay at their mercy for a time. Ibn Al-Dâya (5) relates an anecdote in which he mentions that the Emperor planned revenge against Crete for the continuous raids which caused the Byzantines to suffer severely.

In 227/841 Muslims from this base were ravaging the Asiatic coast and in 248/862 they plundered the Cyclades, devastated the coast of Asia Minor and carried off great

---

(1) Balâdhurî, 236; Ya'qûbî, Hist., II, 560-561; Tabarî, III, 1091; Kindî, Governors, 180, 182, 184; Yâqût, Mu'jam, I, 236 sq.; Ibn Al-Athîr, VI, 135 sq., 209 sq. 281 sq.; Ibn Khaldûn, 'Ibar, III, 253, IV, 221.
(2) Vasiliev, Byzance, I, 56; Byz. Empire, I, 338; Bury, Eastern, 289; Brooks, E.H.R., XXVIII, 440; Schlumberger, 25.
(3) Quoted by Brooks, E.H.R. XXVIII, 433. Information relating to naval activities about Crete is hardly to be found in Arabic and had to be looked for in Byzantine sources.
(4) Quoted by Brooks, ibid, 433.
(5) Mukâfa'a, 112. The anecdote may refer to the expedition of Theoctistus in March 843. v. Brooks, ibid, 436; Vasiliev, Byzance, I, 195; Bury, Eastern, 291.

booty and a number of slaves.(1) According to the Continuator (2) the fleet consisted of twenty **cumbarii,** seven galleys and some **saturae.** The maritime invasions of the Muslims again became a menace during the first years of the tenth century A.D. Their two strong fleets from Syria and Crete frequently acted together.(3) The Byzantine struggle with the Cretan Muslims in the reigns of Leo VI and Constantine VII was unsuccessful(4) and the island remained in Muslim hands until 350/961 when it was reconquered by the Empire.(5)

The failure of Byzantine expeditions to recover Crete and the ravaging of the Aegean islands by Cretan Muslims point to the fact that the island was a naval base of considerable importance. As such it differed from Cyprus which seems to have held a curiously indefinite position between the rival powers. St. Willibard (6) says that the Cypriots dwelt between the Byzantines and Muslims. Muqaddasî, (7) referring to it says: «*It is full of populous cities and offers the Muslims many advantages for their trade... The island is in the control of whichever power is predominant.*» Istakhrî(8) states that the population of Crete was entirely Muslim except for a few Christians, which was usually the case in Muslim countries, whilst that of Cyprus was Christian with no Muslim in it. Ibn Hawqal (9) notes the same difference and adds that raids were continually carried out from both islands against the Byzantines, with disastrous results. Ibn Khurdâdhbih (10) says : «*When the governor ordered an expedition, the governors of Egypt and Syria were commanded to make the necessary preparations. The meeting place for*

---

(1) Vasiliev, Byzance, I, 258, Finlay, II, 190.
(2) Quoted by Finlay, II, 190, n. 2, and Bury, Eastern, 293, n. 5.
(3) v. Const. Porph., quoted by Hill, I, 294.
(4) Vasiliev, C.M.H., IV, 142, 144; Bury, Eastern, 231; Finlay, II, 278, 315-316; Baynes, Byz. Empire, 148; Diehl, Empire Byzantin, 98.
(5) Vasiliev, ibid, I, 57; Runciman, Byz. Civilisation, 151; Giese, E.I., I, 879; Mez, 4. v. Yâqût, Mu'jam, I. 377; Ibn Khaldûn, 'Ibar, IV, 211;Maqrîzî, I.F., III, 185.
(6) P.P.T.S., III, 15.
(7) B.G.A., III, 184.
(8) B.G.A., I, 70.
(9) B.G.A., II, 136; Kramers Edition, 203-204.
(10) B.G.A., VI, 255.

the fleet was Cyprus. The governor of the Syrian frontiers was the commander-in-chief. The expenditure for a maritime expedition of this nature came to some one hundred thousand dinars. »

It can be concluded, therefore, that whereas Crete was an independent naval centre for Cretan Muslims, Cyprus was but a jumping off ground for Muslims and Byzantines alike to attack each other.

CHAPTER III

MATERIALS FOR SHIPBUILDING

I. Timber

Since ancient times the naval power of the Mediterranean peoples depended largely on the proximity of forests providing timber for the keel, planking, mast, yard and oars of a ship. Man must have made many experiments before he learnt to plane planks accurately, caulk them, and fix the mast firmly in its socket, supporting it with ropes. Finally he was confronted with the problem of shaping the hull so that it would rise to the waves. All this must have taken centuries of experimentation. When speaking of the art of carpentry, Ibn Khaldûn (1) says : « *Men living in society cannot do without this art, the material for which is timber. God has given everything certain useful properties so that man may satisfy his needs. Trees, for example, can be utilised in a number of ways, as everyone knows. When they are hard, they provide the most useful timber for shipbuilding...* ».

This interesting account stresses the importance of timber for shipuilding. Ibn 'Abd Al-Hakam (2) relates that, on one occasion, when timber was needed for shipbuilding on the island of Rawda, the manager of finance, Hayyân ibn Shurayh, found it could be obtained from the Copts. Being unwilling to take it by force, he wrote to the Caliph 'Umar ibn 'Abd Al-'Azîz, who bade him offer a fair price for it.

---

(1) Muqaddima, II, 324-326; Fr. Tr., II, 376-379.
(2) 90; reproduced by Maqrîzî, I.F., V. 45.

Different kinds of timber

Lebek.

Kindî (1) says that every kind of tree was found in Egypt. The most valuable timber for shipbuilding was that of the lebek tree. Abû Hanîfa Al-Dînawarî (2) (d. 282/895), says that it was only found in Ansinâ (3) and was in great demand for ships because of certain qualities. He adds that when two pieces were firmly fixed together and left in water for a year, they became indistinguishably joined ; one plank cost fifty dinars. 'Abd Al-Latîf Al-Baghdâdî (4) (d. 629/1232), compares this tree with the sidra for its fine growth and magnificent foliage and say that its wine and black coloured timber was excellent because of its hardness.

Acacia - Sant.

Acacia or sant is among the kinds of timber mentioned in the papyri (5) for shipbuilding. Ibn Al-Faqîh (6) (d. 291/903), speaks of the sant tree as one of the wonders of Egypt and good for fuel as it left very little ash. Al-Jâhiz (7) (d. 255/869), adds that a fire made of its wood was quickly kindled but slowly extinguished; he identifies it with the

---

(1) Quoted by Suyûtî, Husn, II, 227.
(2) Quoted by 'Abd Al-Latîf, 10. v. Qazwînî, Athâr Al-Bîlâd, 100; Maqrîzî, Khitat, I, 204; I.F., II, 108, n. 4; 'Alî Mubârak, VIII, 97; De Sacy, Relation, 18.
(3) The ancient town of Antinoe or Antinoopolis lay on the east bank of the Nile opposite Ushmûnayn. It was founded by the Emperor Hadrian in memory of Antinous. Under the Byzantine rule it became the capital of the Thebaid or Upper Egypt. Upon the site of the city now stands the city of Shaykh 'Abâda, included in the district of Mallawî, in the province of Asyût. v. Idrîsî, Nuzhat Al-Mushtâq, [47]; Yâqût, Mu'jam, I, 381; Qazwînî, ibid, 100; Maqrîzî, Khitat, I, 204; 'Alî Mubârak, VIII, 65 sq.; Amélineau, 48,51.
(4) 9-10; De Sacy, ibid, 18.
(5) For papyri references to **acacia** v. Bell, P. Lond., IV, No. 1414(9), 129; No. 1433, 284; Der Islam, III, 136, 369; IV, 93; P. Ross.-Georg., IV, No. 7 sq.; Grohmann, Aperçu de Pap. Arabe, 68.
(6) B.G.A., V, 66, and XXX; Maqrîzî, I.F., I, 115, 138; II, 108, n. 4.
(7) Quoted by Suyûtî, Husn, II, 232.

ebony tree. 'Abd Al-Latîf (1) states that Egypt provided the acacia tree which was called sant; it was very tall and, according to Dînawarî, its timber was as hard as iron and became black as ebony with age; it grew in the plains and on the mountain side. Abû Sâlih (2) describes a tree which only bore fruit when a man ran towards it with an axe as though to cut it down, but was turned from his purpose by meeting another man who forbade him to do it, guaranteeing that the tree would bear fruit. The following year it would produce a quantity equal to that of two years. This account is but a grossly exaggerated description of the well known sensitive properties of the Mimosa Nilotica, called sant in Arabic. In relating the wonders of Egypt, Maqrîzî (3) says: «*In Upper Egypt there is a hamlet called Dishnâ where the sant tree grows. When it is threatened with destruction it grows smaller and shrinks up, but when they say to it: 'We have forgiven thee, we will spare thee', then the tree recovers*». The same writer adds that in his time there were sant trees which withered when a hand was laid upon them and recovered when it was removed.

Fig and Palm.

Fig (4) and palm trunks (5) for «*the castellated galleys*» are mentinoed in the papyri among the necessary materials required for shipbuilding. In letter No. 1371, dated 92-3/710-11, from the governor to the pagarch, the superintendent of the arsenal on the island of Babylon, Al-A'lâ ibn Abî Hakîm, is to receive a number of requisitions, listed at the end of the

---

(1) 28-29; De Sacy, Relation, 33.
(2) Fol. 17a, 44, n. 1.
(3) Khitat, I, 32; I.F., I, 138.
(4) For papyri references to fig trunks v. Bell, P. Lond., IV, No. 1414(78), 136; No. 1433(24), 284; Der Islam, III, 136, 370.
(5) For papyri references to palm trunks v. Bell, Der Islam, XVII, No. 1441, 5; 1449, 7; Grohmann, Aperçu de Pap. Arabe, 68. From the papyri, it is evident that palm wood was also used for the erection of the Caliph's palace at Fustât. v. Bell, Der Islam, II, No. 1362, 373; P. Lond., IV, 37, where it may be presumed that Bâsiliyûs had sent, or attempted to send, palm trunks of less dimensions than Qurra had ordered; Der Islam, III, No. 1433, 370; P. Lond., IV, 284, where there is mention of 15 palm trunks for the building of the palace at Babylon.

existing portion of the letter. They include beams of palm and fig tree evidently used for shipbuilding : «... *Cleaning and fitting up of the* **acatenaria** *and ... which are in the island of Babylon under the charge of Al-A'lâ ibn Abî Hakîm the superintendent in the present 9th indiction and (for) the raid of the 10th indiction, and having made out the demand notes for these to the people of the separate places we have sent them to you. On receiving the present letter, therefore, in accordance with the powers given by our demand notes embark the said articles and hand them over to the aforementioned 'Abd Al-A'lâ by your faithful and competent men with instructions to deliver them and receive the acquittances for them. Written the... 9th indiction.*

Memorandum

... 1/12 Cloven palm-trunks, 11 at 1/3 S.

... 2 S. 1. c. Untrimmed (?) fig-trunks, 11 at 1/3 S.» (1)

'Abd Al-Latîf (2) says that fig and palm trees were very common in Egypt, that the former were tall, rather like old nut trees, and that the wood was also used for houses, doors and durable implements because it would stand water and sun without damage. Although it was light and not very flexible it seldom wore out.

Lotus.

Among other kinds of trees, 'Abd Al-Latîf (3) mentions the lotus (sidra), as being plentiful and bearing a fruit called nabq. According to Abû Sâlih, (4) there was a church dedicated to the Angel Gabriel at Fustât, outside which grew a lotus tree of considerable height, reaching up to the roof. It was eventually cut down and sold for a good price. Maqrîzî (5) mentions the lotus trees as being extensively cultivated in Egypt.

---

(1) Bell, Der Islam, II, No. 1371, 375; P. Lond., IV 46.
(2) 11-12, 27; De Sacy, Relation, 19-20, 32.
(3) 33; De Sacy Relation, 36.
(4) Fol. 27a, 95.
(5) Khitat, I, 103.

It has been assumed that Egypt was destitute of timber for shipbuilding (1) in historic times but from all that has been stated, there seems little doubt that the country possessed trees providing timber for this purpose during the early period of the Caliphate. Syria also produced a species of pine tree *(sunûbar)*, for which Fort *(Hisn)* Al-Tînât,(2) near Alexandretta, was the centre of trade, whence it was exported to other parts of Syria, Egypt and Cilicia. (3) The forests of Lebanon and Anti-Lebanon had been famous since ancient times for timber for shipbuilding. (4) Muqaddasî (5) describes this country as a land of blessing, the lower province being of even greater value than the upper for the lusciousness of its fruits and abundance of palm trees. Nâsirî Khusrû (6) says that Hayfâ on the seashore abounded in palm gardens and trees from which shipbuilders constructed large vessels. 'Abd Al-Latîf (7) saw fig trees at Ascalon and in the coastal districts of Syria. Phoenix in Lycia is said to have been rich in Cypress trees from which masts were made and ships built. Nicephorus says that the Muslims went there to cut this wood and Theophanes relates that they constructed a fleet there. (8) Venice also supplied the Muslims of Egypt with timber. It is true that the Byzantine Emperor, in the early years of the ninth century A.D., had forbidden this trade, but the prohibition did not by any means prevent the Venetians from trafficking with the Muslims.(9)

---

(1) Pirenne, Economic and Social History,18; Mez, 448; Butler, 112. v. Infra, App. I, 143 sq.

(2) Hisn Al-Tînât is on the gulf of Iskandarûna, between Bayyâs and Al-Massîsa. v. Muqaddasî, B.G.A., 154; Bib. Ind., 252, n. 5.

(3) Istakhrî, B.G.A., I, 63; Ibn Hawqal, B.G.A., II, 121.

(4) For Lebanon forests in Roman times v. Bouchier, I, 159; Dussaud, 68; Rose, 20; East, Historical Geog., 192

(5) B.G.A., III, 179 sq.

(6) Ed. Khashshâb, 18; P.P.T.S., IV, 19-20.

(7) 11, De Sacy, Relation, 19-20.

(8) Theophanes, Ed. De Boor, 385; Nicephorus, Brev., Ed. De Boor, 50. I owe the reference to Prof. R.J. Jenkins. v. Canard, J. As., 1946, 66, n. 5; Brooks, C.M.H., II, 393-415.

(9) Baynes, Byz. Empire, 217; Pirenne, Mohammed and Charlemagne, 178, 179; Mediaeval Cities, 87; Economic and Social History, 18; Bury, Eastern, 327; Guest, E.I., II, 538.

II. Metals

Mediterranean shipbuilding depended not only on timber but also on metals for nails, fastenings and anchors. In the Mediterranean ships the planks were joined by iron nails whereas in the Red Sea and Indian Ocean they were stitched. The Umayyad governor Al-Hajjâj is said to have launched ships of timber, nailed and caulked, while previously the planks had been bound together with ropes. (1) Mas'ûdî (2) writes: «*In the Mediterranean, not far from Crete, planks of vessels of Sâj wood have been found, which were perforated and joined with fibre from the coco-nut tree. It was evident that they belonged to wrecked vessels and had been in water a long time. Ships of this description are only found in the Abyssinian Sea, for the vessels of the Mediterranean and the West are all joined with nails. In the Abyssinian Sea iron nails would not be suitable for shipbuilding as they become thinner and weaker in the water; hence the planks are joined with fibre and besmeared with grease and pitch.*» (3) Ibn Jubayr (4) says: «*No nails are used in the ships of the Red Sea; they are merely stitched together with cords of cocohusk ... The planks are perforated with stakes of palm wood and then saturated with mutton fat, castor-oil or shark oil; the last is the best.*» According to the same traveller, (5) the object in oiling the vessel was to make the wood soft and pliable on account of the numerous eddies in this sea, which were also the reason why they allowed no ships constructed with nails to sail there. When describing the Persian Gulf ships of the 7th/13th century, Marco Polo (6) writes: «*Their ships are wretched affairs and many of them get lost; for they have no iron fastenings, and are only stitched together with twine made from the husk of the Indian nut. They beat this husk until it becomes like horse-hair, and from that they spin twine, and with this stitch the planks of the ships together. It keeps well, and is not corroded by the sea-water,*

---

(1) Jâhiz, Hayawân, I, 41 (10 sq.); Ibn Rusta, B.G.A., VII, 195-196.
(2) Murûj, I, 365.
(3) The Arabic word in the text is **nûra** = pitch. Sprenger, Meadows of Gold, 374, translates it as quicklime.
(4) 70. v. also Idrîsî, Nuzhat Al-Mushtâq, [26].
(5) Ibn Jubayr, 70-71.
(6) I, ch. XIX, 108.

but it will not stand well in a storm. The ships are not pitched, but are rubbed with fish-oil ... They have no iron to make nails of, and for this reason they use only wooden trenails in their shipbuilding, and then stitch the planks with twine... Hence 'tis a perilous business to go a voyage in one of those ships, and many of them are lost, for in that Sea of India the storms are often terrible. »

Constant references to nails are found in the papyri correspondence relating to shipbuilding under the early Caliphate. Letter No. 1408, dated 91/709, is an order to the people of one of the villages of Aphrodito, the Five Fields, to collect fifty **litrae** of unrefined iron from the pagarch Bâsilyûs and make it into nails for the arsenal at Babylon : « *In the name of God. Qurra ibn Sharîk, Governor, to you, the people of the Five Fields in the village of Aphrodito. Receive from your pagarch 50 = fifty litrae of dirty lump iron from the Government stores and make of it when clean 33 1/3 = thirty-three and a third litrae of nails, and pay them over to 'Abd Al-A'lâ Ibn Abî Hakîm for the* **carabi** *and* **acatenaria** *in the present 8th indiction and the raid of the 9th indiction, and if you give the wages (instead), pay for the 50 litrae of lump iron for cleaning 1 1/3 = one and a third nominal solidus only. Written the ... 8th indiction. Total, 50 litrae of dirty iron; for cleaning, 33 1/3 litrae, 1 1/3 S.* » (1)

Another interesting letter is No. 1369, dated 92/710, concerning a quantity of iron which the government has provided for the making of nails for shipbuilding : « *In the name of God. Qurra, etc... We have sent up to you... for the manufacture of nails for the* **carabi** *4 quintals of iron answering to (?) the standard (?) which we stated (?) in the requisition in the present... for the past year 6 litrae per quintal, and behold ! we have appended for you to the present letter the specification of the said iron, stating what we reckon on each kind for waste. On receiving the present letter, therefore, take over the said iron and distribute to the places in accordance with the powers given by our demand notes sent to you, not showing partiality or antipathy to any (place) in the said distribution but assigning to each place proportionately the*

---

(1) Bell, Der Islam, III, No. 1408, 135; P. Lond., IV, 78. v. Becker, P.A.F., Z.A., XX, No. IX, 88 sq.; Grohmann, Aperçu de Pap. **Arabe, 68.**

quota which falls to it of each kind, exhorting them (i.e. the inhabitants) to make it with all speed into good nails, manufactured in accordance with [the specification ?] sent to you. Written..., 9th indic.

    Memorandum (?).

    Specification 4 quintals

        Lumps 4 quintals, to be reduced by a third.

    Scrap iron 2 quintals, thus :

        1 quintal to be reduced by a third,

        1 quintal to be reduced by a fourth.» (1)

The above two letters are very important as they throw light upon the iron industry at this period. It seems there were two classes of iron, unrefined and scrap. An item in the account No. 1434 (2) also refers to this fact and another item, dated 97/715, in the same account, (3) fixes the price of the three quintals of unrefined iron for shipbuilding at 16 2/3 solidi, (4) that is the price of the quintal 5 5/9 solidi. Bell (5) suggests that the unrefined iron might mean pig-iron, but Thomlinson (6) points out that this is a modern product, entirely unknown, as far as has been ascertained, at that time. He therefore suggests that unrefined iron (lumps or blooms), was probably imported from Spain or Elba, even nuder Muslim rule. Amîr Abû'l-Hârith (7) says that Spain possessed great riches and mines of every kind. Muqaddasî (8) also states that there were iron mines in the mountains above Beirut and, according to Ya'qûbî, (9) there

---

(1) Bell, Der Islam, II, No. 1369, 374-375; P. Lond., IV, 43-44.

(2) Bell, P. Lond., IV, No. 1434 (107-118), 314 ; Der Islam, IV, 89 (107-118).

(3) Bell, Der Islam, IV, No. 1434, 93.

(4) The solidus during the time of Justinian II (A.D. 685-95), was equal to 15 dirhems (about 12 shillings). v. Wroth, I, LXXIV sq.; Bell, P. Lond., IV, No. 1414(82), 136 ; Hofmeir, Der Islam, IV, 97 sq.; Balâdhurî, 465 ; Sauvaire, J. As., XV, Sér. VII, 1880, 251 sq.; XIX, Sér. VII, 1882, 25 sq.; Grohmann, A.P.E.L., II, No. 96, 103; Mez, 473 sq.; Gibbon, VI, 5.

(5) P. Lond., IV, 43.

(6) Thomlinson, of the Seaton Carew iron-works, quoted by Bell, P. Lond., IV, 43.

(7) 154.

(8) B.G.A., III, 184.

(9) Ya'qûbî, B.G.A., VII, 334 sq., gives a full account.

were metals in Africa. Extensive iron mines were also found in Sicily (1) and Becker (2) says that in the early Caliphate Pisa used to supply the Muslims with materials, including iron, required for shipbuilding.

The unrefined iron, when cleaned for making nails, was reduced by a third (3) and the manufacture of 33 1/3 litrae of nails cost 1 1/3 solidi. The scrap was divided into two categories : the one, when cleaned, to be reduced by a third and the other by a fourth. It seems that the division was due to some being clean, well-worked small scrap and the other dirty and oxidised. The method of making iron (4) was probably by scooping out a hole in the ground, placing in it a mixture of ores (probably first calcined a little), and charcoal which was then heated by hand or foot. The product was in malleable lumps which were cut into convenient pieces or blooms as required. The pores, however, contained slag which necessitated a refining process in the course of manufacture; this accounted for the considerable wastage through oxidisation and loss of iron in the slag.

An item, dated 92/710 in account No. 1449, refers to a certain Papwônsh who is ordered to collect anchors for « *arrears of requisitions for Clysma.* » (5) Copper chains are also mentioned in the papyri as part of a ship's equipment. In one item of the register No. 1434, the price of one quintal of copper chains is fixed at 8 1/3 solidi (6) and in another at 6 2/3. (7) It seems probable that, as in the case of iron, copper was of two kinds. From ancient times this metal was plentiful in Cyprus, (8) whence it got its name, and Amîr Abû'l-Hârith (9) states that Spain was rich in copper mines. The supplies might have been imported from these two places.

---

(1) Mez, 442; East, Historical Geog., 289.
(2) E.I., II, 19.
(3) v. Bell, P. Lond., IV, No. 1434(107-118), 314 ; Der Islam, IV, 89, (107-118), where 3 quintals of lump iron, when cleaned, are reduced to 2 quintals.
(4) Bell, P. Lond., IV, 43.
(5) Bell, Der Islam, XVII, No. 1449, 7.
(6) Bell, Ibid, IV, No. 1434, 89, 91, 93.
(7) Bell, ibid, IV, No. 1434, 91, 96.
(8) Rose, 23.
(9) 154.

From account No. 1433 (1) chains also seem to have been made of tin, the price of which is given as 1 4/9 solidi for ten litrae of beaten tin and one solidus for the same amount of molten tin.

III. Cables and Other Fittings

The Arabic word for cable is **habl** which, according to Lammens,(2) has passed into the Romance languages. Muqaddasî(3) states that Egypt was famous for ropes made of palm fibre. Cables of palm fibre are mentioned in the papyri and the price of one is given as 7/12 solidus. (4) Egypt produced a special kind of hemp admirably suited for cordage and ship's tackle. Ibn Al-Faqîh (5) speaks of it : « *One of the wonders of Egypt is a kind of hemp called* **duqs** *which is used for ship's tackle; such ropes are called* **al-qirqis**». Papyrus was also used for this purpose and was grown, according to Ibn Hawqal,(6) in a marshy stretch within the town of Palermo. The Muslims made this city their political capital and naval base in Sicily when they had secured a foot-hold there.

There are references in the papyri to a number of fittings for ships. In letter No. 1348, dated 92/710, and in account No. 1414 there is mention of cushions, (7) the latter fixing the price at one solidus for four cushions. Though no clue as to their use is given it is possible they were intended for the rowers' benches. Account No. 1434 includes items, dated 96/714, concerning pads as part of the fittings for the **carabi** and other ships. (8) The price is fixed as one solidus for five pads; if money composition is made it is one solidus for four and a half pads. In No. 1414 there is mention of felt, the price being three and a third solidi for one quintal and No. 1433 contains an item, dated 88-9/706-7, stating one and a half solidi as part of the price of hides for covering the two-

---

(1) Bell, Der Islam, III, No. 1433, 373.
(2) Mots Français, 62.
(3) B.G.A., III, 203.
(4) Bell, Der Islam, IV, No. 1434, 90, 93
(5) B.G.A., V. 66.
(6) Ed. Kramers, 122-123.
(7) Bell, P. Lond., IV, No. 1348(4), 21 ; Der Islam, II, 278 ; No. 1414, III, 139.
(8) Bell, Der Islam, IV, No. 1434, 89-90, 93.

banked **carabi** in the island of Babylon by Paeon the sailor.(1) It appears that the sides of a vessel were first padded with felt and then covered with oxhides sewn together in sheets (2) to protect ships from catching fire or being rammed. Constantine Porphyrogenitos (3) speaks of goat skins, used on Byzantine ships as tarpaulins for awnings to keep off sun and arrows.

Of the skilled workmen mentioned in the papyri caulkers are referred to on several occasions (4) and Constantine (5) explains how planks of ships were caulked on end with cotton fibre and wax. He (6) also speaks of lead sheeting for the part underneath the water line and says that one hundred and ten sheets or three thousand pounds of lead were required for twenty ships, that is, one hundred and fifty pounds per ship. Account No. 1433 (7) mentions yarn which may have been used for stitching pieces of sailcloth together. Constantine (8) gives useful information about sails. He states that they were made of separate pieces of sailcloth sewn together to the length required for each type of ship; the sail of a Russian galley was thirty cubits in length and that of a Dalmatian galley twenty eight cubits. He also refers to sail stitchers and the thread they used.

---

(1) Bell, Der Islam, III, No. 1414, 139; No. 1433, 372.
(2) v. Const. Porph., De Cerem., Ed. Bonn, II, 675. I owe the reference to Const. Porph. for this part to Prof. R.J. Jenkins.
(3) Ibid, II, 675.
(4) v. Infra, 106.
(5) Ibid, II, 675.
(6) Ibid, II, 671.
(7) Bell, ibid, III, No. 1433, 370.
(8) Ibid, II, 674.

CHAPTER IV

NAVAL ORGANISATION

I. **Disposition of Fleets**

The principal feature of the naval organisation was the institution known by the Latin word **cursus** (corsair), that is, the raids which the fleets of the Caliphate regularly undertook against the Byzantine Empire. The papyri make it clear that they occurred every year and that the taxes for each expedition were raised in the previous indiction.(1) This practice of making periodical incursions was, according to Amari,(2) begun by Mûsâ ibn Nusayr in 85/704 and was certainly fully established during the governorship of Qurra ibn Sharîk. Certain passages in the papyri further show that the fleets were despatched during the winter.(3) Brooks'(4) assertion that it was unusual to make expeditions at this time is not supported by evidence from the papyri. The raids are invariably distinguishable, not only by the indiction in which they were made, but by certain place names referring to the three provinces of Egypt, «*Oriens*» and Africa, which incidentally throw some light on the organisation of the Caliphate. It seems that the eparchies still existed as the Mus-

---

(1) Bell, J.H.S., XXVIII, 114 ; P. Lond., IV, XXXII.
(2) Storia, Old Edition, I, 124 ; New Edition, I, 248-249 ; Bell, J.H.S., XXVIII, 114.
(3) Bell, P. Lond., IV, XXXII ; No. 1349(15,16), 23 ; Der Islam, II, 278; Becker, P.S.R., No. I (9-12), 58.
(4) E.H.R., XXVIII, 438.

lims modelled their Empire very closely on that of the Byzantine Emperors even to the retention of the name «*Oriens*» which was no longer appropriate for them.(1)

There can be no question of raids against these districts and when they are mentioned in connection with any expedition the reference must be to the fleets starting from them. By the end of the 1st/beginning of the 8th century, the naval administration of the Caliphate was fairly well organised, the navy being subdivided into distinct self-controlled fleets.(2) Ibn Khaldûn(3) alludes this fact when he says : «*The Muslims built warships and equipped them with fighting men fully armed to meet the infidels overseas; they made their naval headquarters on the coast of Syria, Africa, Maghrib and Spain.*» Thus each province had its own separate fleet to which Egypt and perhaps the other provinces had to contribute.

Accounts Nos. 1433, 1434 and 1449 contain references to the raiding fleet of Egypt(4) which was connected with the two great arsenals of Babylon and Clysma. The «*raiding fleet of the sea*» is mentioned in an item in account No. 1434(5) from which it is clear that Al-Qâsim ibn Ka'b and Yazîd ibn Abî Yazîd were the officials responsible for this

---

(1) The general scheme of Muslim administration as given by Bell, P. Lond., IV, XXIV ; J.H.S., XXVIII, 114-115, was as follows : First came the great provinces, Africa, Egypt, «*Oriens*» etc... under governors; Egypt was divided into Upper and Lower Egypt for financial purposes. Next were the eparchies under duces whose exact functions are not clear, but were especially connected with finance. Then came the pagarchies under pagarchs corresponding directly with the governors and paying taxes directly to the Central Treasury. Lastly there were the village communities. v. also Abbott, 100-101 ; Butler, 450-451 ; Kremer, Culturgesch., I, 162 sq. The dux mentioned very often in the Aphrodito papyri may no doubt be taken as that of the Thebaid. From No. 1440(6) it would appear that he was an Arab. He is frequently mentioned in No. 1412(129) as making payments. He is twice referred to in No. 1438, once in connection with articles ordered for the fleet, and once in connection with a fine imposed upon runaway sailors. Arabs also occur as pagarchs. v. Bell, P. Lond., IV No. 1383 (17), 56; XIX, n. 3; Becker, P.A.F., No. XIV; Wessely, U.K.F., III, 260.

(2) Bell, J.H.S., XXVIII, 114 ; P. Lond., IV XXXIII ; Muir, Caliphate, 362.

(3) Muqaddima, II, 34 ; reproduced by Maqrîzî, Khitat, II, 190.

(4) For papyri referring to the raiding fleet of Egypt v. Bell, Der Islam, III, No. 1433, 371, 372 ; IV, No. 1434, 87(17-26), 91(207) ; XVII, No. 1449, 7, 8. v. also Bell, J.H.S., XXVIII, 114-115 ; P. Lond., IV, XXXIII.

(5) Bell, Der Islam, IV, No. 1434, 91(224-231). v. 95, 96.

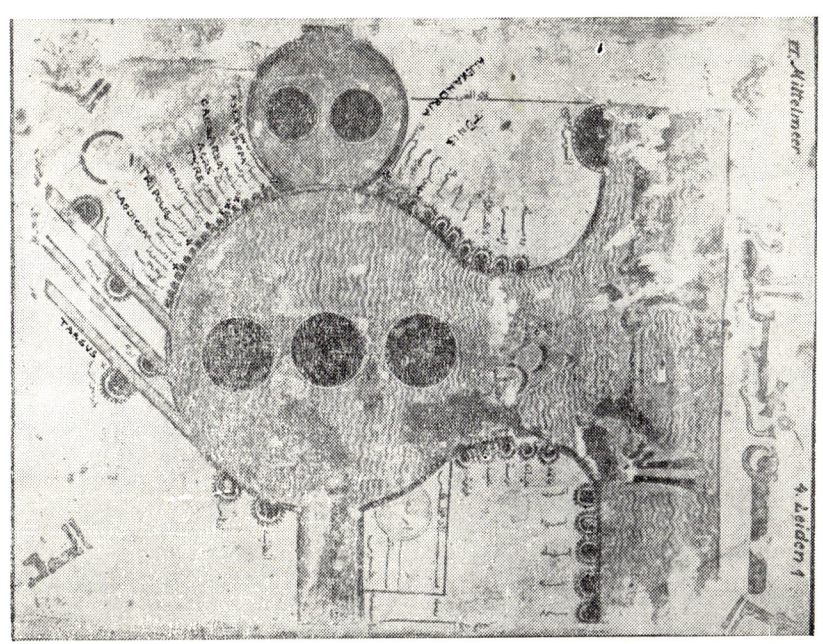

Mediterranean naval centres as shown on Istakhri's map. Original in Leyden, Reichauniv. Cd. 1702. Facsimile, Miller, I. Bd. I, Heft. Tafel I.

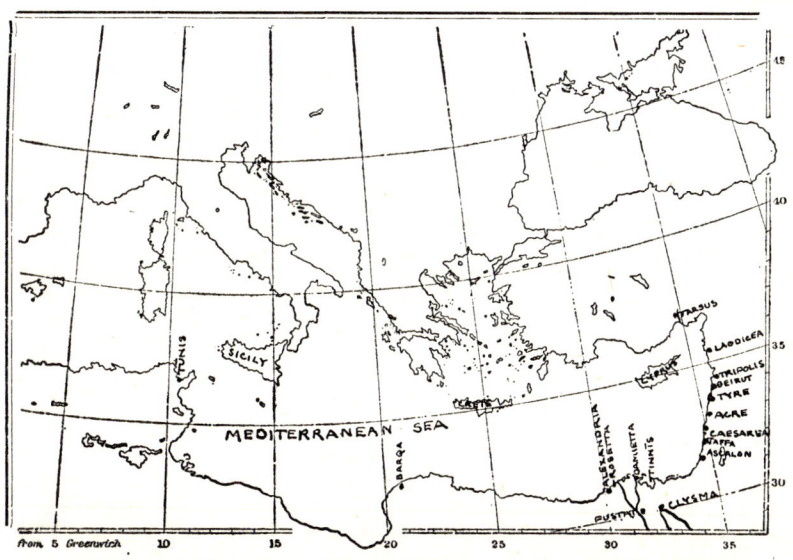

Early Mediterranean Naval Centres of Eastern Muslims.

fleet. The former was superintendent of the dockyard at Babylon and it can therefore be assumed that the fleet was in some way connected with Egypt. Perhaps it was the one stationed at Clysma and the sea referred to was the Red Sea. Both Becker and Bell(1) favour this explanation, though a raiding fleet seemed hardly necessary there at that time.

The third raiding fleet, that of the «*Oriens*», is also mentioned in the papyri. Letter No. 1374,(2) written in 93/711, from Qurra to the pagarch, concerns the wages of seven sailors who were sent to the «*Oriens* » for service on the **acatenaria** in the raid of the 8th indiction, 91/709, and remained there. The allusion here seems to be to a province so called, probably Syria, or at any rate the parts near the coast which were in the old «*Oriens*». The papyri show that Laodicea(3) was one of the chief naval centres of the province. The fourth fleet, that of Africa, had its headquarters at Barqa and Tûnis.(4) Besides the raiding fleets, a squadron was evidently responsible for guarding the mouths of the Nile,(5) a precaution no doubt suggested by the Byzantine attack on Alexandria,(6) after the Muslim conquest.

It will be profitable here to compare the disposition of Muslim and Byzantine navies. Since the end of the sixth century A.D. the Byzantine Empire had neglected to

---

(1) Bell, P. Lond., IV, XXXIII, n. 1. Under the Fâtimid Caliphs, the headquarters of the Red Sea fleet were at 'Aydhâb. v. Bell, J.H.S., XXVIII, 115, n. 75.

(2) Bell, Der Islam, II, No. 1374, 375-376. v. Bell. P. Lond., IV, XVIII; and n. 1. For papyri referring to sailors and their supplies for the raiding fleet of the «*Oriens*» v. Bell, Der Islam, III, No. 1433, 371 IV, No. 1434, 88, 91-92, 94 ; XVII, No. 1441, 4, 6 ; No. 1449, 6.

(3) v. Supra, 53.

(4) Bell, P. Lond., IV, XVII, n. 4, says that the Berlin Qurra Papyrus, dated 95/713, «*seems to prove that Pentapolis (Barqa), which in Byzantine times formed part of the diocesis of Aegyptus, had now been transferred to Africa.*» v. Supra. 64 sq.

(5) For passages in papyri referring to the coast-guard fleet at the mouths of the Nile v. Bell, Der Islam, IV, No. 1434, 87, 93, 95 ; XVII, No. 1441, 6. v. also Bell, J.H.S., XXVIII, 115 ; P. Lond., IV, XXXIII.

(6) For Byzantine attempt to retake Alexandria in 25/645 v. Ibn 'Abd Al-Hakam, 175 ; Balâdhurî, 221 ; Ya'qûbî, Hist., II, 189 ; Tabarî, I, 2809 ; Ibn Khaldûn, 'Ibar, II, Pt. II, 127; Maqrîzî, I.F., III, 159-160.

maintain a strong naval force but the creation of Muslim sea power and the aggressive naval policy of Muʻâwiya forced Constantinople to reorganise the fleet.(1) This was principally the work of Constans II. There was one supreme naval command, that of the admiral (strategos), of the carabisiani, who controlled two districts, each of which had its own fleet commanded by a vice-admiral (drungarius). These were the province of the Cibyrrhaeots, which included Pamphylia and was the more important, and that of the Aegean Sea, consisting of the northern coastline of Asia Minor and the islands.(2) It seems that Muslim organisation at that time was superior to that of the Byzantines.(3) As a protective measure, in the 3rd/9th century, when African Muslims had acquired supremacy over the Mediterranean, Michael II set about reforming the fleet and Basil I continued the work. A new naval province or theme was created, that of Samos, with Smyrna as capital. In addition, there was the imperial fleet stationed at Constantinople. Smaller establishments were maintained in Sicily, the Peloponnese and the entrance to the Black Sea, whilst the theme of Cephallenia became the base for Byzantine operations in the west. When the fleets co-operated there was a single admiral (the great drungarius), in command of all the forces. The Cibyrrhaeot theme formed the Byzantine outpost against the Muslims and engagements with the Amîrs of Adana and Tarsus were constant.(4) Thus, by the end of the 1st/beginning of the 8th century, Muslim naval organisation had reached a high standard which the Byzantines only began to achieve in their efforts of the 3rd/9th century, the effects of which were not fully realised until a later period.

---

(1) Bury, Gibbon Edition, VI, App. V. 538 ; Eastern, 229 ; Centinario, II, 24; Baynes, Byz. Empire, 144; Runciman, Byz. Civilisation, 149.

(2) For this organisation v. Baynes, Byz. Empire, 144-145.

(3) Cf. Reinaud, J.As., September 1848, 232, where he states that Muslim sea power was inferior to that of the Christians all through the Middle Ages and that the Muslims did not dream of equipping the fleets until it was necessary for their defence.

(4) For this reorganisation v. Baynes, Byz. Empire, 145-146; Amari, Storia, Old Edition, I, 175 ; New Edition, I, 301 ; Bury, Administrative System, 108 sq.; Eastern 230; Gibbon Edition, V., App. V, 538; Diehl, Etudes Byzantines, 280 sq.; Schlumberger, 49-50; Gfrörer, Byz. Geschichten, Bd. II, 432.

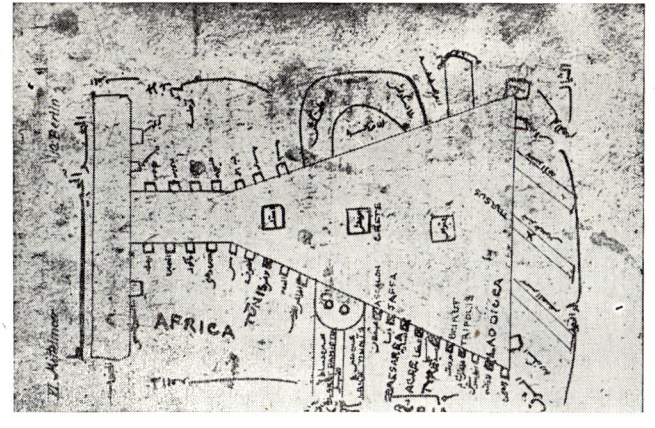

Mediterranean Centres as shown on Muqaddasī's map. Original in Berlin. Pr. Staatsbibl. 6034. Facsimile, Miller I Bd. Heft, Tafel 4.

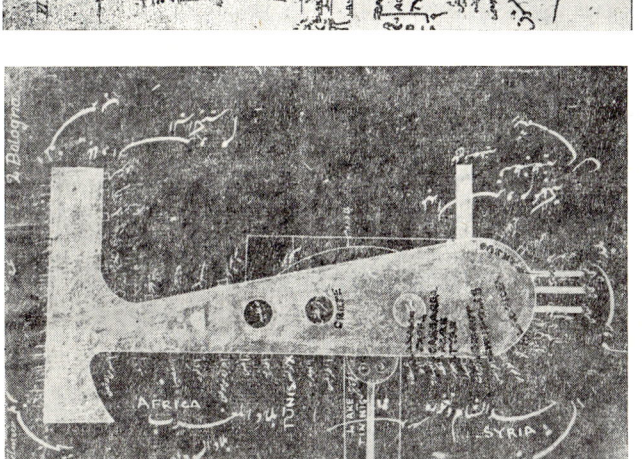

Mediterranean Naval Centres as shown on Balkhī's map. Original Bologna, Univ. Bib. Facsimile, Miller, I Bd. Heft, Tafel 4.

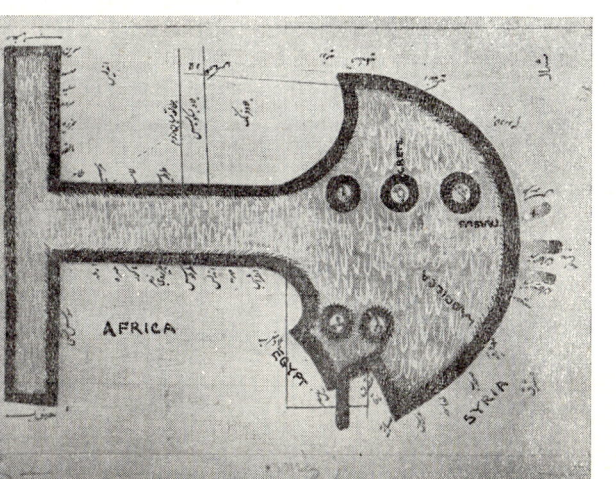

Mediterranean Naval Centres as shown on Jayhānī's map. Facsinile Miller. V. Bd. Beiheft, Tafel, 67.

II. **Maintenance of Fleet**

Naval Expenditure.

The papyri show that the total revenue of Egypt, after deducting local expenditure, founds its way either to the treasury in Alexandria(1) or to that in Fustât. Money for special purposes, naval or otherwise, was sent directly to the officials responsible or through the treasury.(2) Letter No. 1336(3) specified the wages of a carpenter which were to be paid out of the treasury. In the Berlin Qurra papyrus(4) the money for wages and provisions was being furnished by the Central Treasury and local collectors were therefore to pay the amount direct into it.

The expenses of the fleet during the reign of Yazîd ibn Mu'âwiya rose to 7000 dinars yearly.(5) Greater sums seem to have been raised in the 3rd/9th century for Ibn Khurdâdhbih(6) says that the cost of one maritime expedition came to some 100,000 dinars (about £ 30,000).

Figures relating to the expenditure for Byzantine naval undertakings are available for comparison with those of the Muslims. The pay of officers and men for each of the expeditions against Crete in the time of Leo VI and Constantine VII amounted to over £ 140,000.(7) On the first occasion there were 177 ships and 47,127 men. Bury reckons that in the second attempt the fitting out of the ships cost more than £ 1000, according to details of prices

---

(1) Abbott, 97 ; Bell, P. Lond., IV, 174. v. Supra, 29.
(2) Bell, P. Lond., IV, XXX, n. 3 ; Archiv für Papyrusforschung, V. 190.
(3) Quoted supra, 24.
(4) Quoted supra, 64 sq.
(5) Severus, Pat. Or., V, fasc. I, 5-6 [259-260] ; Synaxaire, Ed. Basset, Pat. Or., I, 341[127]; Wiet, Corpus, II, 167.
(6) B.G.A., VI, 255. v. Supra, 73 sq.
(7) v. Official documents of Const. Porph., quoted by Bury, Eastern, 231, n. 1, where the total in the first expedition seems to come to £ 143, 483 and in the second expedition to £ 147, 287.

of articles required for the equipment of the vessels. He(1) further suggests that the expedition against Damietta in 238/853 must have entailed an expenditure of £ 250,000. Thus there was a considerable difference between the cost of a Byzantine naval undertaking and one carried out by the Muslims.

Taxes for Fleet

In his studies of the taxes of the early Caliphate, Becker(2) was obliged to turn to the ancient institutions of the Roman Empire, but Rouillard's recent investigation of Byzantine administration together with the valuable material to be found in the papyri recently discovered, give a fair idea of the situation before and after the Muslim conquest.

The taxes levied in Egypt during the early period of the Caliphate go back to the Byzantine administration and can be divided into two principal groups, ordinary or public, and extraordinary taxes. The former included money payments and the corn tax or embola, payable in kind, a portion being sent to the State granaries at Babylon (Fustât), for exportation or distribution among Arab tribes or for the maintenance of public officials. The latter were raised according to necessity and could be paid in money or in kind; they usually concerned allowances for officials and Arab settlers, provisions for workmen and sailors, naval construction and transport,(3) Papyrus No. 1414(4) shows that there was probably no formal distinction between requisitions in kind and the money equivalent. There was also a tax of personal service which varied from minor, temporary demands to important, responsible liturgies.

In a country where agriculture depended upon artificial

---

(1) Bury, Eastern, 231.
(2) Beiträge, II, 81 sq. v. Grohmann, Aperçu de Pap. Arabe, 60.
(3) On these various taxes, V. Bell, P. Lond., IV, Nos. 1338, 8 sq.; 1339, 10; 1357. 33; 1414, 167-174; XXV sq.; Der Islam, II, 272-273; Byz., Zeit., XXVIII, 282-284; Grohmann, Aperçu de Pap. Arabe, 60, 66; Abbott, 76, 94; Tritton, 197-211; Rouillard, 76 sq., 79-81, 121; Wiet, Précis de l'Hist. de l'Egypte, II, 75 sq.; Muir, Caliphate, 167.
(4) Bell, P. Lond., IV, No. 1414, 124 sq. and XXVI.

irrigation and the flood of the Nile, the corvée for the upkeep of canals and embankments had existed since ancient times and was unpaid labour.(1) The exact date of the introduction of the liturgical system is unknown. When Egypt was incorporated into the Roman Empire, the Romans inherited to the full the Ptolemaic political conception which subordinated the individual to the State. The earliest extant papyrus(2) referring to personal service shows it to have been established in A.D. 91 and relates to a person released from a liturgy «*owing to age and financial inability.*» It was probably adopted fairly early in the Roman period for certain offices and gradually extended to others. By the end of the third century A.D. the principle of compulsory service was fully established. One papyrus(3) contains a complaint by a person charged with the duty of providing rowers for the ducal state galley, who said that one of his rowers had been pressed into a liturgy unsuited to him; he pointed out that this rower inherited his present liturgy from his father. This document also shows that a man could not be appointed to two public services at the same time. The principle of inheritance and compulsion came to be applied to any class whose labours were considered vital for the community.(4) Shippers, for example, whose services were necessary for the transport of corn to Constantinople, came under this ruling. In an earnest request, addressed to a duke of the Thebaid, asking for release from imprisonment, the petitioners declared that they were«*fullers and smiths and carpenters and boat-makers, and they have no other craft from (the time of their) parents and grandparents save only the earning of (their) present calling.*»(5) Craftsmen had become little better than serfs — son succeeded father without choice or hope. The servile state was in being.

(1) Bell, Byz. Zeit., XXVIII, 283; J.E.A., IV, 90; Abbott, 76; Wiet, Précis de l'Hist. de l'Egypte, II, 75; Grohmann, aperçu de Pap. Arabe, 67; Lane-Poole, Hist. of Egypt, 20.
(2) P. Flor., III, No. 312, 45 ; Bell, J.E.A., IV, 91-92 ; Vinogradoff, C.M.H., I, 553.
(3) P. Grenfell, II, No. 82, 131 ; Rouillard, 73, n. 2 ; Bell, J.E.A., IV, 100.
(4) P. Oxy., VI, 904, 241-243; VII, 1042(7), 188-190; P. Grenfell, II, No. 82, 131 ; Gelzer, Archiv. für Papyrusforshung, V, 357, n. 4; Rouillard, 73-74 ; Bell, J.E.A., IV, 100.
(5) P. Cairo, Maspero, I, No. 67020, 45 sq.; Bell ; J.E.A., IV, 101.

Muslim Civil Service

The papyri reveal that the Muslim civil service for the administration of Egypt was highly organised. The procedure regarding personal service was in the main identical with that for taxation. Requisitions from the central government were addressed to the community and not to the individual. The central authorities divided the quotas whilst local officials seem to be responsible for the assignment of service between the taxpayers, in accordance with a register prepared by assessors.(1) The work, though apparently compulsory, was not exactly forced labour in the ordinary sense, but was a form of conscription, the persons requisitioned receiving wages. In some cases in accounts Nos. 1433 and 1434,(2) the labourers were required for work at the village embankments but no wages were stated. It might be suggested that the work may have been forced labour in the strict sense but the inference is not convincing since wages were not always mentioned.(3) The conscripts chosen had to be guaranteed by sureties.(4) Women as well as men might be called on for service.(5) According to a Cairo papyrus, dated 299/911.(6) the public service system under the 'Abbâsids operated in the same way as under the Umayyads. The Muslim civil service adapted to the needs of the time.

Maritime Civil Service

Recruitment of Sailors

The papyri is the main source of information for the maritime civil service of the early Caliphate. They show that

---

(1) Bell, P. Lond., IV, No. 1356 (10, 11), 32 ; No. 1393, 65-66, quoted Infra 99 sq.; XXXI; Abbott, 94; Muir, Caliphate, 167.
(2) Bell, P. Lond., IV, No. 1433(74), 288 ; No. 1434 (71 sq.), 312.
(3) Bell, P. Lond., IV, No. 1433 (16), 283; XXXII ; Muir, Caliphate, 167.
(4) Bell, P. Lond., IV, XXXII. v. Infra, 102 sq.
(5) Crum, P. Lond., IV, No. 1488, 430, and XXXII.
(6) Public Soc. Ital. per la Ricera dei Papieri Greci e Litini in Egitto III, No. 873, quoted by Grohmann, Aperçu de Pap. Arabe, 67.

the maintenance of the fleet was charged upon the inhabitants in three ways : the payment of money for specific purposes,(1) the provision of articles of various kinds and the supply of sailors. It seems that sailors for all the fleets were obtained by government requisitions from all parts of Egypt and not only from the coast towns(2) as might be expected. They were also drawn from various classes of the population including bathmen, fullers and shepherds.(3) The method of recruitment was probably the same as that for the raising of ordinary taxes, the governor stating the number required in his letter to the pagarch, and specifying the quota expected from each village in the demand notes addressed to it. The actual choice of men was left to local officials. Certain references point to the selection being made on the basis of a register, in accordance with which particular persons were listed as liable for service.(4) Although the beginning of letter No. 1393, dated 92/710, is missing, it is certainly from Qurra to Bâsilyûs the pagarch of Aphrodito. It gives the total requisition demanded from the pagarchy and distributes the quotas among the various villages, hamlets and monasteries. These were not left in the hands of local authorities. The calculation was made on the basis of census and tax registers sent by the pagarchs to headquarters, and as each pagarch had his permanent representative at Fustât, the latter may have been called on to co-operate in the work. This was probably done because of the well-founded distrust of local officials. In this letter Qura threatened Bâsilyûs with punishment if he neglected any of his instructions relating to sailors and their suppliers and warned him not to allow anyone to be unjustly treated : «... *(collect) from them all that we directed in our demand notes, while they on their side furnish the amount of their assessment in public and extraordinary taxes;*

---

(1) For example in P.E.R.F., No. 572, 144, the Arab official Ibn Yahyâ informed the inhabitants of the Aperatos Street at Madînat Al-Fayyûm that they had to produce $1/2 + 1/24 \div 1/28$ of a gold solidus as the cost of twenty boats. v. also Becker, P.A.F., Z.A., XX, No. 10; Grohmann, Aperçu de Pap. Arabe, 66.
(2) Bell, P. Lond., IV, XXXIV ; J.H.S., XXVIII, 112.
(3) Bell, P. Lond., IV, No. 1449(73), 375 ; 1449(90), 367 ; 1449(19), 372; XXXII, n. 3.
(4) Bell, J.H.S., XXVIII, 113.

and you are to take from them sureties, who shall be men of means, under obligation to answer for them if it appear that any of them has evaded his obligations, sending to us a register in which are contained the names and patronymics, arranged by hamlets, of the said sailors and artizans. You are to make known to us in the said register those who have (actually) gone out on behalf of their own hamlets, those hired on behalf of others, and the amounts paid for such persons for wages, not allowing to anyone the full amount(?) but sending off ...Let us not find that you have sent a money composition for any ...whatever, but only the person himself; (otherwise) we shall in requital visit you with a retribution which will be to your detriment, since you have no excuse whatever with regard to the personal service...(1)

The service was evidently compulsory, through a form of conscription by which sailors for the raiding fleets both of Egypt and other provinces were requisitioned from the pagarchies.(2) Two systems were followed by which the pagarchy might either pay the wages of men hired from another place or provide the men in person, together with their wages and maintenance.(3) In letter No. 1337, dated 91/709, Qurra informed Bâsilyûs, owing to the latter's neglecting to send the required sailors in person, he had been compelled to hire them from other places and commanded him to raise money for their wages. He further urged Bâsilyûs and the people of his district to show more zeal for maritime service and not always wait for his instruction : « *...and neglect to send out to us the sailors who were requisitioned from your administrative district for the* **carabi** *and* **dromonaria** *and other ships of the raiding fleet of Egypt in the 8th indiction, we have instructed Hayyân ibn Shurayh to hire those with whom you are in arrear in accordance with the rate (of wages) stated in our demand notes. On receiving the present letter,*

---

(1) Bell, P. Lond., IV, No. 1393, 65; Complete Eng. Tr. in J.E.A., XII, 279.
(2) Bell, P. Lond., IV, XXXIV ; Byz. Zeit., XXVIII, 283-284 ; J.H.S., XXVIII, 112.
(3) Bell, P. Lond., IV, Nos. 1433(16), 283; 1449(12), 372; XXXI; J.E.A. XII, 276 ; Crum, P. Lond., IV, Nos. 1508, 444; 1509, 446 sq.

therefore, send with all speed, in accordance with the account enclosed with the present letter, the money for their wages, not keeping back one single solidus of it. For indeed we know that it is no concern to you nor yet to the people of your district to carry out or perform any sort of duty, unless you are importuned for the arrears in your payments, except in accordance with the instructions contained in our demand notes. But we will not allow this to be so ; for we shall not treat the capable and efficient man who zealously performs his duty in the same way as him who through corruption falls short in the tasks entrusted to him by us. Therefore if you have any sense perform the command given by our letter, not sending any of these moneys negligently but discharging your duty zealously. Written ... 8th indiction.» (1)

Adaeratio in Maritime Service

Quarra's letters show that there was great reluctance among the rural population to accept personal service and a marked preference for a money composition, **adaeratio**, *by* which a village might pay the wages of a man hired from elsewhere in place of providing the sailor requisitioned. (2) The persons conscripted were paid according to a regular scale. The papyri establish the fact that when the man and not the **adaeratio** was provided the local authorities were responsible for his wages. There are several cases in the accounts (3) of fractions of men demanded for personal service, as, for example, «*a third of a sailor to serve in person.*» This meant that three small places were called on to provide a man between them, each paying a third of his wages, the man himself being presumably chosen by arrangements between the local chiefs of the hamlets as there is no instance of such a requisition being addressed to the pagarch. (4)

The Coptic papyrus No. 1508 (5) is especially interesting

---

(1) Bell, P. Lond., IV, No. 1337, 7 ; Der Islam, II ,272.
(2) Bell, J.E.A., XII, 276.
(3) For fractions of sailors and labourers demanded v. Bell, Der Islam, III, No. 1433, 372; IV, No. 1434, 87-88, 94; XVII, No. 1441, 6.
(4) Bell, P. Lond., IV, XXXI, n. 4 ; J.E.A., XII, 276.
(5) Crum, P. Lond., IV, No. 1508, 444 ; Bell, J.H.S., XXVIII, 112.

as it concerns the refusal of the government to accept **adaeratio**. It appears that the lashane of «*Keramion*» under Aphrodito paid, through the pagarch Bâsilyûs, the **adaeratio**, instead of providing workmen requisitioned for work at Babylon. The pagarch paid over the money to the tax-collector but when Qurra's messenger arrived he declared that only the workmen themselves would be accepted. The lashane «*went and hired the aforesaid workmen,*» and at his request, Bâsilyûs applied to the tax-collector for the return of the money. The document is a receipt for it from the lashane.

Security for Fulfilment of Service

The sailors having been chosen, the next step was to get security for the due fulfilment of their service. Sureties for sixty nine sailors are mentioned in letter 1393 (1) and among the accounts are lists of sailors and workmen requisitioned for various services, in some cases names being followed by those of sureties.(2) The agreements were probably always in Coptic, several of which are extant.(3) One was a guarantee declaration, dated 90/April 709, and addressed to Qurra by the officials of one of the villages of Aphrodito, the Three Fields, through pagarch Bâsilyûs. They declared themselves responsible for the work and good conduct of three sailors for the next year's raid. «*In the name etc... written, Pharmouthi 13th., 7th indiction. We, Apa Cyrus, son of the late Samuel, the lashane, and Apollo, son of Heraclius, the tax collector, and David, son of John and Phoebammon, son of George, inhabitants of the Three Fields, west of Jkôw (Ashqûh), we write unto the..., namely our lord, the all-famous Qurra, most wonderful governor, through you, most glorious lord, master Bâsîl, by God's will, illustrius and pagarch of Jkôw, with its homesteads and fields. Greeting. We declare, we are willing, we guarantee, we are responsible and we go surety and are liable for the*

---

(1) Bell, P. Lond., IV, No. 1393, 65 ; Complete Eng. Tr. in J.E.A., XII, 279.

(2) Bell, J.H.S., XXVIII, 113.

(3) Crum, P. Lond., IV, Nos. 1495, 437 ; 1496, 438 ; 1497, 439 ; 1498, 440 ; 1506, 443 ; 1511, 447.

persons of these sailors, being those of our fields, whose names we shall display to you at the bottom of this guarantee-declaration. Them we send northward, as sailors of ships, in this 7th year of the indiction, for the cursus of the 8th. indiction, that they may fulfil their expedition as sailors, without turning aside, in the census of Egypt, for the second time, that they may fulfil their expedition without turning aside. But if any one of them shall turn aside, we are ready to undergo any fine that our lord the allfamous governor may decree for us. For we are willing and responsible for them, ere ye had sent them. As an assurance therefore unto the ..., through you most glorious lordship, we have drawn up for you this guarantee-declaration, being responsible unto you with all our substance for this affair, swearing by the name of God Almighty and the health of our lords that bear rule, that we will keep and observe (it) as we have already written. We have been questioned and have agreed.

Here follows the ... of the names and residences of the three sailors; then a repeated declaration by the four sureties, to the same effect as before, and including the sailors' names. Since the sureties cannot write, George, son of Psate,, acts as their scribe. Then the signatures of five witnesses, a list of the sureties and Theodore the notary's subscription.»(1)

Another such document,(2) relative to the supply of sailors to be sent north, states that if they proved unsatisfactory the consequences would fall upon «*the heads of the guaranteed*» so that the guarantors in this case were not wholly responsible.

Fighting Men

In addition to Greek and Coptic sailors obtained by conscription, there were two other groups of persons connected with the fleet, the Muhâjirûn and Mawâlî. These were the military part of the crew as distinct from rowers and helmsmen.(3) It appears from Tabarî's(4) account of

---

(1) Crum, P. Lond., IV, No. 1494, 435-437.
(2) Crum, ibid, No. 1506, 443.
(3) Bell, P. Lond. IV, XXXIV; J.H.S., XXVIII, 113.
(4) I, 2870. v. Ibn Al-Athîr, VII, 244 (18 sq.); Levy, II, 332.

the battle of Dhât Al-Sawârî, 54/654-5, that the Coptic sailors were distinct from Muslim warriors and not concerned with the actual fighting.

The Muhâjirûn originally consisted of Arabs who had taken part in the Hijra or flight from Mecca to Medina, but by this time it also included those who had left their homes subsequently, so that Hijra now meant emigration.(1) These emigrants had settled in the new military capitals established in various parts of the Caliph's dominions such as Qayrawân in North Africa and Fustât in Egypt. The original Muslim theory was that the whole of a conquered country became the property of the victorious army, but the practice was soon given up owing to the impossibility of putting it into effect, and the Arab settlers received an allowance for their support(2) in lieu of the unmanageable booty. The allowance was of two kinds, corn from the embola, referred to by Becker(3) as *al-rizq*, and a money allowance. Other supplies, such as clothing,(4) were also granted. The papyri show that large numbers of the Muhâjirûn were employed in the fleet(5) and, according to No. 1447,(6) those of Egypt consisted chiefly of Ansâr and Quraysh. There is no evidence that the crews of Muslim ships were recruited from the inhabitants of the South Arabian coasts and the Persian Gulf. Lammens'(7) assertion that *«Mu'âwiya was especially indebted to the Yemenites and that it was from them that he preferred to recruit the crews for his fleet»*, is not supported by evidence from the papyri.

These documents, however, show that the Arabs were above all land fighters and that those serving in the fleet were not so much mariners as troops intended for landing on the coastal districts of the Byzantine Empire, as they are never

---

(1) Wellhausen, Ar. Reich, 16; Becker, P.A.F., Z.A., XX, 93; Bell, J.H.S., XXVIII, 113 ; P. Lond., IV, XXXIV.

(2) Wellhausen, ibid, 19 sq.; Bell, J.H.S., XXVIII, 113 ; Levy, II, 332.

(3) P.A.F., Z.A., XX, 93 ; Bell, J.H.S., XXVIII, 113.

(4) Becker, Beiträge, II, 85; Bell, ibid, 114.

(5) Bell, Der Islam, III, No. 1433, 372 ; IV, No. 1434, 93 ; XVII, No. 1449, 7-8, where supplies and allowances for Muhâjirûn are mentioned.

(6) Bell, P. Lond., IV, No. 1447, 360, and XXIV, n. 2.

(7) Mo'âwiya, 52-53. Cf. 279, where he says that the Muslim sea power depended on the obstinate landholders of Quraysh.

mentioned in connection with a purely naval squadron.(1) The inexperience of the Arabs in naval battles compared with the Byzantines may have been the reason why the Caliph 'Umar is said to have refused to consider naval action.(2) A tradition related by Tabarî(3) says that in the battle of Dhât Al-Sawârî the Muslims offered to fight on land but the Byzantines preferred the sea. It is worth noting here that when 'Uthmân is said to have allowed Mu'âwiya to carry out a naval enterprise he stipulated that no Muslim was to be pressed for sea service, which was to be on a voluntary basis.(4)

It seems to have been the custom for fighting men to take their wives with them. According to Balâdhurî(5) Mu'âwiya, in compliance with the Caliph's order, was accompanied by his wife Fâkhita(6) on the first expedition against Cyprus. 'Ubâda ibn Al-Sâmit also had his wife Umm Harrâm(7) with him on the same occasion. Ibn 'Abd Al-Hakam(8) relates that the wife of Ibn Abî Al-Sarh was with her husband at the time of the battle of Dhât Al-Sawârî and admired a certain 'Alqama ibn Yazîd for saving the admiral's ship which had been carried off by a Byzantine vessel.

The Mawâlî were of non-Arab race converted to Islam;(9) doubtless chiefly Greeks or Copts in Egypt. They were affiliated to Arab tribes and employed in various capacities, some serving in the fleet, as shown in the papyri.(10) The

---

(1) Bell, P. Lond., IV, No. 1351(5), 26, refers to the military members of the crew. v. Becker, P.S.R., No. 1(9), 58; Bell, P. Lond., IV, XXXIV, n. 4.
(2) Tabarî, I, 2820- 2821 ; Ibn Khaldûn, Muqaddima, II, 33 ; Maqrîzî, Khitat, II, 190.
(3) I, 2868.
(4) Tabarî, I, 2824 ; Maqrîzî, Khitat, II, 190.
(5) 153.
(6) Tabarî, II, 205, mentions her sister Katwa bint Qaraza whom Mu'âwiya also married.
(7) Balâdhurî, 154 ; Tabarî, I, 2820 ; Ibn Al-Athîr, III, 75 ; Ibn Taghrî Birdî, I, 85. v. Delaval, J.R.A.S., 1897, 81 sq. According to Isfahânî, Aghânî, XI, 100, Bakra, the daughter of Al-Zubirqân ibn Badr was the first Arab woman to go on a ship.
(8) 190-191 ; Maqrîzî, Khitat, I, 169 ; I.F., III, 164.
(9) v. Bell, J.H.S., XXVIII, 114, n. 66, where he refers to Wellhausen, Goldziher and Kremer.
(10) Bell, P. Lond., IV, Nos. 1353 (6, 29), 28 ; 1392(21), 64-65 ; 1393 (59), 67; 1435(87), 329; XXXIV, n. 6; 26, n. 5; J.H.S., XXVIII, 114.

Muhâjirûn of Fustât are mentioned several times as receiving an allowance of money and corn annually but no reference is made to the Mawâlî in this connection. However, in No. 1447(1) there are names of many Mawâlî receiving an allowance for their maintenance, the provision of their food and wages being chargeable to the taxpayers. Expenses and supplies for the «*Mawâlî of the* **acatia** *and* **dromonaria** *of the raiding fleet of the Orient*» are mentioned in Nos. 1441 and 1449 respectively.(2) It is not clear whether there was any difference in the amount alloted to Muhâjirûn and Mawâlî.

Workmen

Industry seems to have flourished only in Egypt at the time of the Muslim conquest and the Caliphs took steps to re-establish it on the Syrian littoral, especially at Acre and Tyre.(3) Ibn Khaldûn,(4) in his account of Arab navigation, says : « *When the Arab Empire was established and become predominant..., men of different trades offered their services to them* (Arabs) *who employed boatmen and sailors to help them to improve nautical knowledge and activities.*» The fact mentioned by Ibn Khaldûn is confirmed by the papyri which contain references to the equipment of the navy and show that large numbers of artisans, such as carpenters, skilled workmen, caulkers, fullers and blaksmiths were required.(5) They were employed in the dockyards of Babylon, Clysma and other naval centres. Letter No. 1393(6) mentions sailors as well as artisans who were also raised by levy. Severus(7) relates that Theodore, the governor of Alexandria during the Caliphate of Yazîd ibn Mu'âwiya,

---

(1) Bell, P. Lond., IV, No. 1447 (32 sq.), 361 and XXXIV ; J.H.S., XXVIII, 114.
(2) Bell, Der Islam, XVII, No. 1441, 4-5 ; No. 1449, 8.
(3) Bartold, Mussulman Culture, 12, 14.
(4) Muqaddima, II, 34 ; reproduced by Maqrîzî, Khitat, II, 190.
(5) For papyri references to these artisans v. Bell, P. Lond., IV, No. 1336, 6 ; No. 1410. 79 ; No. 1449 (90), 376; Der Islam, II, 271, 279; III, 132-133, 370, 371-372 ; XVII, 5-6 ; Bell, P. Lond., IV, No. 1391, 63 ; Becker, P.A.F., Z.A., XX, No. VIII, 84 ; Jernstedt, P. Ross. — Georg., IV, No. 6, 22 ; Bell, J.H.S., XXVIII, 114 ; J.E.A., XII, 276 ; Grohmann, Aperçu de Pap. Arabe, 67.
(6) Bell, P. Lond., IV, No. 1393, 65 ; Complete Eng. Tr. in J.E.A., XII, 279.
(7) Pat. Or., X, fasc. V, 372-373 [486-487].

compelled the monks in Egypt to build ships for the fleet and that Usâma, the governor of Egypt under Sulaymân ibn 'Abd Al-Malik, threatened them with service on board the ships if they did not pay a certain sum of money.(1) According to the same writer, the method of conscription was used also during the 'Abbâsid Caliphate. He states(2) that in the reign of the Caliph Abû Ja'far Al-Mansûr, the Patriarch and bishops in Egypt were not compelled to pay any sum of money for the fleet but had «*to perform the task allotted to them daily in the arsenal at Misr, working with their own hands at whatever was required for the ships for a whole year, with their faces exposed to the sun all day during the summer.*»

Supplies and Provisions

The fleet was furnished with supplies of all kinds by means of the taxes. Aphrodito regularly provided money and supplies in kind. The latter included timber, iron, copper, ropes, cushions, pads and yarn(3) for ships; bread, butter, wine, oil and salt (4) for the maintenance of artisans and sailors. Wheat of the embola paid to the granaries of Babylon is mentioned in No. 1386(5) and a boat holding one hundred artabas of wheat is demanded in No. 1351.(6) In one case nine measures of butter were to be sent to Alexandria and delivered to the Augustal for a fleet apparently on the verge of departure.(7)

For some inexplicable reasons, local authorities seemed to have preferred **adaeratio** even in the case of supplies. Letter

---

(1) Pat. Or., V, fasc. I, 70-71 [324-325].

(2) Ibid, X, fasc. V, 374 [488].

(3) For these materials v. Supra, Ch. II, 75 sq.

(4) For oil, sour wine and salt for the maintenance of skilled workmen v. Bell, Der Islam, III, No. 1414, 137 ; IV, No. 1434, 95. For provisions in general v. Bell, J.H.S., XXVIII, 114 ; P. Lond., IV, XXXVIII.

(5) Quoted supra, 25 sq.

(6) Bell, Der Islam, II, No. 1351, 279. v. also IV, No. 1434, 95.

(7) No. 1392, quoted supra, 28.

No. 1348(1) is an order to Bâsilyûs to send supplies and not «*to collect money composition*» and in letter No. 1393(2) Qurra insisted that the supplies ordered must all be paid in kind except in the case of boiled wine for which **adaeratio** was demanded. This explains why the schedule appended to the second letter only gave rate and quantity of all supplies save for boiled wine, for which rate, quantity and total cost were given.

In letter No. 1353, dated 92/710, Qurra ordered Bâsilyûs not to accept money composition for wheat, bread or other articles unless the person was really unable to pay in kind : «*Do not delay any thing at all of the wheat and bread nor yet collect from the places any money composition whatsoever in lieu of them but the articles themselves. And of the remaining supplies whatever article among them the people of the places have ready send at once, and if, anyone is unable to pay in kind collect his money composition in accordance with the rate of prices contained in our demand notes, and send it to us by your faithful agent with instructions to pay it to us, not giving to the supercargoes(?) who receive the said supplies any money payment whatever. And do not neglect to send quickly the sailors and workmen and the supplies or give ground of complaint against you.*»(3)

Another interesting letter is No. 1354(4) which gives details concerning supplies for a raiding fleet. Unfortunately, the beginning of the letter is missing so that the object of the correspondence is a little uncertain. Bâsilyûs was instructed to return the supplies, which had apparently been embarked for transport, to the taxpayers and not to make any claims upon them until after the harvest. The order refers only to wheat and bread. The reason for the unloading of the wheat is not clear but it was probably a relief measure for the taxpayers on account of some temporary need having arisen. This supposition is supported by the order to return the money composition for the supplies to the full. There might have been

---

(1) Bell, P. Lond., IV, No. 1348, 21 ; Der Islam, II, 278.
(2) Bell, J.E.A., XII, 276, 279.
(3) Bell, Der Islam, II, No. 1353, 280-281 ; P. Lond., IV, 27.
(4) Quoted supra, 30 sq.

a shortage in the preceding year's harvest and as the officials could not raise the full amount of corn required, they might have collected the balance in money at a reduced rate. Thus Qurra, finding that the taxpayers were exhausted, decided to overlook the deficit for this year and to collect it out of the ensuing harvest. In any case the letter illustrates to some extent his care for the interests of the people and is a vindication of his character which had suffered from 'Abbâsid historians. Although the measure may not have been entirely due to kindness he preferred to have the whole amount in kind at the next harvest to taking part of it in cash at a reduced rate immediately. He evidently disapproved of local officials accepting a lower rate without his authority.

Wages and Cost of Supplies

These are best compared in tabular form and the following details taken from the papyri give an idea of the cost of living and the rate of wages at this period.

A — Wages of Sailors and Artisans

Date	Workmen	Rate of Wages Per Month.	Papyrus	Remarks
97/715	1 Sailor	1 2/3 S.	No. 1434	Bell, Der Islam, IV, 92.
91/709	1 Carpenter	2/3 S.	No. 1336	Bell, ibid, II, 271. The wages are said to be defrayed out of the funds in the Central Treasury.
91/709	1 Carpenter	1 1/3 S.	No. 1410	Bell, ibid, III, 132-133. v. Becker, P.A.F., No. VIII, 84.
98/716	1 Carpenter	1 1/4 S.	No. 1434	Bell, ibid, IV, 93. The same wages in No. 1366, Bell, ibid, II. 374.
91/709	1 Shipbuilder	2 S.	No. 1410	Bell, ibid, III, 132-133.
91/709	1 Caulker	1 1/2 S.	No. 1410	Bell, ibid, III, 132-133. The same wages in No. 1434, Bell, ibid, IV, 92, 93.
92/710	1 Sawyer	1 5/6 S.	No. 1341	Bell, ibid, II, 274.
97-8/715-6	1 Blacksmith	3/4-1 3/4 S.	No. 1435	Bell, ibid, IV, 92, 93. The wages for the manufacture of two quintals of iron nails are 2 S. v. Bell, ibid, III. No. 1433, 370.

109

B — Cost of Provisions for Men.

Date	No. of Men	Cost of Provisions	Papyrus	Remarks
95/713	2 1/2 (sailors)	11 1/6 S. (4 1/2 S. per man).	Berlin	Archiv für Papyrusforschung V, 189 sq. The journey from Antinoopolis to Pentapolis. v. Bell, P. Lond., IV, XXXVII.
97/715	4 (sailors)	2 S. (1/2 S. per man)	No. 1434	Bell, P. Lond., IV, 309 (21, 24), XXXVIII; Der Islam, IV, 87. The journey from Aphrodito to the mouth of the Nile.
Uncertain	1 (skilled workman).	11 1/4 Carats = 1/2 S. for 6 months.	No. 1414	Bell, P. Lond., IV, 152 (304), XXXVIII, n. 1; Der Islam, III, 137. Probably only oil and salt.

C. — Cost of Provisions.

Date	Article	Price	Papyrus	Remarks
80/699	Wheat	1 S. per 20 artabas	P.E.R.F. No. 587	148. v. Bell, P. Lond., IV, XXXVIII. These prices included probably the cost of carriage from the local centre to Babylon and may have been different from the market prices, though the variations show that they depended on the market to some extent. Cf. Severus, Pat. Or., V, fasc. I, 67 [321], 69 [323].
88-9/ 706-7	Wheat	1 S. per 12 artabas	No. 1433 (119)	
91/709	Wheat	1 S. per 13 artabas	No. 1435 (11,12)	
97-8/ 715-16	Wheat	1 S. per 10 artabas	No. 1435 (128)	
92-3/ 710-11	Butter	1 1/6 per measure	No. 1392	Bell, P. Lond., IV, 64; Der Islam, II, 381.
93/711	Oil	1/2 S. per metron (= 10 Xestae)	No. 1375	Bell, P. Lond., IV, XXXVIII ; Der Islam, II, 376.
Uncertain	Oil	1 S. per 20 Xestae (1/2 S. per metron).	No. 1414	Bell, Der Islam, III, 137.
Uncertain	Oil	1 S. per 12 Xestae.	No. 1414	Bell, P. Lond., IV, XXXVIII.

C — Cost of Provisions (Cont.)

Date	Article	Price	Papyrus	Remarks
Uncertain	Salt	1 S. per 12 Collatha	No. 1414	Bell, Der Islam, III, 137, 140.
Uncertain	Vin ordinaire	1 S. per 60 Xestae	No. 1414	Bell, P. Lond., IV. XXXVIII.
Uncertain	Sour Wine	1 S. per 72 Xestae	No. 1414	Bell, Der Islam, III, 137, 140.
Uncertain	Boiled Wine	1 S. per 4 metra (48 Xestae)	No. 1414	Bell, P. Lond., IV. XXXVIII ; Der Islam, III, 140.
Uncertain	Boiled Wine	1 S. per 3 metra	No. 1414	Bell, P. Lond., IV. XXXVIII.

D — Cost of Materials.

Date	Material	Price	Papyrus	Remarks.
92-3/ 710-11	Cloven palm trunks.	1/3 S. per 11	1371	Bell, Der Islam, II, 375.
92-3/ 710-11	Untrimmed fig trunks.	1/3 S. per 11	1371	Bell, ibid, II, 375.
97/715	Unrefined iron	16 2/3 S. per 3 quintals=5 5/9 S. per quintal	1434	Bell, ibid, IV, 93.
97/715	Copper chains	8 1/3 S. per quintal.	1434	Bell, ibid, IV, 89 91, 93
97/715	Copper chains.	6 2/3 S. per quintal.	1434	Bell, ibid, IV. 91, 96.
88-9/ 706-7	Beaten tin	1 4/9 S. per 10 litrae	1433	Bell, ibid, III, 373
88-9/ 706-7	Molten tin	1 S. per 10 litrae	1433	Bell, ibid, III, 373.

D. — Cost of Materials. (Cont.)

Date	Material	Price	Papyrus	Remarks
96/714	Cables of palm fibre.	4 2/3 S. per 8-7/12 S. per cable	1434	Bell, Der Islam, IV, 90, 93.
Uncertain	Felt	3 1/3 S. per quintal.	1414	Bell, ibid, III, 139.
96/714	Pads.	1 S. per 5 pads.	1434	Bell, ibid, IV, 90, 93.
96/714	Pads.	1 S. per 4 1/2 Pads.	1434	Bell, ibid, IV, 89-90 if mony composition is made.
Uncertain	Cushions	1 S. per 4	1414	Bell, ibid, III, 139.
88-9/706-7	Yarn.	5 S. per 2 quintals = 2 1/2 S. per quintal	1433	Bell, ibid, III, 370.

III. Fugitives and Passports

Among the papyri are also letters[1] concerning fugitives. It is worth while considering whether these were trying to escape from naval conscription or not . The flight of the farmer to town is not a modern evil. The liturgies had been burdensome from the beginning[2] and the only way of escape was by flight. There is frequent mention of peasants fleeing from their homes and liturgies, often to become brigands. The Muslims did not originate the system of conscription for securing a supply of sailors; the

---

(1) Bell, P. Lond., IV, Nos. 1333, 1343, 1384; Der Islam, II, 269-271, 274 sq., 379; P. Ross.-Georg., IV, Nos. 1, 2.
(2) Bell, J.E.A., IV, 92; Abbott, 97.

Byzantines had instituted this method for government work.(1) It seems that the question of fugitives was vitally connected with that of taxation in general. There were times and conditions, however, which made their numbers assume large proportions, as was the case in Egypt in the first century of Islam.

To control these fugitives more effectively a system of passports was introduced. Papyri dealing with permission to stay in Egypt or travel abroad have been published since a long time.(2) From the very early days of the Muslims in Egypt insistence on passports was strictly adhered to, and no one was allowed to leave his district without permission of the authorities. About 100/720 the governor is said to have issued orders that anyone found without a passport *(sijil)* either on the march or removing from one place to another, or embarking or disembarking, was to be arrested, and the vessel with its contents seized and burned.(3) Severus(4) mentions a fine of ten dinars, imprisonment, mutilation and even death as punishment. Bernard the Wise,(5) who visited Egypt during the 3rd/9th century, emphasises this fact when he says: *«But if in the city, or at sea, or on a journey, they were to find a man walking by night, or even by day, without a parchment or seal of some king or prince of the country, forthwith he would be ordered to be shut up in prison until the day should come when he could give an account of himelf, as to whether he was a spy or not.»*

A passport cost five dinars and was hard to secure; if it was lost or damaged it could be only replaced by a further payment of five dinars.(6) The country and sea-ports were well policed. Under the Tûlûnids a passport *(Jawâz)*, was required to leave Egypt; even a slave accompanying his master had to be mentioned. Ibn Al-Dâya gives an

---

(1) Bell, Byz. Zeit., XXVIII, 284.
(2) v. Rogers, B.I.E., IIème Sér., No. 1, 1880, 9-23; Becker, Der Islam, II, 369. For the treatment of enemy subjects in Islamic territory and the passport granted to them v. Hamîdullâh, 250.
(3) Becker, Der Islam, II, 369. v. P.E.R.F., Nos. 601, 602; Moritz, Ar. Pal., Pl. 106; Becker, P.S.R., 1 sq., 40 sq.
(4) Pat Or., V. fasc. I, 68-70 [322-324].
(5) P.P.T.S., III, 11.
(6) Abbott, 99.

interesting example of a merchant and his slave who were not allowed to pass through the customs at Al-'Arîsh, the frontier town between Egypt and Syria, until instructions were received from Ibn Tûlûn whether the slave ought to have a separate passport or not.(1)

---

(1) Ibn Sa'îd, Ed. Vollers, 13, 53.

CHAPTER V

MEDITERRANEAN MUSLIM WARSHIPS.

I. Characteristics of Mediterranean Ships

Since ancient times the Mediterranean Sea had an individuality and importance of its own. Although it separated three continents it was the chief means of contact and spread of the civilisations along its shores. Man did not take naturally to the sea but was tempted to the Mediterranean because its waters were so safe and climatic conditions so favourable(1) for vessels propelled by oars. Here trade, piracy and organised sea warfare seem to have flourished, especially in the eastern part.(2)

The collection of models of ships in the Science Museum, London, provides a chronological record of types of sailing vessels. It appears that the squaresail was by far the oldest

---

(1) Newbigin, Mediterranean Lands, 27 ; Rose, 3 ; Stevens and Wescott, 2.

On the geography and history of Mediterranean lands v. Bibliography under Newbigin, Parain, Semple, East, Rodgers, Tarn. On the strategical problems of Mediterranean v. Richmond, Gomme, ch. X.

(2) Pirenne, Mediaeval Cities, 3 ; Rose, 3. According to Prof. Batt, quoted by Ormerod, 120, n. 6, piracy means the practice or crime of robbery and depredation on the sea or navigable rivers, or by descent from the sea upon the coast by persons not holding a commission from an established civilised state. A complete history of piracy in the Mediterranean as understood by this definition either in ancient or medieval times has still to be written. The task would be a fascinating one and its completion of no small service to the historian. For the treatment of pirates according to Muslim law v. Qur'ân, V: 33-34; Tabarî, Tafsîr, VI, 132-133, 135 ; Hamîdullâh, 117 sq.

115

sail known(1) and was used in Egypt and the eastern Mediterranean at a very early date. From the beginning of historic times Egyptian wooden boats were already large enough to be fitted with mast and sail.(2) The Phoenicians were also shipbuilders and navigators.(3) Their galleys show one square sail but judging by the number of oars indicated, they may have been considerably longer.(4)

The Greeks built warships with several banks of oars, the most common type being the **trireme** which had three decks.(5) The squaresail was a help to a galley during long journeys but only oars were used when actual fighting was taking place.(6) Pictorial representations of Greeks and Roman galleys show that there was no essential difference between them. In course of time the Romans built the **liburna** with two banks of oars; this generic term was gradually applied to all their warships, of one to five decks. In the East their largest vessels were only of two banks.(7) About A.D. 500 the Byzantines introduced **dromon** as a generic term for warships, distinguishing them from merchant ships because of their greater speed. Some of their vessels had only one bank of oars but those built at Ravenna were of three decks.(8)

Brought by conquest to the shores of the Mediterranean the Muslims had to face the new maritime problems. As soon as they had conquered the old Phoenician cities and acquired Egyptian ports they quickly realised the vital importance of sea power(9) to a conquering and rapidly expanding Empire and decided to use the same weapons as their enemies

---

(1) Clowes, Story of Sail, 51. The survey of ancient ships is mainly based on the collection in the Science Museum, London, and on secondary sources such as: Brindley, Clowes, St. Denis, Hornell, Torr, v. Bibliography.
(2) Clowes, Sailing Ships, 18; Hornell, Water Transport, 225; Torr, 3. v. Herodotus, II, par. 159, 135.
(3) Rawlinson, ch. IX, 271 sq.; Fleming, Preface, IX.
(4) Clowes, Sailing Ships, 26; Hornell, Water Transport, 286.
(5) Appian and Aelius Aristeides, quoted by Torr, 16, n. 43.
(6) Clowes, Sailing Ships, 33.
(7) Vegetius, quoted by Torr, 16. v. n. 44.
(8) Procopius, De Bello Vandalico, I, 11; Torr, 17, n. 45 .
(9) Wellhausen, N.G.W. Gött., 1901, 418 says, «*The Arabs made the change from the desert and the camel to the sea and ship with astonishing rapidity.*» v. East, Historical Geog., 188-189.

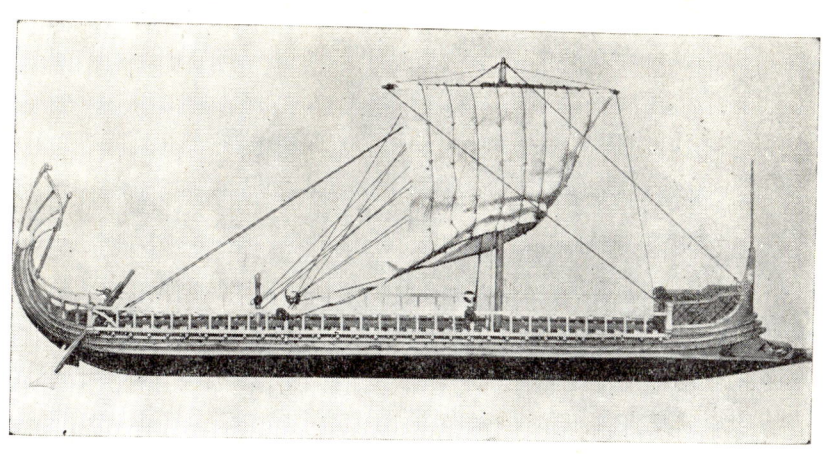

Greek war galley of 4th century B.C.

The model shows a reconstruction made by Mr. A.C. Jackson based on sculptures at Athens and The Piraeus. In action the sail and mast were lowered and oars only were used for propulsion (the Science Museum. London. No. 319).
Reproduced by courtesy of the Director of the Science Museum, London.

Roman Merchant Ship.
2nd Century A.D.

Reproduced by courtesy of the Director of the Science Museum, London.

employed. They began to advance in the art of shipbuilding and in navigation and became familiar with the Mediterranean, for the establishment of suitable land bases, an indispensable condition of sea power, roused their maritime ambitions. Maqrîzî,(1) in relating the building of the fleet in Egypt after the sack of Damietta in 238/853, says that «*warships* (**shawânî**) *were built and mariners given equal pay with soldiers. The Amîrs employed bowmen in the navy and Egyptians tried to teach their children to shoot arrows and other missiles. Only men well experienced in fighting the enemy were chosen as leaders and the fleet no longer accepted a man of dull mind or untrained in the art of warfare. Moreover, people were animated with a zeal for fighting God's enemies and assuring the victory of their religion. The naval service commanded respect and consideration so that everyone wanted to join the maritime army and belong to the fleet.*» When referring to the Fâtimid fleet Maqrîzî(2) also states that those serving in it were regarded as fighters for God's sake *(al-mujâhidûn fî sabîl Allâh)*, and that people were blessed by them. Ibn Khaldûn(3) has given a most graphic account of Muslim navigation. He says that when the Muslim Empire became a dominating power it produced expert navigators and their enthusiasm for naval *jihâd* rose high. They built warships, equipped with fully armed fighting men, to attack the infidels overseas. The same author also says that in the days of their glory the Muslims held complete sway over the Mediterranean, so that the Christian fleet counted but little. As a result the Muslims made naval conquests everywhere and became lords of most of the islands. Their ships regularly sailed in the Mediterranean and pounced upon the Christians as a lion seizes its prey. The whole sea was full of Muslim ships in time of war and peace, whilst the Christians could no longer float a plank upon it.(4) The poet Ibn Hâni'(5) relates in verse what Ibn Khaldûn says in prose. Istakhrî(6) writes: «*There is no sea more beautiful*

---

(1) Khitat, II, 191.
(2) Ibid, II, 194 (21).
(3) Muqaddima, II, 34 ; reproduced by Maqrîzî, ibid, II, 190.
(4) Ibn Khaldûn, Muqaddima, II, 35-36.
(5) v. His verses quoted by Nîfir, Rev. Tun., 1946, II, 29.
(6) B.G.A., I, 71.

than the Mediterranean which has a chain of populated sites on either side ... Here Muslim ships sail from one side to the other, often encountering those of the Byzantines.» By the tenth century A.D. the Mediterranean had become, for the most part, a Muslim sea and European navigation seemed to be a wretched affair.(1)

Muslim ships of the early Caliphate were probably similar in general type to those of the Greeks and Romans. The evidence afforded by the papyri shows them to have been of considerable size, capable of carrying large drafts of sailors.(2) Once the Muslims established themselves in the Mediterranean there came a quick and surprising change. By taking Syrian and Egyptian shipwrights into their service they were enabled to create a powerful war fleet. They followed the technical traditions favoured by the Greeks and by the Syrian successors of the Phoenicians, probably adopting the hull construction common in the Mediterranean at that period. The nimble minds of the enthusiastic Muslims made them apt pupils and their energy enabled them to gradually surpass and replace their teachers. Maqrîzî(3) says that the ships were divided into two groups: the warships, equipped with fighting men and weapons for waging war against the enemy, and the Nile ships used for carrying corn and other goods across the river.(4) Whatever may have been the type and size of vessels, the part of the hull below the water was modelled on the shape of a whale. Ibn Khaldûn(5) mentions this point in his chapter on carpentry:

---

(1) Mez, 508.
(2) Bell, P. Lond., IV, XXXV. v. Nos. 1433(48), 286; 1450(5), 377; Crum, P. Lond., IV, No. 1497, 439, refers to 46 sailors destined for service in the raid of 8th indiction, 91/709.
(3) Khitat, II, 189.
(4) For Nile navigation v. Arculf, P.P.T.S., III, 52; Bernard the Wise, P.P.T.S., III, 6; Istakhrî, B.G.A., I, 54; Mas'ûdî, Murûj, I, 208-210; Sprenger, Meadows of Gold, 235-236; Ibn Hawqal, B.G.A., II, 106; Amîr Abû'l-Hârith, 152, 416, n. 8; Muqaddasî, B.G.A., III, 208; Ibshîhî, Mustatraf, II, 305-306, where there is a chapter about nautical terms, a document of great importance as shown by Goldziher, Z.D.M.G., 1881, 528-529. For different names of fishing boats v. Shams Al-Dîn ibn Bassâm Al-Tinnîsî, Kitâb Anîs Al-Jalîs fî Akahbâr Tinnîs, MS., Cairo Library, Adab No. 1852, 72 sq. The monograph of Colin, B.I.F.A.O. XX, 1921, 45 sq., is valuable for fresh investigations. v. also Faulkner, J.E.A., XXVI, 3-9; Mez, 491.
(5) Muqaddima, II, 325. v. The description of Abû 'Amr Al-Qurtubî in Nuwayrî, Cairo Edition, I, 258.

Fragment of faience with painted underglaze decoration. The naive scene of the two figures in a boat with a chequered sail is treated in blue and black. Arabic Museum, Cairo. No. 5379/25.
Reproduced by courtesy of the Director of the Arabic Museum, Cairo.

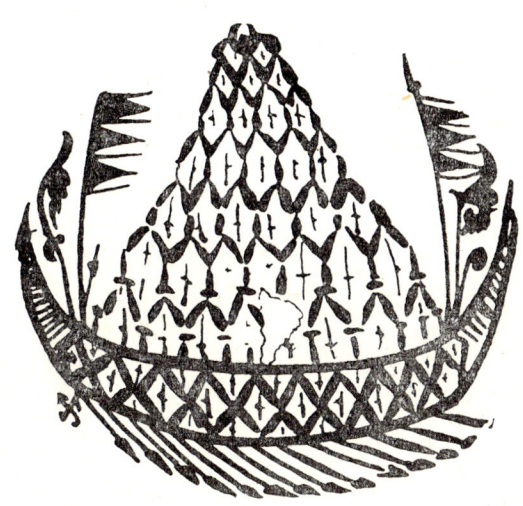

Faience dish with metallic reflections. The decoration represents a galley with rigging, oars and oriflammes. Faience of Samarra or Egypt, 3rd/9th century. Arabic Museum, Cairo. No. 7900.
Reproduced by courtesy of the Director of the Arabic Museum, Cairo.

«*This art is also required for building ships with planks and nails to sail on the open sea. They are large frames based on geometrical principles for which the whale is the model. To make them, one must study the way in which this fish moves along by means of its fins and chest, as its shape is most suitable for cutting through the water. In place of the natural means of movement the fish possesses, we make use of the wind, probably aided by oars as in the case of warships* **(asâtîl)**».

The use of the lateen sail by the Arabs proved a stimulus to further progress when they were thoroughly established in the Mediterranean. The passage from Cameniates,(1) describing how Leo of Tripolis took Thessalonica in 291/904, gives valuable information about the construction of Muslim warships. It suggests that they were lateen rigged, had at least two masts and were steered by oars of extraordinary size. The lateen sail was fixed to a long sloping yard hoisted to the mast-head. Its shape and position made it more effective than the small squaresail of the Romans, and the two-masted lateen rigged vessels would probably have had greater speed than the earlier Roman ships when the wind was on, or slightly before, the beam. This constituted a very definite advance in the art of navigation. Belloc(2) gives the following interesting account of the use of the lateen sail by the Muslims : «*Now when during that great renaissance of theirs in the seventh century, the Arabs left their deserts and took to the sea; they became for a short time in sailing, as in philosophy, the teachers of their new subjects. They took this sail which they had found in all the parts they had conquered along this coast — in Alexandria, in Cyrene, in Carthage, in Caesarea — they lightened and lengthened the yard, they lifted the peak up high, they clewed down the foot, and very soon they had that triangular lateen sail which will, perhaps, remain, when every other evidence of*

---

(1) De Ex. Thess., M.P.G., CIX, 525-538. I owe the translation of the passage to Mr. R.H. Dolley. For a poetical description of the mast, rudder and sail of Muslim ships v. Al-Ayâdî and Ibn Hâni', quoted by Nîfir, Rev. Tun., 1945, IX, 13; 1946, I 26; V, 10.
(2) Essays, 340. The history of the lateen sail is obscure. I have been unable to find out whether the Muslims introduced or developed it. Clowes, Story of Sail, 16 ; Sailing Ships, 12, says that the lateen sail arrived in the Mediterranean in the wake of the conquering Arabs. v. Hornell, Antiquity, XIII, 41.

their early conquering energy has disappeared. With such a sail they drove that first fleet of theirs which gave them at once the islands and the commerce of the Mediterranean.»

The two-masted lateen rigged vessels were confined almost entirely to this sea. Muslim navigation was divided into the two separate areas of the Mediterranean and the Indian Ocean. Mez,(1) quoting a Chinese source, says the ships of the former were larger than those of the latter. On the Mediterranean there were vessels with two rudders;(2) those on the ocean never had more than one deck, and in most cases, only one mast. Marco Polo,(3) describing the Persian Gulf ships of the 7th/13th century says : «*They have one mast, one sail, and one rudder, and have no deck, but only a cover spread over the cargo when loaded. This cover consists of hides, and on the top of these hides they put the horses which they take to India for sale.*» In the Red Sea vessels which were easy to handle and especially adapted to its conditions, were employed; they were broad and of small draught on account of the numerous reefs.(4) Muslim warships in the Mediterranean were comparatively large and slow as is shown by Leo VI(5) when addressing his admiral : «*The size of the ships you build will depend on the enemy you are fighting. The Saracen and the Russian navies are very different propositions. The Saracens use large and comparatively slow ships, while the Russians light, swift, and hardy craft not unlike pirate ships. The reason is that the Russian raids into the Black Sea are made down the rivers where it is impossible to use ships of more than a certain tonnage. Therefore you have to take these facts into consideration when planning operations.*»

(1) 506. Chapters 27 and 29 in Mez are richer in information on the Indian Ocean than on the Mediterranean. The study of Astronomico-nautical treatises published by Ferrand also provides valuable information for the Indian Ocean. v. Bibliography.
(2) The reference to Ibn Jubayr, quoted by Mez, 506, is not found in the old or new edition on the page stated (235). v. Ibn Jubayr, 320(22).
(3) I, ch. XIX, 108 ; v. III, ch. I, 250.
(4) Mez, 506, quoting Idrîsî; East, Historical Geog., 198.
(5) D.P.N., ch. 78. v. ch. 4, where Leo VI advises his admiral that the **dromon** should not be slow or too heavy but of nicely balanced construction.

II. Types of Muslim Warships.

Ibn 'Abd Al-Hakam(1) mentions **safîna, markib,** and **qârib** as names of ships used in the early naval battle of Dhât Al-Sawârî. **Safîna,** plural **sufun, safâ'in, safîn,** is a very common word for ship and occurs in Pre-Islamic Arabic poetry(2) and in the Qur'ân.(3) Fraenkel(4) says that «*all indications seem to point to the fact that it is a borrowed word*» and concludes it is Aramaic. According to Kindermann(5) the word often has the more specialised meaning of transport ship and the word **spanu,** which means to cover, may indicate that the original meaning was a ship with a deck.

Markib, plural **marâkib,** is used in the widest sense and means a thing on which one rides, such as an animal or even a saddle. The usual meaning is ship and in this sense it is the commonest expression in the Arabic language. In Kindermann's(6) opinion the word is definitely an Arabic term and, like **safîna,** came to be used gradually with the specific meaning of galley or warship.

Qârib, plural **qawârib,** is defined by the dictionary(7) as a small boat — a ship's boat used by seafarers to facilitate the conduct of their business. A hadîth(8) states that «*they sat in* **aqrab safîna**» which means the ship's small boats. Jal(9) quotes Meninsky as saying that it means an auxiliary boat which performs the service of plying between the ships and the port for loading and unloading.

Among the ships mentioned in the papyri are **dromonaria** and **acatia.** They occur, for example, in connection with the coast-guard fleet at the mouths of the Nile in 96/714, the raiding fleet of Egypt in the same year and that of the Orient

---

(1) 190 (8, 15, 20).
(2) v. The poems of Tarafa, and 'Amr ibn Kalthûm in Zûzanî, 30-31, 94 ; Jones, 17, 88.
(3) XVIII : 70, 78 ; XXIX : 14.
(4) 216 sq.
(5) Schiff, 40, 108 ; E.I., Supp., 192.
(6) Schiff, 95. v. Fraenkel, 215 ; Dozy, Supplément, I, 554 ; Lane, I, 1145.
(7) Tâj Al-'Arûs, I, 425(12).
(8) Quoted ibid, I, 425(13).
(9) Under **karb.**

in 97/715.(1) Theophanes(2) states that **dromones** formed part of the Muslim fleet during the second siege of Constantinople in 99/717. The word is a generic term for warship and is used by Leo VI;(3) it may be a synonym for **shalandî**,(4) the name applied to later types.

The papyri refer to **acatenaria** for the raid of the 9th indiction, 92/710.(5) The **acatia** and **acatenaria** were probably auxiliary vessels for carrying stores for the fleet and may have corresponded to the **katinae** mentioned by Theophanes(6) as storeships for the Muslim fleet during the second siege of Constantinople. They therefore may signify the later type known as **tarrîda**.(7)

Various references are made to the **carabi** in the papyri. They are named in connection with the island of Babylon for the raid of the 15th indiction, 97/715.(8) Sometimes they are spoken of as castellated(9) which indicates that they were of two kinds, with and without castles. The castle may have been a turret having wooden sides, erected halfway up the mast, to protect the soldiers raining down stones and arrows upon the enemy.(10) **Carabi** may mean ships in the sense of the Arabic word **qârib** which is said to be derived from the Greek(11) and may signify the later type known as **ghurâb**.(12)

Galleys are also referred to in the papyri and appear to have been of two varieties, the two-banked, mentioned for the raiding fleet of Egypt in 96/714(13) and the castellated.(14) These boats may have been used for scouting pur-

---

(1) Bell, Der Islam, IV, No. 1434, 87, 95, 96 ; XVII, No. 1449, 8.
(2) Ed. De Boor, 395-396. I owe the reference to Prof. R. Jenkins.
(3) D.P.N., chs. 8, 82.
(4) v Infra, 129 sq.
(5) Bell, ibid, XVII, No. 1449, 6.
(6) Ibid, 395-396, I owe the reference to Prof. R. Jenkins.
(7) v. Infra, 136 sq.
(8) Bell, ibid, IV, No. 1434, 90.
(9) Bell, ibid, IV, No. 1434, 88, 96. **Carabi** only are mentioned in Bell, ibid, No. 1434, 95 ; XVII, No. 1441, 5.
(10) v. Leo, D.P.N., ch. 7.
(11) v. Fraenkel, 218 ; Kindermann, Schiff, 76.
(12) v. Infra, 132 sq.
(13) Bell, ibid, IV, No. 1434, 88, 96.
(14) Bell, ibid, XVII, No. 1441, 5.

poses.(1) Leo VI(2) describes the Byzantine galley as only having a single bank of oars.

During the 'Abbâsid period many new words for ships came into use. Muqaddasî(3) mentions thirty six different vessels and Wüstenfeld(4) says : «*In spite of the nature of the Arabic language, which can offer two hundred different names for the camel and four hundred for the lion, it is nevertheless a source of wonder that there should be as many as well over a hundred for the ship.*» He further explains that a large number of them are words which came from outside Arabia. The Arabs had picked up foreign words easily so that new terms rapidly became part of the Arabic vocabulary.(5)

Ustûl. Khafâjî(6) maintains that this Arabic word, used in the sense of war fleet, is apparently found for the first time in Arabic poetry, and quotes as evidence a verse written in the 3rd/9th century by Buhturî where the poet praises Ahmad ibn Dînâr, the commander of the fleet despatched against the Byzantines.(7) The word is later used by the poets Ibn Hâni' (d. 362/972), and Al-Ayâdî (d. 365/975).(8) Maqrîzî(9) does not regard the word as authentically Arabic and some lexicographers(10) include it in the Arabised words. Mas'ûdî(11) definitely states that it is of Greek derivation and signifies the combined warships. In

---

(1) v. Leo, D.P.N., ch 10.
(2) D.P.N., ch. 10. v. Torr, 19 ; Bury, Gibbon Edition, VI, App. V, 539.
(3) v. Infra, App. III, 155 sq.
(4) N.G.W. Gött, 1880, 135.
(5) Wüstenfeld, N.G.W. Gött., 1880, 135-136.
(6) 38, 119. v. Buhturî, Dîwân, I, 258(7) ; reproduced by Nuwayrî, Cairo Edition, VI, 198(21).
(7) This expedition seems to have escaped the contemporary Muslim historians and appears to have been exaggerated by the Byzantines. v. Bury, Eastern, 274 ; Vasiliev, Byzance, I, 192. Little is known about Ibn Dînâr; perhaps he was the son of Dînâr ibn 'Abdallah who, according to Ibn Taghrî Birdî, II, 243(8), was governor of Damascus in 225/840.
(8) Nîfir, Rev. Tun., 1945, II, 14, quotes their verses.
(9) Khitat, II, 189(14).
(10) Tâj Al-'Arûs, VII, 375(29) ; Lane, I, 1359(b). Kindermann, Schiff, I, says that the word is not found in Jawharî, Sihâh, nor in Fîrûzâbâdî, Qâmus.
(11) B.G.A., VIII, 141(14-15). For Greek origin of word v. Watt, J.R.A.S., April 1834, 7; Kindermann, Schiff, 1; Gateau, Rev. Afr., 1946, 146; Wüstenfeld, N.G.W. Gött., 1880, 135; Vollers, Z.D.M.G., LI, 294 ; Quatremère, Mamlouks, Ia, 157, n. 33.

addition to the meaning of fleet, **ustûl** indicated galley or warship «*for fighting the infidels on the sea.*»(1) Ibn Khaldûn, for example, writes : «*He left Al-Mariyya and joined him with ten* **asâtîl** *(ships),*» and further on : «*He equipped one hundred and eighty* **ustûl** *(ship)*», and «*they were seventy* **ustûl,** *(ship).*»(2) On another occasion the same author speaks of the **asâtîl,** plural of **ustûl** which relied upon sails and oars.(3)

It must be noted that the explanation of Tâj Al-'Arûs goes back to Maqrîzî and the examples cited are taken from Ibn Khaldûn. Mas'ûdî, on the other hand, who was about four hundred and sixty years earlier than Ibn Khaldûn, clearly defines the word as meaning the combined warships. It seems likely, however, that the word was originally borrowed to signify fleet(4) and that it was later used for single ships which formed a part of it. The adjective **ustûlî** is used as a noun to designate one who belongs to the fleet, that is, a soldier of the fleet, in contrast with **jundî,** a soldier of the army.

The word **ustûl** is synonymous with the Arabic word **'imâra,**(5) plural **'amâ'ir,** which is found with this meaning in modern dictionaries but not in the old ones.(6) Bustânî(7) refers to the word in this sense and Ibn Dînâr(8) uses it in connection with the year 481/1088, when the **'imâra** of the Genoese and Venetians attacked Al-Mahdiyya and the neighbouring Zawîla with about three hundred ships. Ibn Mamâtî(9) uses the word **sinâ'at al-'amâ'ir** to signify the ar-

---

(1) Tâj Al-'Arûs, VII, 375(29).
(2) These examples are quoted by Quatremère, Mamlouks, Ia, 157, n. 33, and 'Alî Mubârak, XIV, 82. v. Ibn Khaldûn, B.A.S., 462(9, 13) ; Dozy, Supplément, I, 22(a).
(3) Muqaddima, II, 325(19). v. Supra, 123.
(4) v. Ibn Jabayr, 337(6) ; Ibn Al-Athîr, VI 236(1) ; B.A.S., 304(14); Nuwayrî, B.A.S., 454(14 sq.), where the word is used to signify a fleet.
(5) Gateau, Rev. Afr., 1946, 146.
(6) Kindermann, Schiff, 2, says that it is not given in this sense even in Vocabulista, Ed. Schiaparelli.
(7) Muhît, 1469 (a, 25).
(8) B.A.S., 530(14).
(9) 339(2).

senal where the fleet was built. Ibn Duqmâq(1) gives **sinâ'at al-'imâra**, and Qalqashandî (2), **sinâ'at al-'amâ'îr**.

Qit'a. The term **qit'a**, plural **aqtâ'** (3) but usually **qita'** and **qatâ'i'**, means a kind of vessel, a piece or part of the fleet. Ibn Al-Athîr uses it in this sense when he says: «*In the mouth of the river of Abî Al-Khasîb, he had five hundred qit'a* (pieces) *carrying his treasure.*» Ibn Khaldûn writes: «*They put out to sea with thirty two* **qit'a** *as many from their fleets as from his*», and further on: «*He sent two pieces for his aid.*» (4) The word seems to have been more usually employed to indicate a number of ships. It is used for ships of war as well as for transport vessels for troops and horses: «*In 557/1162 'Abd Al-Mu'min along the coast of Maghrib armed four hundred* **qit'a** *for war against the Byzantines.*»(5) It occurs in the Vocabulista(6) as galley. Ibn Al-Athîr(7) speaks of **qit'a** as serving for the transport of troops, horses, goods and chattels. The word is also mentioned with other names of ships(8) and in this case it may signify a special type of vessel.

Harbî. Ibn Al-Athîr (9) uses **harbî** as an elliptic expression for **markib harbî** to signify warship, and both he and Mas'ûdî(10) use **harbiyya** in the same way. Dozy(11) gives the word the same meaning. The plural form **harâbî** is found in Idrîsî and **harbiyyât** in Nuwayrî and Maqrîzî.(12) It should be noted that **markib harbî** is used for warship today.

---

(1) IV, 35(25) ; 82(20) ; V, 38(3).
(2) III, 339.
(3) Used by 'Imâd Al-Dîn Al-Isfahânî, B.A.S., 207(7).
(4) These examples are quoted by Quatremère, Mamlouks, Ia, 143, n. 16. v. 'Alî Mubârak, XIV, 82.
(5) Ibn Abî Zar', 91(24) ; 131(4 sq.) ; 224(27 sq) ; Fr. Tr., 284 sq. v. Ibn 'Idhârî, I, 282(13). In R.H.C., the word for warship occurs more than 20 times : v. Ibn Al-Athîr, R.H.C., I, 351(3 sq.), 213(7), 354(14), 708(4) ; Ibn Shaddâd, R.H.C., III, 57(1) ; îbn Al-Adîm, R.H.C., III, 578(6) ; Kindermann, Schiff, 82 ; Quatremère, Mamlouks, Ia, 143, n. 16.
(6) Ed. Schiaparelli, under **galea**, 414; v. Kindermann, Schiff, 81.
(7) R.H.C., I, 351(3) ; II, 43(3).
(8) In Amarî, I Diplomi Arabi, 192(1), 199(7), 041, there is mention of **marâkib** and **qatâ'i'**. v. Kindermann, Schiff, 82.
(9) VII, 349(16).
(10) Murûj, I, 283(2) ; Ibn Al-Athîr, VII, 350(16).
(11) Supplément, I, 265.
(12) Idrîsî, Ed. Dozy, I, 90, 112 ; Nuwayrî, B.A.S., 454(16) ; Maqrîzî, Khitat, II, 197(17).

Shalandî. Constantine Porphyrogenitos(1) mentions in the «*Life of Basil*» the Greek names of three types of Muslim warships for which the Latin equivalents are: **cumbarii** the largest and heaviest ships; **saturae,** small fast vessels; **galeae,** single decked warships. Unfortunately he gives no details. The **cumbarii** may probably signify a type of ship for which the usual Arabic term is **shalandî** plural **shalandiyyât.** Fraenkel(2) discusses the origin of the word and whether **shalandî** came direct into Arabic through the Byzantines. The word is to be found in the works of several Arab writers of the 4th/10th century when referring to Byzantine warships. Tabarî(3) mentions a hundred Byzantine **shalandî,** carrying about five thousand men who landed at Damietta in 238/853. Ibn Hawqal (4) uses **sharandî,** plural **sharandiyyât** to signify a type of Byzantine warship. Muqaddasî(5) speaks of Byzantine **shalandî** frequenting Syrian ports and bringing Muslim captives for exchange. In the accounts of the wars against Sicily these ships are often mentioned. Ibn Al-Athîr(6) says that in 244/858-9 a large Byzantine army came from Constantinople in three **shalandî** to Syracuse and that Al-'Abbâs ibn Al-Fadl captured one hundred of them. In other passages he mentions **ashâb al-shalandiyya,** the people of the **shalandî,** signifying the Byzantines,(7) and speaks of a fleet of seventy ships comprising three types, including the **shalandî** (8) Maqrîzî(9) states that from the time of the accession of the Fâtimid Caliph Al-Mu'izz and during the reigns of his sons, great preparations were made for the construction of warships in Cairo, Alexandria and Damietta. They included **shawânî, shalandiyyât** and **musattahât** intended expressly for Sûr, 'Akkâ and Ascalon for the war against the Byzantines.

---

(1) M.P.G., CIX, 315. I owe this reference to Mr. R.H. Dolley .v. Supra, 73.

(2) 219-220. For origin of French word **chaland** v. Lammens, Mots Français, 83 ; Devic, 90 ; Defrèmery, J. As., August 1867, 183, n. 3.

(3) III, 1417(12), 1418(4). v. Gloss., CCXV.

(4) B.G.A., II, 132(2, 19). In Kramers Edition, 198(17), it is written **shalandiyya.**

(5) B.G.A., III, 177(3). v. His list, 32(3) ; Supra, 55 sq.

(6) VII, 42(5 sq.) ; B.A.S., 232.

(7) VII, 4(14), 258(20) ; B.A.S., 244(10).

(8) XI, 159(20 ; B.A.S., 304(14). v. B.A.S., 166 ; Ibn Miskawayh, Ed. Margoliouth, II, 211(14) ; V, 225, n. 2,; Wiet Corpus, II, 166.

(9) Khitat, II, 193(4 sq.).

Ibn Mamâtî,(1) in describing the Ayyûbid fleet, uses the word **musattah** to indicate a type of ship similar to **shalandî**, The editor Suryâl (2) merely says that **musattah** is a kind of ship. It really denotes a large decked warship(3) and is often mentioned at the time of the Crusades.(4) Ibn Mamâtî(5) speaks of the **shalandî** as a decked ship on which the soldiers fought whilst the rowers plied their oars beneath them. It was equipped in such a way that a number of fighting men could have sufficient space for action at a moment's notice, should the enemy come alongside.(6)

Shîni, shîniyya or **shânî**, plur. **shawânî**, was a term commonly used for galley.(7) Dozy(8) is uncertain of its being of Arabic origin. According to the dictionaries(9) it signifies a vessel equipped for naval warfare. Tâj Al-'Arûs(10) regards it as an Egyptian expression and speaks of a **shîn** as a long ship. The use of the word seems to be confined to the Mediterranean. Ibn Hawqal and Muqaddasî(11) mention Byzantine **shawânî** on the coasts of Syria and Palestine. Idrîsî(12) says that **marâkib hammâla**, transport ships, and **harâbî** warships, as well as **shawânî**, frequented the port of Waqqûr near Tûnis. In 303/915 'Ubaydallah established the shipyard at Mahdiyya and built nine hundred **shawna** there. (13) Details of their size are uncertain. Maqrîzî(14) states that by the

---

(1) 340(2). v. Wüstenfeld, N.G.W. Gött., 1880, 139.
(2) Edition to Ibn Mamâtî, 458.
(3) v. Amari, I Diplomi Arabi, 401 ; Kindermann, Sciff, 99 ; Wüstenfeld, N.G.W. Gött., 1880, 140.
(4) v. Abû Shâma, R.H.C., V. 48(7) ; Ibn Al-Athîr R.H.C., II, 80, n. 2. According to Lammens, Mots Français, 166, it gave rise to the Spanish **mistico**, and the French **mistique.**
(5) 340 ; Wüstenfeld, N.G.W. Gött., 1880, 139.
(6) Ibn Al-Athîr, VII, 41(9). v. Kindermann, Schiff, 52. Cf. Dozy, Supplément, 1, 738; Defrèmery, J. As., August 1867, 183; Devic, 90; Lammns, ibid, 83.
(7) Quatremère, Mamlouks, Ia, 142, n. 15 ; Gateau, Rev. Afr., 1946, 346 ; Wüstenfeld, N.G.W. Gött., 1880., 140 ; Kinderman, Schiff, 53.
(8) In the glossary to Idrîsî, 331, and Supplment, I, 793(a).
(9) Lisân Al-'Arab, XVII, 110 (16 in margin) ; Tâj. Al-'Arûs, IX,
(10) IX, 257(34), 258(6). v. also Lane, I, 1635(c).
(11) Ibn Hawqal, B.G.A., II, 132 (2, 19); Muqaddasî, B.G.A., III, 177(3).
(12) Ed. Dozy, 112(6). **Shawânî** seems to be the correct reading in place of nawâshî. v. Gloss., 331.
(13) Ibn 'Idhârî, I, 130(3), 192(20), 318(8). The form **shawna** often occurs in Maqrîzî, Khitat, I, 351(14). Ibn Al-Athîr, VIII, 70(15), writes **shîni**. v. Kindermann, Schiff, 53.
(14) Khitat, I, 94(36).

end of the Fâtimid dynasty, ten **shawânî** carried ten thousand soldiers. Abû Shâma(1) gives a much smaller number. On each of the two hundred **shînî** comprising the fleet, there were only one hundred and fifty foot soldiers, but such a vessel was regarded as «*a large* **shînî** *with many people*». (2) According to Ibn 'Idhârî (3) the **shînî,** which Ziâdatallah had brought in 291/903 to the island of Al-Kurrâth (twelve miles from Tûnis) could not have been very large.

Ibn Mamâtî(4) gives some details of this type of ship in his description of the Egyptian war fleet. He says that the **shînî** was also known as **ghurâb,** that it had one hundred and forty oars and carried soldiers as well as rowers. Abû 'Amr Al-Qurtubî(5) describes, in a literary Arabic prose, a **shînî** as being painted with tar and having large white sails, whilst the hull resembled the form of a whale and the stern that of a swallow. The Sicilian poet Ibn Hamdîs(6) gives a picture of **shawânî** in his poem in praise of Abû Yahyâ Al-Hasan ibn 'Alî. It shows that they contained towers from which white naphtha was thrown against the enemy. The editor of Nuwayrî(7) explains **shînî** as a type of merchant vessel or warship. Kindermann (8) gives the meaning according to more modern dictionaries as pirate ship, privateer, an armed ship. It seems that the meaning of the word has undergone changes in the course of time and that, owing to their sporadic nature, it is difficult to trace the details of its development.

Ghurâb is a name for galley and in this sense Vollers(9) thinks that it was not essentially an Arabic word but was derived from the Greek term signifying **carabus.** Fleischer(10) remarks that the word has passed into the Romance languages

---

(1) R.H.C., IV, 165(2 sq.).
(2) Abû Shâma, R.H.C., V, 12(3, 4, 6).
(3) I, 130(3).
(4) 340(3) ; Wüstenfeld, N.G.W. Gött., 1880, 139, 140. v. Quatremère, Mamlouks, Ia, 142, n. 15 ; Lammens, Mots Français, 91.
(5) Reproduced by Nuwayrî, Cairo Edition, I, 258-259.
(6) v. His verses quoted by 'Ibâda, Hilâl, XXI, 1912, 362.
(7) Cairo Edition, I, 258, n. 1.
(8) Schiff, 54.
(9) Z.D.M.G., L,624. v. Lammens, Mots Français, 91, 120.
(10) Quoted by Kindermann, Schiff, 69. v. Amari, I Diplomi Arabi, 397; Lammens, Mots Français, 91 ; Moritz, in Festchrift Ed. Sachau, 439. For history of use of word since 17th cent. A.D. v. Kindermann, Schiff, 69.

as **corvetta** and **corvette**, Wüstenfeld (1) uses the word **ghârib** in his list of ships and Brunot(2) identifies it as the Algerian form of **qârib**. Kindermann(3) says that the similarity in meaning between the Arabic **ghurâb** and the Latin **corvus,** which is raven, is, in the opinion of Lokotsch, «*merely accidental.*» One suggestion is that the name raven was given them because of their lightness and length.(4) Perhaps they may signify the **saturae,** one of the three types of Muslim vessels mentioned by Constantine and referred to as small fast ships. In Arabic, the resemblance between bird and ship is stressed. Al-Khafâjî(5) wonders if the word **ghurâb** is the result of a comparison with the raven and restricts its use to Al-Maghrib. He quotes some verses of Ibn Al-Sa'âtî (d. 604/1207), Ibn Al-Abâr (d. 658/1259), and Ibn Abî Hijla (d. about 762/1360), describing the **ghurâb** as painted with tar, having white wings (sails), which would give them the appearance of ravens. Gildemeister(6) remarks that the wings, **ajniha,** can hardly indicate anything but swords. The manuscript translated by him(7) shows that this type of ship carried troops and was propelled by sail and oars, the latter varying in number up to one hundred and eighty. Ibn Mamâtî(8) calls them **shînî** and says that they carried fighting men and were rowed by one hundred and forty oars. Ibn Khaldûn mentions them with **shînî** and Maqrîzî (9) classifies them with **tarrîda** under **shînî.** Ibn Abî Zar' (10) regards them as the largest Muslim ships, which were overwhelmingly conquered by the **Qurqûrs** of the Christians in 678/1279.

According to passages in «*Recueil des Historiens des Croisades*» the term **ghurâb** seems to be confined to the Mediterranean.(11) In Amari(12) it means corsair ships. Thus

---

(1) N.G.W., Gött. 1880, 138.
(2) La Mer, 249. v. Notes Lexicologiques, 94.
(3) Schiff, 68.
(4) v. Kindermann, Schiff, 69.
(5) Shifâ' Al-Ghalîl, 162.
(6) N.G.W. Gött, 1882, 435. v. Kindermann, Schiff, 69.
(7) N.G.W. Gött., 1882, 435. v. Nuwayrî, Al-Ilmâm, Ahlwardt, 9815. fol. 124a, quoted by 'Alî Ibrâhîm, 319-320.
(8) 340(2); Wüstenfeld, N.G.W. Gött., 1880, 139, 140.
(9) v. Quatremère, Mamlouks, Ia, 144, n. 18 ; 157, n. 33.
(10) 225(1).
(11) Badr Al-'Aynî, R.H.C., II, 241-242, n. 1, and Abû Shâma, R.H.C.,
(12) I Diplomi Arabi, 8(7), 193(5), 194.

in 577/1181 one such vessel from Tripolis captured a merchant ship and in 902/1496 the piracy carried out by these ships is mentioned by Muslims and Franks.

Harrâqa. The dictionaries explain **harrâqa,** (less frequently found as **harrâq),** (1) plural **harrâqât** and **harârîq** as meaning fireboat. (2) **Harrâqa** is fairly common in the sense of a warship filled with combustible materials for firing the enemy ships.(3) Ibn Mamâtî(4) says that there were **harrâqât** in the Egyptian war fleet, smaller than **shawânî** and having probably only a hundred oars, whereas **shawânî** had a hundred and forty.

The word seems to have been used so indiscriminately that it lost much of its original meaning and even its Arabic derivation from **haraqa** to burn, has been called into question.(5) In Kindermann's(6) opinion it is impossible, owing to the multiplicity of its usage, to identify the term, of which the development is difficult to trace with any chronological exactitude, with any type of ship. **Harrâqât** are often mentioned as smaller war vessels on the Nile serving as auxiliaries to the large ships and galleys.(7) Moritz(8) connects them with the original meaning and refers to their being used for firework displays at festivals in Cairo. Quatremère (9) says that these ships, when disarmed, were used for transport on sea and rivers. The Caliph Al-Amîn had them constructed in the form of lions, elephants, eagles, dolphins and snakes. In

---

(1) Given by Dozy, Supplément, I, 274(a), according to Vocabulista, Ed. Schiaparelli, 86 and 267, where the ending kâf instead of qâf is a mistake.

(2) Lisân Al-'Arab, XI, 326(4); Tâj Al-'Arûs, VI, 312(20); Bustânî, Muhît, 38(a,16).

(3) Ibn Shaddâd, R.H.C., III, 178(7); Abû shâma, R.H.C., IV, 342(7), 475(8); 'Alî Mubârak, XIV, 81-82; Suryâl, Notes to Ibn Mamâtî, 453-454 ; Quatremère, Mamouks, Ia, 143, n. 17 ; Jal, under **brulôt;** Gateau, Rev. Afr., 1946, 142. Zaydân, I, 161, states that they carried catapults for throwing naphtha against the enemy.

(4) 340. Wüstenfeld, N.G.W. Gött., 1880, 140. Kindermann, Schiff, 23, applied 100 to the number of **harrâqât,** whereas the original text means the number of oars.

(5) Quatremère, Mamlouks, Ia, 143, n. 17; Kindermann, Schiff, 22.

(6) Schiff, 22.

(7) Maqrîzî, Khitat, I, 222(2); Ibn Al-Athîr, R.H.C., II, 123(6).

(8) In Festschrift Ed. Sachau, 439.

(9) Mamlouks, Ia, 143, n. 17.

this connection the contemporary poet, Abû Nuwâs, wrote verses praising the Caliph. They are quoted by Tabarî : (1)

> «People wonder to see you pass by them,
> On a lion as swift as a cloud.
> They call upon God when you ride it.
> What cry will they raise when they see you
> Proudly borne on the back of an eagle,
> With a beak, mighty wings and talons,
> Cresting wave upon wave in the storm ?»

In the following lines the same poet again praises the Caliph and describes his **harrâqa** which was in the form of a dolphin :

> «As the full moon in the darkness
> Rides the Caliph on the dolphin.
> Never saw I a ship that was like it
> So beauteous in motion and rest.
> God kept it for the Caliph Al-Amîn,
> Blessed with the diadem of Empire.» (2)

On another occasion he says :

> «Thou has not seen the gift to Al-Amîn.
> No eye has seen it — no mind can conceive it —
> The lion, the eagle and the dolphin.» (3)

Tabarî (4) states that the **harrâqa**, which was to transport the Caliph Al-Amîn to Baghdad after his capitulation, was attacked on the way by Tâhir. Yâqût (5) says that pirates attacked a company of high officials, including the Vizir Ibn Abî Al-Rayyân, and the two chiefs, Al-Râdî and

---

(1) III, 952.
(2) Quoted by Tabarî, III, 953.
(3) Quoted by Yâsîn Al-Hamawî, 29.
(4) III, 917 (4, 5).
(5) Irshâd, I, 235 (1 sq.). v. Isfahânî, III, 178 (3), who mentions the Caliph Al-Rashîd sailing in his **harrâqa**.

Al-Murtadâ, who were sailing in their **harrâqât** to meet another magnate. Mez(1) is of the opinion that these boats were a sort of river craft. Ibn Khallikân(2) says that the boats called **shabbâra** by the people of Mosul were known as **Harrâqa** in Egypt. Maqrîzî(3) speaks of the Sultan riding to Al-Miqyâs in order to embark on the **harrâqa.** The various examples given above suggest that the term **harrâqa** evolved from the idea of a fireship to that of a pleasure boat.(4) It was first used in the latter sense in Iraq but was eventually replaced by **shabbâra.** In Egypt it signified pleasure boat until the Ottoman Turks introduced the **'aqaba.** (5)

Tarrîda, plural **tarâ'id,** was a common term. (6) Other forms, according to Kindermann, (7) were **tarrâd** and **tarrâda,** (derived from the verb **tarada,** to push), meaning, that which pushes. Tâj Al-'Arûs (8) explains **tarrâd** as a swift boat and adds **tatrîda** which Lane (9) attempts to emend: «*Perhaps a mistranscription for* **tarîda,** *which is a post-classical term*». The two words **tarrîda** and **tarrâd(a)** are often confused and Gildemeister (10) already encountered the difficulty of identifying them. **Tarrîda** was only used in the Mediterranean where it was found in many languages, and, as Quatremère (11) states, still exists there today as **tarrâd** and probably gave rise to the Spanish and Italian **tartana** and the French **tartane.**

---

(1) 490.
(2) De Slane Tr., I, 175. v. n. 6, where De Slane identifies **harrâqa** as a boat or barge.
(3) v. Quatremère, Mamlouks, IIa, 24 and n. 25.
(4) Gateau, Rev. Afr., Mamlouks, IIa, 24 and n. 25.
(5) Quatremère, Mamlouks, Ia, 144, n. 17; IIa, 24, quotes the description of **al-'aqaba** from Jabartî. v. 'Alî Mubârak, XIV, 82 (6 sq).
(6) Quatremère, Mamlouks, Ia, 144, n. 18.
(7) Schiff, 56-57.
(8) II, 408 (I).
(9) I, 1839 (c).
(10) N.G.W., Gött., 1882, 447. For the use of **tarrâda** in the eastern Islamic world v. Kindermann, Schiff, 57, and Quatremère, Mamlouks, Ia, 144, n. 18, where they quote accounts of some modern travellers; Clowes, Story of Sail, 37; Kâzim Al-Dujaylî, Lughat Al-'Arab, II, 101.
(11) Mamlouks, Ia, 144, n. 18. v. Kindermann, Schiff, 14, 57, 59; Lammens, Mots Français, 267; Jal, under **taride.**

Tarrîda was, above all, a Mediterranean transport ship, used particularly for horses. When speaking of the Egyptian war fleet Ibn Mamâtî (1) says : « *The* **tarrîda** *is specifically for carrying horses; the greatest number taken is forty.* » The manuscript translated by Gildemeister (2) shows that the **tarrîda** was equipped to transport war-horses and opened at the back to facilitate the embarking and disembarking of the animals. There are frequent references to these boats carrying horses,(3) together with many people (men and women), provisions, wood and war equipment.(4) **Tarrîda bahariyya** also signified transport ship.(5) The fact that **tarrîda** is mentioned in conjunction with other ships such as **shînî** and **shalandî** helps to determine the types of vessels which comprised the fleet.(6) Jal (7) thinks that it was generally used for transporting all kinds of cargoes: troops, horses, supplies and arms.

It may be concluded from this study of ships that the Muslim navy not only had a variety of names for a single type, but a single name for a variety of types. Technical progress not only caused new words to be included in the vocabulary but also brought about a change in meanings. A new class of ship did not necessarily have a new name but might retain that of the type from which it was evolved. The numerous words used in the Arabic language probably only cover some dozens of types; it is practically impossible to work out any reduction as it would only hold good for a definite period in a certain district.

---

(1) 340; Wüstenfeld, N.G.W. Cött., 1880, 139. v. 'Alî Mubârak, XIV, 81; Gateau, Rev. Afr., 1946, 146, 147.

(2) N.G.W. Gött., 1882, 435. v. Nuwayrî, Al-Ilmân, quoted by 'Alî Ibrâhîm, 319-320.

(3) Passages in Quatremère, Mamlouks, Ia, 144, n. 18; Ibn Al-Athîr, R.H.C., I, 612 (4); Abû Shâma, R.H.C., IV, 164 (12).

(4) Ibn Shaddâd, R.H.C., III, 214 (9).

(5) Quatremère, Mamlouks, Ia, 212 (28).

(6) v. Ibn Al-Athîr, R.H.C., I, 510 (1), 513 (2); II, 80, n. 2; Ibn Shaddâd, R.H.C., III, 57 (1); Abû Shâma, R.H.C., 167(10), 203(4); B.A.S., 335 (13); Quatremère, Mamlouks, Ia, 144, n. 18.

(7) Under **taride**.

III. Staff of Ships and Responsibilities of Commander of Fleet

Staff of Ships

Mas'ûdî (1) makes it clear that there were various grades in the staff of Mediterranean warships. The greater part of the crews consisted of **nawâtiya,** then the **ru'asâ'** and those entrusted with the command of vessels of war, as for example, Leo of Tripolis.(2)

The **nawâtiya,** singular **nûtî,** were the sailors. Jawharî(3) says that the word was borrowed from the Syrians but it is obviously of Latin or Greek origin, **nauta.** The ru'sâ', singullar **ra'îs,** were the captains. Sprenger (4) accepts this meaning whilst Nadvi, (5) on one occasion, says it denotes superior officers, and on another, states that it signifies sea captains, corresponding to the term **mu'allim** used in the Indian Ocean.

In the same passage Mas'ûdî uses the term **ashâb al-arhul** which Sprenger (6) mistranslates as the officers of men and Nadvi (7) incorrectly gives the meaning of servants of lower ranks who were probably called **banâniya** in the Indian Ocean. Lammens, (8) quoting Eguilaz, says that the fleet which maintained communications between Africa and Spain was called **al-rahl al-Andalusî,** of which the shortened form, **al-rahl,** meant transport. Ibn Khaldûn (9) says that when an important expedition was in question in North Africa, the command of the squadron was entrusted to an amîr who held

---

(1) Murûj, I, 282.
(2) v. Supra, 62, n. 7. Both Sprenger, Meadows of Gold, I, 306, and Nadvi, Is. Cult, April 1942, 188-189, mistranslated this passage.
(3) Sihâh, under nût. v. Nadvi, Is. Cult., Oct. 1941, 437; Gateau, Rev. Afr., 1946, 146.
(4) Ibîd, I, 306
(5) Is. Cult., Oct. 1941, 437-438; Oct. 1942, 411.
(6) Meadows of Gold, I. 306.
(7) Is. Cult., Oct. 1942, 411.
(8) Mots Français, 24.
(9) Muqaddima, II, 32, 35; Fr. Tr., II, 37, 41. Maqrîzî, Khitat, II, 193, when speaking about the Fâtimid fleet, says that it was entrusted to an amîr of the highest rank. It seems that the Fâtimids introduced this position in Egypt.

the position **almilland.** Lammens (1) explains this word by pointing out that, in the time of Ibn Khaldûn, the Arabs had already borrowed **almirante** from the Spanish and had changed it to **almilland,** the leader so called taking the title of **Amîr-Al-Rahl.** (2) which signified commander of the convoy of the Spanish fleet. It seems probable that Mas'ûdî used the term **ashâb al-arhul** for the commandants of the fleets maintaining communications between Africa and Spain. These fleets may have consisted of merchant ships as Mas'ûdî distinguishes them from the warships, **al-marâkib al-harbiyya.** He calls them **al-marâkib al-'ammâla,** which Kindermann (3) defines as something resembling merchant or cargo ships ; the term was also used by Abû'l-Qâsim (4) in the same sense.

Mas'ûdî (5) also makes it clear that each of the Mediterranean and Eastern seas had separate sailors and experts. Muqaddasî (6) mentions the following as being attached to a ship in the Idian Ocean : **rubbâniyyûn** (singular, **rubbânî**) ; **ashâtima** (singular, **ashtiyâm**), **riyâdiyyûn** (singular, **riyâdi**), the mathematicians ; **wukalâ'** (singular, **wakîl**), the factors ; and **tujjâr,** the merchants.

Ibn Khaldûn (7) devotes a chapter to the command of the fleet, in which he outlines, in a masterly way, the responsibilities attached to the various naval ranks. The duties of the chief sailor, **qâ'id al-nawâtiya,** included the care of wea-

---

(1) Mots Français, 24, n. I. v. De Slane, Ibn Khaldûn Tr., II, 37, n. 4.
(2) For a long time the meaning of the modern word admiral has been explained by the Arabic word **amîr al-bahr** which means the commander of the sea. But the trouble is the ending **al** for which Devic, 32, could not find an explanation. Eguilaz has found a solution in the Spanish word **almirante** to which Lammens, Mots Français, 24, agrees and finds it fits admirably with Portugese, French, Italian and Spanish forms.
(3) Schiff, 67-68.
(4) v. B.G.A., Closs., IV, 231.
(5) Murûj, I, 281-282. v. D'Abbadie, J, As., May 1841, 585 sq.
(6) B.G.A., III, 10. The word **rubbânî** was the most common word for the ship's captain in later Arabic literature. v. Ibn Manzûr, I, 389. According to Nadvi, Is. Cult., Oct. 1942, 411, the term **riyâdi** was later called **mu'allim** who was the expert in maps and terrestrial instruments. Tabarî, III, 1582 (13), uses the expression **ashtiyâm** for the chief of the sailors in the warships, **bawârij,** employed in the fight against the Turks in Basra in 251/865. Ibn Manzûr, XV, 211 (14), says it was later used to denote the supervisor of the passengers. v. Ferrand, Astronomie Arabe. I 235.
(7) Muqaddima, II, 32 sq.; Fr. Tr., II, 37 sq.

pons and direction of naval action. The captain, **ra'îs,** had charge of the warship's course, whether by wind or oars, and its anchorage. The commander of the fleet, on whom the final responsibility for everything rested, gave the order for sailing. He was one of the dignitaries of the Empire.

Responsibilities of the Commander of the Fleet

A consideration of the responsibilities of the commander of naval forces in the 4th/10th century, as given in the official instructions of the 'Abbâsid Caliph issued in Qudâma's (1) time, seems to be a fitting conclusion to this study.

Selection of Men.

The responsibility of selecting the men, irrespective of their ranks, rests with the commander. Naphtha throwers, sailors, oarsmen, artisans and workmen on the ships must be highly skilled, patient and able to carry out repairs. As far as possible, only experienced sailors are to be distinguished so that they may not be mistaken for those unfit for the service. None but the best soldiers, who have a high moral standard and are fearless in face of the enemy, are to be taken on board. The commander is to choose for his police officers men who will satisfy his sense of justice and deal strictly with suspected and debauched persons.

Treatment of Men.

The Caliph advises the commander to thoroughly understand his troops and their particular qualifications by reviewing them continually and keeping contact with their ships. He must make it easy for the men under his command and those who have complaints or needs to have free access to

---

(1) Kitâb Al-Kharâj, MS. in Kuprili Library, Istanbul, reproduced without translation by Hamîdullâh, App., 306-308.

him. He himself has to be an exemplary leader of the soldiers and all who look to him for guidance, inciting and correcting them by the best methods. He must deal with each case justly, treating the obedient with leniency and the disobedient with severity. Full allowances(1) are to be paid generously and without delay.

Construction and Anchorage of Ships.

An important duty of the commander is to supervise shipbuilding, striving to obtain not only better quality in materials such as timber, iron and pitch, but a better selection of oars, masts and sails. He must inspect the new ships to ensure their being well built, the methods of construction and implements improved and the artificers selected. These vessels must be guarded in the harbour and beached in safe places during the winter to protect them from the winds.

Men well known to him for their bravery and sound advice are to be put in charge of ships in ports of anchorage so that no vessel leaves the harbour without his knowledge. The Caliph urges him to constantly watch over them and see that they are in good repair, ready against the hour of need. He must keep an eye on their equipment, including naphtha, cables and other materials, lest they deteriorate in any way.

Secret Service and Prevention of Leakage of Naval Information.

It is the commander's responsibility to see that spies, who gather information about the enemy, are trustworthy, able to give good advice, religious and honest. They must have experience of the sea, its ports, secrets and hiding places so that they may bring true reports and correct movements.

---

(1) The Arabic word used is **al-rizq** which literaly means wages and allowances. v. Supra, 104.

If they encounter enemy ships which they cannot resist they will be able to go to places which they know well and where they will be safe. The commander must supervise outposts and control stations so as to keep check on those in charge. A sharp look-out is to be kept for enemy spies and every city is to be placed in the hands of a man thoroughly acquainted with it, whose duty is to see that gatekeepers and guards do not allow anyone to enter until they know all about him, whence he comes, his features, his attitude of mind and his intention.

Of the many heavy obligations laid upon the commander of the fleet, precautions against leakage of information about naval warfare are among the most important. Care must be taken that enemies have no means of securing weapons, articles of war or knowledge of naval tactics from Muslim territory and that merchants do not carry anything to them or direct them. Anyone found guilty of such an offence must be punished severely as an example to others.

The Caliph concludes his instructions by admonishing his commander not to betray his trust and wishing him success and good guidance in the task assigned to him.

APPENDIX I

PORESTS IN EGYPT

According to Ibn Sîna (1) and 'Abd Al-Latîf, (2) the lebek was a deadly poison in Persia, but having been transported to Egypt, it became an aliment. It was known as the « *persea* ». In the time of Dioscorides (3) it flourished in Upper and Lower Egypt and from the time of Galien, (4) as he himself states, it was common in the region of Alexandria and in the gardens of the city. He does not speak of having seen this tree in any other country under Roman domination. However, the fact that he only mentions Alexandria because he lived there is no proof that the tree was not found in other parts of the country. Pausanias, (5) writing in A.D. 174, gives its habitat as the borders of the Nile, an expression which could mean the whole of Egypt. Elien, (6) at the beginning of the third century A.D., confirms having seen a forest of these trees in Alexandria. From a law of the Emperors Arcadius and Honorius (beginning of fifth century A.D.), given in the Justinian code, (7) it seems very probable that the number of perseas began to increase in Egypt at that time.

---

(1) Quoted by 'Alî Mubârak, VIII, 99.
(2) 9-10, on the authority of Aristotle. v. De Sacy, Relation, 54. Cf. 'Alî Bahgat, B.I.E., 1900, 153, where he traces the origin of the lebek tree to the Fâtimid period.
(3) Quoted by De Sacy, ibid, 49, 64; and by 'Alî Mubârak, VIII, 99.
(4) Quoted by De Sacy, ibid, 50, 64, and by 'Alî Mubârak, VIII, 99.
(5) Quoted by De Sacy, ibid, 50, 64, and by 'Alî Mubârak, VIII, 100.
(6) Quoted by De Sacy, ibid 64, and 'Alî Mubârak, VIII, 100.
(7) Quoted by De Sacy, ibid, 64, and 'Alî Mubârak, VIII, 100.

Much interesting information about forests in Egypt under Muslim domination is supplied by Ibn Mamâtî. He asserts that they existed at an early date and that sant trees flourished in some parts of Upper Egypt but were rare in Lower Egypt. The Treasury controlled the forests and an administration was later set up to preserve what was left. He speaks of them under the name hirâj (1) which, he says, (2) « *were found in Upper Egypt, in Bahnasâ(3) at Saft Rashîn,(4) and others in Ushmûnayn,(5) Asyût, Ikhmîm(6) and in Qûs.(7) Rulers were constantly issuing orders for the preservation of the forests so that they might be protected from all depredation. Trees might only be cut down when necessary so that timber for shipbuilding would be assured. Nevertheless, in course of time, rulers failed to impose*

---

(1) Not Al-Kharâj as it is often misprinted. v. Casanova, Description de l'Egypte, III, 62, 138, 268; Becker, E.I., I, 578; 'Alî Mubârak, X, 2-3; XIV, 115.

(2) Ibn Mamâtî, 344 sq., reproduced by Maqrîzî, I.F., II, 108; 'Alî Mubârak, X, 2; Wüstenfeld, N.G.W. Gött., 1880, 140-141 ; 'Alî Bahgat, B.I.E., 1900, 142 sq.

(3) The classical name of Al-Bahnasâ is Oxyrhynchus. It stands on the west bank of the Nile, some distance from the river. It was famous in antiquity even in the early Muslim period. It was one of the most important towns in Central Egypt. Under Muslim rule it remained the seat of government of a district (Kûra). When the division into provinces was carried out under the Fâtimid Al-Mustansir, it gave its name to the province of Al-Bahnasâwiyya. The town is now an unimportant village in the district of Banî Mazâr in the province of Al-Minyâ. v. Ibn Mamâtî, 17 ; Yâqût, Mu'jam, I, 771 ; Maqrîzî, Khitat, I, 237 sq., 272 (7) ; 'Alî Mubârak, X, 2; Amélineau, 90 sq.; Baedeker, 202, 207 ; Becker, E.I., I, 578.

(4) Saft Rashîn is a considerable distance to the north of Al-Bahnasâ, and to the south of Banî Suwayf, in which province it is now included. Yâqût, Mushtarak, 249, includes it in the province of Al-Banhasâ. v. Abû Sâlih, fol. 57b, 217; Ibn Duqmâq, V, 8.

(5) The classical name of Ushmûnayn is Hermopolis, on the west bank of the Nile, between Minyâ and Manfalût. It is now in the province of Asyût. v. Idrîsî, Nuzhat Al-Mushtâq, [47]; Yâqût, Mu'jam, I, 283; Ibn Duqmâq, V, 15; Maqrîzî, Khitat, I, 238-239; Amélineau, 167. sq.

(6) The classical name of Ikhmîm is Panapolis. It was formerly famous for its temple which was reckoned among the wonders of Egypt but few remains exist. It is in the district of Sûhâj. v. Idrîsî, Nuzhat Al-Mushtâq, [48]; Abû Sâlih, 204, n. 3; Yâqût, Mu'jam, I, 165 ; Ibn Duqmâq, V, 25; Maqrîzî, Khitat, I, 31, 239 ; Suyûtî, Husn, I. 38; Amélineau, 18-22.

(7) Qûs was formerly the capital of a province but is now in the province of Qinâ. It was of great commercial importance, halfway between Qinâ and Luxor. v. Idrîsî, ibid, [48-49]; Benjamin., 69, n. 2; Yâqût, Mu'jam, IV, 201; Ibn Duqmâq, V, 28; Maqrîzî, Khitat, I, 236 ; 'Alî Mubârak, XIV, 140-141 ; Amélineau, 400.

restrictions and the forests were devastated to a great extent; at Qûs only scattred groups of trees remained. I was ordered by the Sultan to appoint an officer to go to the forests of Bahnasâ and hold an enquiry to ascertain to what extent they had been overrun. The report showed that an area of thirteen thousand feddans was affected. The wonder is not so much the quantity that was taken, but the fact that it made no appreciable difference to the forests. I hear that trees required for oil mills and sugar cane presses used to be found there and that one plank of this wood cost a hundred dinars. The people of the localities paid a special duty known as sant tax in return for wood for building or wages of the men who felled the trees. The tax still exists but is not so high, the cost of felling and transporting a hundred himls (1) *being one dinar. Forest keepers received orders that trees suitable for shipbuilding were not to be felled whilst only branches and brushwood might be cut for fuel. The administration for forest (Dîwân), used to sell firewood from Ushmûnayn, Asyût, Ikhmîn and Qûs, at the rate of four dinars for a hundred loads for which the keepers gave merchants a receipt, stating the quantity of wood bought. When the boats arrived at Fustât central government officials examined the timber, confiscating any suitable for shipbuilding and weighing the remainder for firewood. If the weight exceeded that shown on the receipt, the surplus had to be paid for at the agreed price. Wood from the forest of Bahnasâ was only sold when there happened to be more than was needed for the* (Caliph's) *kitchens and then the price was from eight to ten dinars for a hundred loads. Although the forest was near Cairo and the cost of transport less, the good quality of the wood created a demand for it which accounted for its high price... Officials attached to the Sâhil Al-Sant* (the quay of disembarkation at Fustât), *had to price, sell and deliver the loads upon arrival from the forests to the Dîwân for shipbuilding.»*

Amîr Fakhr Al-Dîn 'Uthmân Ibrâhîm Al-Nâbulsî, governor of the Fayyûm, explains the causes of the devastation of the forests. He gives the following account(2)

---

(1) The **himl** or load was equal to about 168 pounds. v. 'Ali Bahgat, B.I.E., 1900, 143, n. 2.
(2) Nâbulsî, Lam' Al-Qawânîn, quoted by 'Alî Mubârak, XIV, 114-115; 'Alî Bahgat, ibid, 148 sq.

in his treatise written in the form of a report for the Sultan Al-Sâlih Najm Al-Dîn Ayyûb, (638-47/1240-9): «*The hirâj were plentiful in Egypt and, like the mines, were the exclusive property of the Public Treasury (Bayt Al-Mâl). There was a special administrative office (Dîwân), for them but when rulers neglected the administration, people cut down what they wanted and brought it to Sâhil Misr (Fustât). In lieu of paying the tax of a third of the selling price, they bribed the officials of the Sâhil with a small present and sold the wood, which they received at a low price, for considerable sums of money. The general governor ought to appoint, for each forest, a director and supervisor authorised to cut down trees and despatch them to Fustât so that some wood would be saved for time of need and the rest sold to those requiring it. The public Treasury would thereby gain great profits without wronging any person.*» The same writer says that there were sant trees valued at one thousand dinars at Matariyya,(1) in the neighbourhood of Cairo. The indifference of the forestry administration encouraged people to attack the forest of Qalyûb (2) although they had not dared to cut down a single tree during the reign of the Sultan Al-Kâmil. He was so anxious to preserve not only monuments, but palm and other trees peculiar in Egypt, that he even went so far as to order gardens to be laid out in Cairo, Fustât, Jîza and other places. He also ordered sant trees to be counted and recorded in the archives of the Dîwân.

Al-Nâbulsî makes it clear that the prime cause of the destruction of the forests was the negligence of governors of provinces and the corruption of the forestry administration and officials of Al-Sâhil. His account further confirms that sant trees flourished north of Cairo at Matariyya and that there were others south of Qalyûb.

'Abd Al-Latîf Al-Baghdâdî (3) says that the lebek fruit was rare and dear owing to the scarcity of the trees. Maqrîzî(4) says that they were one of the finest products of

---

(1) Al-Matariyya is a few miles to the north of modern Cairo. v. Abû Sâlih, 86, n. 2; Yâqût, Mu'jam, I, 111-112; Maqrîzî, Khitat, I, 31 (31); Amélineau, 287.

(2) Qalyûb was about ten miles to the north of Cairo in the province of Qalyûbiyya. v. Ibn Duqmâq, V, 47 sq.; 'Alî Mubârak, XIV, 114; Amélineau, 390.

(3) 9-10; De Sacy, Relation, 17, 65.

(4) Quoted by De Sacy, ibid, 65, and 'Alî Mubârak, VIII, 100.

Egypt but became scarce before 700/1300. Ibn Iyâs(1) also writes of a fruit called lebek which resembled a green almond but which disappeared from Egypt about 700/1300. Among modern travellers, Vansleb(2) refers to the rarity of this tree for he did not see a single one in all his travels. Baedeker(3) says there were no wild trees nor forests.

Conclusion

From the various references it seems that there were forests throughout Egypt in ancient times and that Egyptian boats were made of the lebek wood(4) which began to be rare at the end of the fourth or the beginning of the fifth century A.D., in the time of Arcadius and Honorius. From the time of the Muslim conquest, forests were rare in Lower Egypt but still existed in parts of Upper Egypt. During 'Abd Al-Latîf's time the number of trees decreased considerably, until only the memory of them remained in the following century.

---

(1) I, 5.
(2) Relation de l'Egypte, 96, 111.
(3) Egypt, LVII, v. Maqrîzî, I.F., II, 108, n. 4.
(4) Heredotus, II, 111, par. 96, says that Egyptian ships were made or acacia. v. also Theophraste, Historia Plantarium, IV, par. 2 8; Clowes, Sailing Ships, 17.

APPENDIX II

NAMES OF SHIPS OF TULUNID FLEET

Madaynî (1) mentions a fleet Ibn Tûlûn built to defend his capital. It consisted of one hundred large Arabic ships, **marâkib 'arabiyya,** (2) and one hundred warships, **marâkib harbiyya,** (3) besides **'ulâbiyyât, hamâ'im, 'ushâriyyât, sanâdîl** and **qawârib al-khidma,** (4) (service boats).

'Ulâbiyyât.

In the enumeration of the vessels comprising Ibn Tûlûn's fleet both Madaynî and Maqrîzî place **'ulâbiyyât,** together with the other ships' names, after warships. They may, therefore, have been smaller craft, perhaps pleasure boats.(5)

Hamâ'im.

Hamâma, plural **hamâ'im,** literally means dove, hence Moritz (6) suggests a fast sailer. The word occurs in Maqrîzî(7) when he mentions Ibn Tûlûn's fleet and is found

---

(1) 87 (1 sq.).

(2) Probably **shînî** or **shalandî**. For **shînî** v. Supra, 131 sq. and for **shalandî** v. Supra, 129 sq. Maqrîzî, Khitat, II, 180 (7), gives the same account of the Tûlûnid fleet as Madaynî, with the exception of the hundred Arabic ships, and gives **sanâbik** in place of **sanâdîl**.

(3) For **markib harbî** v. Supra, 129.

(4) For **qârib** v. Supra, 125.

(5) v. Kindermann, Schiff, 67.

(6) In Festschrift Ed. Sachau, 439; Kindermann, Schiff, 24.

(7) Khitat, II, 180 (7).

in Muqaddasî's (1) list of names. Kindî,(2) speaking of Fâtik's journey to Fustât in 293/906, uses **hamâma** but the editor emends it to **hammâla** in a note. The glossary(3) shows, however, that he got this latter rendering from Dozy(4) who gives it the meaning of transport ship. **Markib hammâla** is found in Idrîsî (5) as an antonym for **markib harbî,** warship. Marcel and Hélot's (6) modern term is **markib hamla,** a merchant vessel or transport ship. Maqrîzî(7) uses **hammâla** in this sense. Ibn Mamâtî (8) employs this last word to mean a transport ship for corn.

'Ushâriyyât.

According to Kindermann (9) the word **'ushâriyyât,** singular **'ushârî,** may well be an Arabic word, and Amari (10) suggests that the Italian **usciere** may have been derived from it. This type of ship formed part of Ibn Tûlûn's fleet. In 307/919, at the time of the 'Abbâsid Caliph Al-Muqtadir, 'Ubaydallah threatened Rosetta with a warfleet of eighty **humûl** and twenty **'ushârî.** (11) The manuscript translated by Gildemeister (12) shows that these shallow boats, **'ushâriyyât,** were propelled by twenty oars and served to transfer goods and people from the shore. They were chiefly used as lighter boats and shallops to larger vessels. When the latter sank,

---

(1) B.G.A., III, 32.
(2) Governors, 263 (3) and n. 1.
(3) Kindî, ibid, Gloss., 62.
(4) Supplément, I, 328 (a).
(5) Ed. Dozy, I, 112. v. Abû Shâma, B.A.S., 333 (14).
(6) Marcel, Dict. Français-Arabe, under «vaisseau» ; Hélot, Dict. de Poche Français-Arabe, 257. v. Brunot, La Mer, 250.
(7) Khitat, II, 193 (13).
(8) 340 ; Wüstenfeld, N.G.W. Gött., 1880, 138-139.
(9) Schiff, 64.
(10) I Diplomi Arabi, 397, f. v. Dozy, Supplément, II, 130 (b).
(11) Eutychius, Ed. Pocock, II, 506 (16), uses **ghusharnî,** and in Corp. Script. Christ., VII, 80 (13), gives **'usharnî. 'Ushârî** seems to be the correct reading for both words mentioned.
(12) N.G.W. Gött., 1882, 436. v. Nuwayrî, Al-Ilmâm, quoted by 'Alî Ibrahîm, 319-320.

through some defect (1) or attack, (2) the passengers saved themselves together with goods and chattels (3) in the **'ushâriyyât**.

The term **'ushâriyyât** was also especially used to designate the gorgeously fitted out **gondolas** seen on the Nile, and mentioned during the Fâtimid period. In this sense they can be compared with the **harrâqât** used on the Tigris and Euphrates. Fantastic sums were spent on these pleasure craft. Maqrîzî (4) estimates the building of thirty six such luxury boats, all in all, at four hundred thousand dinars. Naturally they were used by the Caliphs, particularly for the Nile festivals. The Caliph and the distinguished people of his kingdom went on these pleasure boats to the Nilometer at the time of high floods to take part in the ceremony.(5) The best description of the **'ushâriyyât** in this sense is that of 'Abd-Al-Latîf Al-Baghdâdî (6) who says: «*In Egypt they have ships of many shapes and various kinds. I have seen nothing more unusual than a sort of barge called* **al-'ashîrî**. *It is shaped like the* **shabbâra** *(7) seen on the Tigris, but it is much wider, longer, better proportioned and of a more pleasing shape. These boats are decked with solid planks and have projections in the form of balconies of about two cubits. Above deck is a room built of wood and crowned by a dome, in which are windows and openings, furnished with shutters, commanding a view of the river on all sides. In it is a private closet and water-closet, and the room is*

---
(1) Ibn Jubayr, 312(15).
(2) Amari, I Diplomi Arabi, 8(9).
(3) Ibn Jubayr, 312(13); Ibn Battûta, Voyage, II, 251(6).
(4) Khitat, I, 475(35 sq.), 476. v. also I, 469(35 sq.).
(5) v. Supra, 49, n. 8.
(6) 95-97. v. Description of this type of ship by Ibn Al-'Amîd, quoted by Nuwayrî, Cairo Edition, I, 260.
(7) According to Fraenkel, 220, **shabbâra**, plural **shabbârât**, is a «*word of Aramic appearance.*» De sacy, Relation, 309, n. 27, would like to read it **bashshâra**, « *which would signify a vessel for carrying news, a look-out,*» which is, according to Kindermann, Schiff, 45, extremely unlikely, since the spelling given above has long been unquestioned. The word denotes a sort of boat mentioned several times by Tabarî, III, 1563(11), 1589(14), as being used on the Tigris in the fighting against the Turks in 251/865. They appeared in the form of warships which were manned with soldiers, and on which catapults were erected. v. Tabarî, III, 1590(5, 7), 1626(10), 1627(1). They are mentioned with the **sumâyriyyât**, (v. Tabarî, III, 1563 and Gloss., CCCIV), and there seems to be no clear evidence of any great difference between the two types of ships.

decorated in various colours, with gilt and the finest varnish. This sort of boats is made for kings and important people. When one of them is on board he sleeps on his cushion; he has people of his own society round him. His men and slaves, wearing their belts and swords, stand on the balconies. The provisions and all the baggage are in the hold. The sailors are under the deck and all over the ship, working it by means of oars, without knowing anything of what the passengers are doing, and without the latter troubling themselves about what the members of the crew are doing. Furthermore, sailors and passengers are completely isolated from one another and each minds their own affairs. If the chief wants to be alone and to separate himself from his companions, he retires to the private room.»

Sanâdîl.

According to Vollers (1) **sandal,** (plural **sanâdil** and **sanâdîl),** is of Persian origin and is defined as a kind of auxiliary boat — one by which water, food and other necessities were brought to a larger ship. Barbier de Meynard(2) says that **sandâl** was a long, solid boat rather like the fishing boats in the Mediterranean. The true origin of the word has been the subject of lively discussion. In Jal's (3) opinion *«it is the name of a small ship, like a launch, of which the origin is uncertain. Some critics maintain that this craft owes its name to the relation its form bears to the footwear called sandal; others think that the* **sandal,** *masculine or feminine, is thus called on account of the use made of it for transporting grain. On this last hypothesis sandal would have come from the Latin* **sandalum,** *a variety of wheat. The other supposition suggests the Greek word for a woman's shoe which may be merely a transcription of the Turkish,* **sandal.»** Kindermann(4) says that it is nevertheless, possible that the meaning of boat developed out of the already known Greek word especially as this is found in many Mediterranean languages, and is evidently not a primitive word in Turkish, Persian or Arabic.

---

(1) Z.D.M.G., L. 644.
(2) Quoted by Kindermann, Schiff, 55.
(3) Under **sandale.**
(4) Schiff, 56.

Theophanes (1) mentions **sandalia** as service boats for the **katinae** (2) in the Muslim fleet during the second siege of Constantinople. When speaking of the reinforcements that came from Egypt and Africa on this occasion he says that some Coptic sailors deserted one night in **sandalia** and escaped to Constantinople where they gave the Emperor valuable information. Tâj Al-'Arûs (3) gives **sandal** the meaning of a vessel — a small boat in the body of a larger one, which is brought out in cases of emergency. The author adds that it is perhaps similar, in its small size, to the footwear called **sandal**. It is often met with, in this sense, in the descriptions of European travellers (4) and is in use on the coast of North Africa as well as along the Euphrates. Dozy (5) gives a wide choice for the meaning of the word: **«canoe, launch, barge, nacelle»**, adding that the name is located in North Africa and is found in various forms in comprehensive dictionaries. (6)

Sanâbîk.

In Maqrîzî's (7) description of the Tûlûnid fleet, **sanâbîk**, singular **sunbûk**, is used instead of **sanâdîl** found in Madaynî. (8) Kindermann (9) thinks the word is certainly the Persian **sunbuk**, a small ship. According to Al-Sâghânî, (10) it is current in the speech along the whole Yemen coast but Tâj Al-'Arûs (11) regards it as an expression of Hijâz. The word does not only occur in the region of the sea of Yemen and its neighbouring waters, for Ibn Shahriyâr (12) speaks of a sailor who travelled to China on such a boat. Ibn Batt-

---

(1) Chronog., Ed. De Boor, 395-396, 397. I owe the reference to Prof. R. Jenkins.
(2) v. Supra, 126.
(3) VII, 383 (28 sq.).
(4) v. Dozy, Supplément, I, 846(a); Kinderman, Schiff, 56; Brunot, Notes Lexicologiques, 80.
(5) Supplément, I, 846(a).
(6) Kindermann, Schiff, 56, says that **filûka** is usually given as a synonym.
(7) Khitat, II, 180(7).
(8) 87(3).
(9) Schiff, 43.
(10) v. Tâj Al-'Arûs, VI, 385(23).
(11) VII, 146(12).
(12) 'Ajâ'ib Al-Hind, 190.

ûta, (1) who spells it as **snnbûq,** plural **sanâbiq,** describes it in two places as **qârîb saghîr,** a small boat, and speaks of it on the journey from Basra to Ubulla.

To-day the evidence of modern travellers (2) shows **sunbuk or sumbuk** to be a largish, usually two-masted ship, confined to the Red Sea and the Persian Gulf. Brunot (3) says that the word means a flat-bottomed boat not known in Rabat, and is synonymous with **sandal.** It seems that **sanâdîl,** as used by Madaynî to describe Ibn Tûlûn's fleet, is more correct than **sanâbik,** as used by Maqrîzî.

---

(1) Voyage, II, 17(3).
(2) v. Burton, I, 263, 276 ; Neimans, Z.D.M.G., XII, 1858, 420 sq. ; Burchardt, I, 43 ; II, 341 ; Ritter, Der Islam, IX, 1919, 137; Kâzim Al-Dujaylî, Lughat Al-'Arab, II, 100.
(3) Notes Lexicologiques, 79

APPENDIX III

NAMES OF SHIPS MENTIONED BY MUQADDASI

Thirty six different kinds of ships are mentioned by Muqaddassî.(1) More information is needed to explain their structure and to classify them. In some cases there is no further elucidation of the name beyond the meaning of ship ; the type, design and distinctive characteristicts are lacking. (2)

Safîna, qârib, markib, shalandî, shînî, and hamâma have already been described. (3) It has been impossible to find any detailed information about **burma, 'irdâs, malqûta** (4) and **shamût.** The following ships are those which have not been discussed and about which there is some information :

Barka.

This ship is mentioned by Istakhrî (5) who says that in 324/935 a merchant of 'Umân lost four hundred **barka** by fire. The word is explained as meaning a little ship and was the name used there for a **zawraq** of fifty **wiqrs'** capacity.(6) Lammens (7) ascribes it to the dialect of 'Umân. According to Kindermann, (8) the Spanish-Arab, **la barca, labarka,** noted by Fischer as **barke,** « *flat-bottomed boat on rivers*», surely had another development.

---

(1) B.G.A., III, 31-32.
(2) Wüstenfeld, N.G.W. Gött., 1880, 136.
(3) v. Supra, 125, 129, 131, 149 sq.
(4) **Malqûta** is mentioned by De Goeje, B.G.A., IV, Gloss., 349, as a kind of ship.
(5) B.G.A., I, 139. v. Gloss., IV, 188.
(6) Lammens, Mots Français, 46; Kindermann. Schiff, 4. One **wiqr** usually equals one mule load.
(7) Ibid, 46.
(8) Schiff, 4.

Bîrja.

De Goeje (1) considers Muqaddasî's spelling to be **bârija,** plural **bawârij,** which was probably of Indian origin (2) and was the name given to pirate vessels of the people whom the Arabs encountered in the Indian Ocean in the parts of Sind.(3) Under the Caliphate of Al-Mansûr they overpowered Jedda in 151/768 and the sight of their ships was so dreaded that the name **bawârij,** in the terminology of some writers, came to mean the pirates themselves.(4) The sinister connotation of this word led to its further development to mean **sharr,** signifying evil in Arabic. In Tâj Al-'Arûs and Al-Mukhassas,(5) the world **bârija** when applied to a person means «*full of evil.*»

On the other hand, etymologists are very puzzled about the origin of the Romance term **barge.** Lammens (6) compares it with the Arabic **bârija** = warship, but Gamillscheg (7) thinks that this Arabic word was not its source but, on the contrary, was borrowed from it. Baydâwî's (8) explanation, that **bârija** indicated an open vessel, one not decked, because its derivation is the Arabic verb **tabarraja** = to show, has already been proved erroneous by Dozy and De Goeje.

Balâdhurî (9) sometimes uses **bârija** for pirate vessel. Mas'ûdî's (10) **bawârij** might be compared with **shawânî,** singular **shînî,** used in the Mediterranean regions. Balâdhurî(11) speaks of seventy **bawârij** used by Muhammad ibn Al-Fadl when fighting the Indian tribes. Tabarî (12) gives the crew

---

(1) B.G.G., IV, 195.
(2) Kindermann, Schiff, 3, says that according to Pott, the gipsies still have the words **bero, ber.**
(3) Balâdhurî, 440(12-13), calls the people **Al-Mid,** *the «freebooters»* of the sea v. Minorsky, E.I., III, 236-237.
(4) Bîrûnî, in Reinaud, Fragments, 91, 120. v. Kindermann, Schiff, 3.
(5) Tâj Al-'Arûs, II, 7(25); Ibn Sîda, X, 26(17).
(6) Mots Français, 45.
(7) Quoted by Kindermann, Schiff, 3.
(8) II, 30(23). v. Lammens, ibid, 45 ; Kindermann, Schiff, 3.
(9) 435(14 sq.). For references to the piracy of these ships v. Mas'ûdî, Murûj, III, 37; Muqaddasî, B.G.A., III, 14(5) ; Yâqût, Mu'jam, III, 102(15); Ibn Shahriyâr, 114(9), 115(1).
(10) B.G.A., VIII, 55(9), 355(4). v. Ibn Shahriyâr, 130(3).
(11) 446(8), 445(1).
(12) III, 1582(13).

of such a ship, ten of which were employed against the Turks in 251/865 in Basra, as consisting of forty five men, including the captain «*ashtiyâm*», three naphta throwers, one carpenter, one baker and thirty nine rowers, who were also soldiers. In this last sense the word is used at the present time.(1)

Burâkiyya.

The dictionaries (2) give the meaning of ship for this word. Moritz (3) says that **burka** = duck, is the name of a class of ship similar to **hamâma** and **ghurâb**. Kindermann,(4) on the other hand, thinks that **burka,** as mentioned by Moritz, is perhaps an error for **barka.**

Bur'ânî.

This term corresponds very closely with **barsânî** which is found in Kahle. (5) Kindermann (6) says that **barânisa** occurs in «*Firmâns Selîm's I*», published by Moritz, as a ship in which fruit and honey are transported and that **barsâniyyât** is mentioned by Zâhirî as a type of ship.

Dûnîj.

De Goeje (7) vocalises this word as **dawnîj**, plural **dawânîj**. Ibn Shahriyâr (8) uses it on several occasions and connects it with districts in India, Ceylon and Sofâla. It seems to have signified a boat of moderate size, and may have

---

(1) Badger, Lexicon, under «*man-of-war*», 604.
(2) Tâj Al-'Arûs, VII, 107(25) ; Maydânî, 99(2).
(3) In Festschrift Ed. Sachau, 439(2).
(4) Schiff, 4.
(5) Der Leuchtturm von Alexandria, quoted by Kindermann, Schiff, 7.
(6) Schiff, 6.
(7) B.G.A., Gloss., IV, 240.
(8) Quoted by Kindermann, Schiff, 29.

been a synonym for **qârib**. Yâqût (1) relates that the king of the island of Qays or Kîsh enjoyed the esteem and respect of the king of India on account of his many **marâkib** and **dawânîj**. The term may have meant a ship or boat which was very common along the coastal strip of 'Umân, Bahrayn, the Persian Gulf generally and the Indian waters bordering it. (2)

Jabaliyya.

The expression belongs to the category of ships' names indicating places. (3) De Goeje (4) regards it as signifying a type of ship probably so called from the town of **Jabala**, in Syria. Mas'ûdî, (5) mentions 'Abdallah ibn Wazîr, the governor, as being a highly experienced sea captain of the Mediterranean in 332/943, whose advice was followed by all captains of warships and merchant vessels. The word may therefore be regarded as referring to this place on the coast of Hims where good seamanship was held in high esteem.

Jâsûs.

The name appears in Muqaddasî's and Abû'l-Qâsim's (6) lists of ships. The literal meaning of the word suggests that it may mean a special boat used for scouting or secret service purposes. (7)

Kârawâniyya.

Dozy (8) mentions **kârawâniyya** as «*a sort of ship* ». Kindermann (9) says that the word is etymologically related

---

(1) Mu'jam, IV, 216(3).
(2) v. Kindermann, Schiff, Article **Dûnî**, 28-30.
(3) Kindermann, Schiff, 15-16; Wüstenfeld, N.G.W. Gött., 1880, 136.
(4) B.G.A., IV, Gloss, 202.
(5) Murûj, I, 282.
(6) B.G.A., III, 31 (14) ; IV, 231.
(7) v. Kinrermann, Schiff, 15; Fraenkel, 243.
(8) Supplément, II, 434.
(9) Schiff, 88.

to the Persian **kârawân**. A caravan was not exclusively a land expedition and Jal (1) defines the word as « *a company of Turkish merchants or pilgrims, who travelled together, usually under cover, either by land or water.*» The **kârawâniyya** may have been used for such journeys.(2)

Khaytiyya.

This name, plural **khaytiyyât**, is found in both Muqaddasî's and Abû'l-Qâsim's (3) collections of ship's names. De Geoje (4) defines it as «*a sort of ship... perhaps getting its name from its construction,*» and refers to the passage in Ibn Jubayr (5) where he states that they were stitched together with cords made of coco-nut fibre. Ya'qûbî (6) speaks of **marâkib khaytiyya** as being built in Ubulla, and in which voyages were made to China. De Goeje (7) also says that they were ships made of firm wooden planks of **sâj** wood which were joined with thread made from palm bark instead of being nailed. This type of ship may therefore resemble the **jalba** mentioned particularly in connection with the Red Sea and the Gulf of Aden.(8)

Mi'bar.

There are two other forms of this word, the plural **ma'âbir** and the feminine (9) **mi'bara**. The dictionaries (10) explain it as meaning a thing put over a river, such as a ferry-boat, a pontoon or even a bridge. It may indicate a ship

---

(1) Under **Caravane**.
(2) Kindermann, Schiff, 88, 97.
(3) B.G.A., III, 32(1) ; IV, 231.
(4) B.G.A., IV, 231.
(5) 70(18). v. Supra, 80.
(6) B.G.A., VII, 360(5).
(7) B.G.A., VIII, Gloss., XX.
(8) v. Kindermann, Schiff, 19, 26 ; Lammens, Mots Français, 84.
(9) Lisân Al-'Arab, VI, 204(7); Tâj Al-'Arûs, III, 378(16).
(10) Lisân Al-'Arab, VI, 204(6) ; Tâj Al-'Arûs, III, 376(33).

used to span a river.(1) According to De Goeje (2) the term has a more specialised use in Muqaddasî's list of ships, in addition to the general meaning of ship. Tabarî (3) uses it for freight or transport ship and in various other ways, in conjunction with the **shadhawât** and **sumayriyyât** in the years 258/872, 267/880-1 and 269/882-3. From the context it is clear that the Arabs used them on the canals of the Tigris for transporting troops.(4) Even to-day the ferries on the Tigris and Euphrates, «*propelled across with the help of a suspended rope* », are called **me'êbir.** They are sometimes coarse, primitive wooden boats, with a wide gang-board for animals and vehicles. (5)

Makkiyya.

De Goeje (6) is of the opinion that the word denotes a kind of ship used for transporting pilgrims to Mecca, with which the name is associated.

Musabbahiyya.

The idea of ship is closely connected with the root meaning **sabaha** = to swim, but it is rarely used in this sense. (7)

Muthallatha.

The term belongs to the category of ships' names derived from numbers and to those mentioned by Ibn Battûta(8) as **rub'î,** one quarter, **thulthî,** one third and **nisfî,** one half. They

---

(1) v. Kindermann, Schiff, 102; Fraenkel, 213.
(2) B.G.A., IV, Gloss., 295.
(3) III, 1871(13), 1948(5), 1961(7), 1968(8), 2001(9), 2094(3, 11, 13).
(4) Including the Qâ'id, Tabarî, III, 1871(13); the infantry, III, 1948(5); the cavalry and foot soldiers, III, 2074(14). These ships are mentioned before **sufun,** III, 1961(7).
(5) Ritter, Der Islam, IX, 1919, 141; Kindermann, Schiff, 102.
(6) B.G.A., IV, Gloss., 355. v. Wüstenfeld, N.G.W. Gött., 1880, 136.
(7) Kindermann, Schiff, 98.
(8) Voyage, IV, 92(2).

signified three smallish rowing boats which followed a larger Chinese ship or **junk**. Yule (1) suggests that the names indicated their relative size.

Raqqiyya.

The plural form is **raqqiyyât**. De Goeje (2) says that the name might quite possibly be derived either from the town of **Raqqa** or from the fact that it was here that they were adapted for sailing in shallow water, (**mâ' raqîb — riqqat al-mâ'**). Tabarî (3) uses the plural form when speaking of the fleet of Al-Muwaffaq in 269/882 and also in conjunction with **shadhâ** and **sumayriyyât** as being used on the Tigris for transporting horses.

Shabûq.

Moritz (4) maintains that **sanbûq** is the correct rendering of this word. Lammens (5) prefers to derive **chebec** from **shabûq**, used by Muqaddasî.

Shadhâ.

The term has two plural forms, **shdhawât** and **shadha'ât**. (6) According to the dictionary (7) it means a *«sort of ship»*, a small ship like a **zabzab**, or even a warship. Al-Azharî (8) doubted whether it was a genuine Arabic word.

---

(1) Cathay and the Way Thither, IV, 25 ; Kindermann, Schiff, 94.
(2) B.G.A., IV, 249.
(3) III, 2074(6).
(4) In Festschrift Ed. Sachau, 439. v. Supra, App. II, 153 sq.
(5) Mots Français, 86. v. Kindermann, Schiff, 45.
(6) Tabarî and 'Arîb, 28(5), 55(3 sq.), use **shadhawât** ; Kitâb Al-'uyûn uses **shadha'ât.**
(7) Tâj Al-'Arûs, X, 195(15 sq.).
(8) Quoted in Tâj Al-'Arûs, X, 195(15). For the discussion of the origin of the word v. Fraenkel, 220.

The name often occurs in the reports of the Zinj wars in Tabarî (1) where **shadhâ** and **sumayriyyât**, or **shadhawât** and **sumayriyyât**, are frequently mentioned. It can be assumed that it was a type of ship similar to the **sumayriyya**, though the references give no indication of its nature. Tabarî(2) also relates that when Mansûr ibn Ja'far was arming against the Zinj in 257/870-1, he added the **shadhâ al-jannâbiyyât** and the **sufun**, transport ships, to the **shadhâ** he already had. It seems likely that they were made in **Jannâba** on the north coast of the Persian Gulf. (3)

Shankûliyya.

De Goeje (4) regards this word as the « *name of a ship, derived from the Persian* **shankûl** = *thief, and hence meaning a 'pirate ship'* ».

Sûqiyya.

This ship may have been a « *trading vessel* » belonging to the merchant service, as the literal meaning of **sûq** is market. De Goeje (5) merely calls it a «*type of ship*» and makes no attempt to describe it further.

Talawway.

The word is used by Muqaddasî and the lexicographers. The dictionary (6) describes it as a sort of small ship. It may have got its name because it follows the large ships. (7)

---

(1) III, 1948(4, 14, 16); 1949(11 sq.); 1961(7 sq.); 1965(13 sq.); 1966 (15).
(2) III, 1844(13 sq.).
(3) v. Kindermann, Schiff, 48.
(4) B.G.A., IV, Gloss., 277.
(5) B.G.A., IV, Gloss., 267. v. Kindermann, Schiff, 45.
(6) Bustânî, Muhît, 171(b, 1).
(7) v. Kindermann, Schiff, 15. Cf. the discussion in Tâj Al-'Arûs, X, 53(22), and Lisân Al-'Arab, VIII, 112(1).

Tayra.

This word can hardly be thought of as a corruption of **tayyâr.** Kindermann (1) says that one of the meanings given in the dictionary is a kind of fish. It may indicate a kind of fishing boat.

Tayyâr

The plural form is **tayyârât.** According to Maydânî (2) it is a kind of ship whilst Vullers (3) describes it as a sort of ship having very swift movement which corresponds with the real meaning of **tayyâr** = flier. The name is included in the list of Muqaddasî and Abû'l-Qâsim (4) and is mentioned by Dhahabî. 'Arîb (5) refers to a **tayyâr** used in Baghdad for the journey of the Vizir Ibn Khâqân after his stay at Bâb Al-Shammâsiyya. It is stated that the general Ibn Râ'iq said «*To sail in a* **tayyâr** *on the Tigris and hear the cries of the boatmen is dearer to me than domination over all Syria*». (6) Al-Muhassin intended to throw Ibn Qarâba into the water as he sailed with him in his **tayyâr** on the **Tigris,** but he did not succeed in doing so. (7) The fighting fleet of the Barîdî in Basra 329/941, included **tayyârât,** as is mentioned by Mas'ûdî. (8) The same information is found in Lughat Al-'Arab, (9) quoted from Hamdânî, where the order given is **zabâzib, tayyârât, hadîdiyyât** and **shadhâ'ât.** Mas'ûdî (10) says that in 333/945, the Caliph Al-Mustakfî embarked on a **ghazâl** called **tayyâr.** Tanûkhî, (11) used the word **tayyâr** for a Tigris boat favoured by the nobility. In 399/1008-9 Ibn

---

(1) Schiff, 61.
(2) Sâmî, 99(2).
(3) Lexicon Persico-Latinum, under **tayyâra.**
(4) B.G.A., III, 31(15) ; IV, 231 ; Dhahabî, Tabaqât, X, 61.
(5) 37(14).
(6) Ibn Sa'îd, Ed. Tallqvist, 29(22).
(7) 'Arîb, 114(13, 17).
(8) Murûj, VIII, 345.
(9) V, 464(1, 5).
(10) Murûj. VIII, 377(7, 8).
(11) Nishwâr, Margoliouth Edition, I, 16(12), 39(3).

Taghrî Birdî (1) recorded the death of the mother of the Calpih Al-Qâdir who was taken on a **tayyâr** to Al-Rusâfa to be buried.

From the foregoing examples the word seems to mean a comparatively small fast type of ship. According to Mez, (2) the wealthy citizen of Baghdad was obliged to have an ass in his stable and his flier, **tayyâr,** on the river. This vessel was found in the region of Baghdad, Basra and its neighbourhood (3) and was used for war purposes if neccessary.

Walajiyya.

De Goeje (4) thinks the term is perhaps derived from **walaja,** plural **awlâj,** in the sense of **litus** = shore, landing place or bank. In this case it may indicate a coasting vessel.

Wâsitiyya

The word belongs to the category of ship's names indicating places where ships were built. (5) It may have been connected with Wâsit where shipbuilding was highly important on account of the busy river traffic there. (6) **Wâsitiyya.** is still used today. (7)

Zabarbâdhiyya.

According to the manuscript translated by Gildemeister, (8) the ships of Baghdad on which men and animal crossed

---

(1) IV, 221.
(2) 488.
(3) Kindermann, Schiff, 61.
(4) B.G.A., IV, Gloss., 379.
(5) Wüstenfeld, N.G.W. Gött., 1880, 136; Kindermann, Schiff, 107.
(6) Zayyât, Lughat Al-'Arab, V, 463.
(7) For Wâsit v. Streck, E.I., IV, 1128-1132. For description of other articles made in Wâsit v. B.G.A., IV, 375.
(8) N.G.W. Gött., 1882, 439.

from one bank to the other, were called **zabzabiyyât**. Remarking on this he says: «*This would correspond to zabzab as being a large ship; as, however, Jawharî and Qâmûs have* **zanbariyya** *with the meaning of a full-bottomed ship, it may be that it should be so interpreted.*» Kindermann (1) thinks that the **zabarbâdhiyya**, occurring in Muqaddasî's list, looks as if it were a misprint for one of the words already mentioned.

Zabzab.

This name, plural **zabâzib**, is included in the lists of Muqaddasî and Abû'l-Qâsim. (2) The dictionaries (3) define it as a sort of ship. Under the Caliphate of Al-Muttaqî, the Barîdî in Basra had two considerable forces at his disposal, one on land and the other on sea; the latter was composed of **shadhawât, tayyârât, sumayrîyyât** and **zabâzib** — large and small ships on which men could fight. (4)

Zawraq.

The word has two plural forms, **zawâriq** and **zawârîq**. To-day it is still in common use for a small vessel. (5) The dictionaries call it **safîna saghîra** or **qârib saghîr** = a small boat. (6) The **zawraq** could be used for a variety of purposes. According to Sindbad the Sailor, (7) a ship, **markib** had a **zawraq** on board for landing purposes. It was customary for the pilgrims from the north to come by water. In

---

(1) Schiff, 34.
(2) B.G.A., III, 31(15); IV, 231.
(3) Lisân Al-'Arab, I, 429(23); Tâj Al-'rûs, I, 285(38 sq.).
(4) Mas'ûdî, Murûj, VIII, 345. The **sumayriyyât** were also employed in passenger and goods transport. v. Mez, 488; Dozy, Supplément, I, 682(b); Kindermann, Schiff, 42.
(5) v. Schiaparelli, Vocabulista, under **Barca**, 267, and **Navis**, 488-489.
(6) v. Tâj Al'Arûs, VI, 369(15) Lisân Al-'Arab, XII, 5(13); Ibn Sîda Mukhassas, X, 26(7).
(7) Ed. Machuel, 101.

348/959 a thousand of them were drowned while sailing down the Tigris in ten large boats named **zawraq**. (1) They were invaluable for traffic on the Mesopotamian rivers and canals. Istakhrî (2) and Ibn Hawqal (3) both noticed a number of these boats on the many small rivers of Basra. Tabarî (4) often mentions them in connection with this district. The Franks produced a Muslim **zawraq** in A.D. 1190-1 which sailed with troops and money to Acre. (5) In the manuscript translated by Gildemeister, (6) **zawâriq** are mentioned after **qarâqîr** which are referred to as cargo boats in the Mediterranean.

---

(1) Ibn Miskawayh, Ed. Caetani, VI, 234(5), Ed. Amedroz, II, 167-177.
(2) B.G.A., I, 80(9).
(3) B.G.A., II, 159(7).
(4) III, 1168(13), 2074(10.).
(5) Ibn Shaddâd, R.H.C., III, 190(13).
(6) N.G.W. Gött., 1882, 433. v. Nuwayrî, Al-Ilmân, quoted by 'Alî Ibrâhîm, 319-320.

BIBLIOGRAPHY

OF WORKS WHICH HAVE BEEN CONSULTED

D'Abbadie, A.M. — *Lettre à M. Garcin de Tassy, sur les termes de marine en Arabe (Mer Rouge).* J. As., 3e Sér., May 1841, 585-591.

Abbott, N. — *The Kurrah Papyri from Aphrodito in the Oriental Institute.* Chicago, 1938.

'Abd Al-Latîf Al-Baghdâdî. — *Al-Ifâda wa Al-'I'tibâr.* Ed. J. White. Tubingae, 1789.

Abû Dâ'ûd. — *Al-Sunan. A Collection of Traditions.* 2 Vols. in one. Cairo, 1348/1930.

Abû'l-Fidâ. — *Taqwîm Al-Buldân.* Ed. Reinaud and Slane. Paris, 1840.

Abû Sâlih. — *The Churches and Monasteries of Egypt and some neighbouring countries.* Ed. and Tr. B. T. Evetts, with notes by A. Butler. Oxford, 1895.

Abû Ya'lâ Al-Farrâ'. — *Al-Ahkâm Al-Sultâniyya.* Ed. Muhammad Hâmid Al-Fiqî. Cairo, 1938.

Adler, E. N. — *Jewish Travellesrs.* Ed. with an introduction by E.N. Adler. London, 1927.

Agapius of Manbij. — *Kitâb Al-'Unwân.* Ed. and Tr. A. Vasiliev, Pat. Or. V, VII, VIII, XI, 1901—.

'Alî Bey Bahgat. — *Les Forêts de l'Egypte.* B.I.E., Séries IV, No. 1. Cairo, 1900.

'Alî Ibrâhîm Hasan. — *Dirâsât fî Ta'rîkh Al-Mamâlîk Al-Bahariyya wa fî Al-Nâsir Muhammad.* Cairo, 1944.

Alî Mubârak Pâshâ. — *Al-Khitat Al-Tawfîqiyya.* 20 Vols. in 4. Cairo, 1306/1889.

Amari, M. —
  (1) *Storia dei Musulmani di Sicilia.* 1st. Ed. 3 Vols. Firenze, 1854. 2nd Ed., revised by C.A. Nallino. 3 Vols. Catane, 1933.

(2) *Bibliotheca Arabo-Sicula.* Leipzig, 1857.

(3) *I Diplomi Arabi del R. Archivio Fiorentino.* Florence, 1863-7.

Amélineau, E. — *La Géographie de l'Egypte à l'Epoque Copte.* Paris, 1893.

Amîr Abû'l-Hârith — *Hudûd Al-'Alam. The Regions of the World — A Persian Geography* 372/982. Translated and explained by V. Minorsky, with Preface by W. Bartold. Gibb Memorial Series, N.S. XI Oxford, 1937.

Anna Comnena.— *The Alexiad of the Princess Anna Comnena.* Tr. E.A.S. Dawes. London, 1928.

Arculf. — *Narrative about the Holy Places, written by Adamnan.* P.P.T.S., III. London, 1887.

Arîb Ibn Sa'd. — *Silat Ta'rîkh Al-Tabarî or Continuation of Tabarî's Chronicle.* Ed. De Goeje. Leyden, 1887.

Arnold, T.— *Arab Travellers and Merchants,* A.D. 1000-1500. *Travel and Travellers of the Middle Ages.* Ed. A.P. Newton. London, 1926, 88-103.

Badger, G.P. — *An English-Arabic Lexicon.* London, 1881.

Baedeker, C. — *Egypt. Handbook for Travellers.* Leipzig and London, 1895.

Bakrî.— *Al-Mughrib fî Dhikr Bilâd Ifrîqiyya wa Al-Maghrib. Description de l'Afrique Septentrionale.* Ed. De Slane. Paris 1911.

Balâdhurî —

(1) *Futûh Al-Buldân.* Ed. De Goeje. Leyden, 1866.

(2) *Ansâb Al-Ashrâf.* Ed. S.D.F. Goitein. V. Jerusalem, 1936.

Bartold, V.V. —

(1) *Turkestan down to the Mongol Invasion.* Gibb Memorial Series. V. London, 1928.

(2) *Mussulman Culture.* Eng. Tr. S. Suhrawardy. Calcutta, 1934.

(3) *Der Koran und das Meer.* Z.D.M.G., VIII., 1929, 37-43.

Bauer, H. — Fulk. E.I., II, 117.

Baumstark, A. — *Geschichte der Syrischen Literatur.* Munich, 1922.

Baynes, N.H. —
- (1) *The Byzantine Empire.* Home University Library. London. 1935.
- (2) *Some Aspects of Byzantine Civilisation.* Journal of Roman Studies. XX. London, 1930, 1-14.

Beal, S. — *Budhist Records of the Western World.* 2 Vols. London, 1884.

Beazley, C.R. —
- (1) *The Dawn of Modern Geography.* 3 Vols. London, 1897-1906.
- (2) *Sindbad the Sailor.* E.B., XXV, 1911, 143-144.

Becker, C.H. —
- (1) *Beiträge zur Geschichte Aegyptens unter dem Islam.* Strassburg, 1902-3.
- (2) *Papyri Schott-Reinhardt.* I. Heidelberg, 1906.
- (3) *Arabische Papyri des Aphroditofundes.* Z.A. XX. 1907, 68-104.
- (4) *Papyrusstudien.* Z.A., XXII, 1909, 137-154.
- (5) *Neue Arabische Papyri des Aphroditofundes.* Der Islam, II, 1911, 245-268.
- (6) *Historische Studien über das Londoner Aphroditowerk.* Der Islam, II, 1911, 359-271.
- (7) *Joseph von Karabacek.* Der Islam, X, 1920, 233-238.
- (8) *The Expansion of the Saracens.* C.M.H. II. Cambridge, 1936, 329-390.
- (9) *'Abdallah ibn Sa'd.* E.I., I, 30.
- (10) *Ahmed ibn Tûlûn.* E.I., I, 190-191.
- (11) *Babylon.* E.I., I, 550.
- (12) *Bahnasâ.* E.I., I, 578.
- (13) *Balâdhurî.* E.I., I, 611-612.
- (14) *Cairo,* E.I., I, 815-826.
- (15) *Damietta.* E.I., I, 910-911.
- (16) *Dâr Al-Sinâ'a.* E.I., I, 918.
- (17) *Egypt.* E.I., II, 4-23.

Bell, I.H. —
- (1) *Greek Papyri in the British Museum. The Aphrodito Papyri.* IV. Ed. I.H. Bell., with an Appendix of Coptic Papyri, Ed. W.E. Crum. London, 1910.
- (2) *Greek Papyri in the British Museum. Catalogue with Texts.* V. London, 1917.

(3) *Translations of the Greek Aphrodito Papyri in the British Museum.* Der Islam :
II, 1911, 269-283 and 372-384.
III, 1912, 132-140 and 369-373.
IV, 1913, 87-96.
XVII, 1928, 4-8.

(4) *The Aphrodito Papyri.* J.H.S., XXVIII. London, 1908, 97-120.

(5) *The Byzantine Servile State in Egypt.* J.E.A., IV. London, 1917.

(6) *Two Official Letters of the Arab Period.* J.E.A., XII. London, 1926, 265-281.

(7) *The Administration of Egypt under the Umayyad Khalifs.* Byz. Zeit., XXVIII, 1928, 278-286.

Belloc, H. — *Stories, Essays and Poems,* with an Introduction by A.G. Macdonell. Everyman's Library. London, 1938.

Benjamin of Tudela. — *Itinerary.* Ed. and Tr. M.N. Adler. London, 1907.

Bernard the Wise. — *Itinerary.* Tr. J.H. Bernard. P.P.T.S., III. London, 1893.

Berthelot, M. —
(1) *Histoire des Sciences. La Chimie du Moyen Age.* 3 Vols. Paris, 1893.

(2) *Feu Grégeois.* Grande Encyclopédie, 1893, 367-368.

Blachère, R. — *Extraits des Principaux Géographies Arabes du Moyen Age.* Paris, 1932.

Bouchier, E.S. — *Syria as a Roman Province.* Oxford, 1916.

Brindley, H.H. — *Primitive Craft. Evolution or Diffusion. Report of Meeting.* Mariner's Mirror, XVIII, No. 3, July 1932, 303-317.

Brockelmann, C. —
(1) *Geschichte der Arabischen Litteratur.* 2 Vols. Weimar, 1898-1902.

(2) *Supplemantband.* 3 Vols. Leyden, 1937-42.

Brooks, E.W. —
(1) *A Syriac Chronicle of the year 846.* Z.D.M.G., LI, 1897, 569-588.

(2) *The Arabs in Asia Minor (641-750), from Arabic Sources.* J.H.S., XVIII, 1898, 182 sq.

(3) *The Campaign of 716-718, from Arabic Sources.* J.H.S., XIX, 1899, 20-33.

(4) *Byzantines and Arabs in the time of the early Abbasids.* E.H.R., XV, October 1900, 728-747.

(5) *The Arab Occupation of Crete.* E.H.R., XXVIII, 1913, 431-443.

(6) *The Relations between the Empire and Egypt from a new Arabic source.* Byz. Zeit., 1913.

(7) *The Successors of Heraclius to 717.* C.M.H., II. Cambridge, 1936, 391-417.

Browne, E.G. —

(1) *A Literary History of Persia.* 4 Vols. London, 1902-24.

(2) *Some Account of the Arabic Work entitled «Niháyatu'l-irab fi Akhbár'l-Furs wa'l-ʿArab ».* J.R.A.S., 1900, 195-259.

Brunot, L. —

(1) *La Mer dans les Traditions et les Industries Indigènes à Rabat et Salé.* Paris, 1920.

(2) *Notes Lexicologiques sur le Vocabulaire maritime de Rabat et Salé.* Paris, 1920.

Brutzkus, J. — *Trade with Eastern Europe.* Economic History Review, XIII, Nos. 1, 2. London, 1943, 31-42.

Buhl, F. —

(1) *ʿAkkâ.* E.I., I, 241.

(2) *Tarabulus.* E.I., IV, 660.

(3) *Tarsûs.* E.I., IV, 679.

Buhturî. — *Dîwân.* 2 Vols. in one. Constantinople, 1300/1882.

Bukhârî. — *Al-Jâmiʿ Al-Sahîh.* Ed. Muhammad Munîr Al-Dimashqî. 9 Vols. in 3. Cairo, 1348/1930.

Burchardt, J.L. — *Travels in Arabia, comprehending an account of those territories in Hedjaz which the Mohammedans regard as sacred.* Ed. with a Preface by W. Ouseley. London, 1829.

Burton, R.F. — *Personal Narrative of a Pilgrimage to El-Medinah and Mecceh.* Ed. with a Preface by T. Wolley. 3 Vols. London, 1855-6.

Bury, J.B. —

(1) *A History of the Later Roman Empire.* 2 Vols. London, 1889.

(2) *The Imperial Administrative System in the 9th Century.* London, 1911.

(3) *The Ceremonial Book of Constantine Porphyrogenitos.* E.H.R., XXII, No. LXXXVI, April 1907, 209-227 ; No. LXXXVII, July 1907, 417-439.

(4) *The Naval Policy of the Roman Empire in relation to the Western Provinces from the 7th to the 9th Century.* Centinario della Nascita di Michele Amari. II. Palermo, 1910, 21 sq.

(5) *A History of the Eastern Roman Empire from the fall of Irene to the accession of Basil I, 802-67.* London, 1912.

(6) *The Treatise De Administrando Imperio.* Byz. Zeit., XV, 517-577.

Bustânî.— *Muhît Al-Muhît.* 2 Vols. Beirut, 1870.

Butcher, E.L. — *The Story of the Church of Egypt.* 2 Vols. London, 1897.

Butler, A. — *The Arab Conquest of Egypt and the last thirty years of the Roman Dominion.* Oxford, 1902.

Caetani, L. —
(1) *Chronographia Islamica.* 5 Vols. Paris, 1912.
(2) *Annali dell'Islam.* 10 Vols. Milan, 1905-26.

Cahen, C. —
(1) *La Syrie du Nord.* Paris, 1940.
(2) *Les Chroniques Arabes concernant la Syrie, l'Egypte et la Mésopotamie.* Revue des Etudes Islamiques, V, 1936, 333-362.

Canard, M. — *Les Expéditions des Arabes contre Constantinople dans l'Histoire et dans la Légende.* J.As., 1926, 61-62.

Carra, Vaux De — *Les Penseurs de l'Islam.* 5 Vols. Paris 1921-6.

Carter, T. — *The Invention of Printing in China and its Spread Westward.* New York, 1925.

Casanova, P. —
(1) *Description Historique et Topographique de l'Egypte* M.I.F.A.O., III, IV. Cairo, 1906, 1920.

(2) *Essai de Reconstitution Topographique de la ville d'Al-Foustât ou Misr.* M.I.F.A.O., XXXV. Cairo, 1919 [1913].

(3) *Les Noms Coptes du Caire et Localités Voisines.* B.I.F.A.O., I. Cairo, 1901.

(4) *De Quelques Légendes Astronomiques Arabes. Considérées dans leurs rapports avec la Mythologie Egyptienne.* B.I.F.A.O., II, 1902.

Champollion, J.F.— *L'Egypte sous les Pharaons.* 2 Vols. Paris, 1814.

Charlesworth, M.P. — *Trade-Routes and Commerce of the Roman Empire.* Cambridge, 1924.

Clowes, L. —
(1) *The Story of Sail.* Illustrated by C.G. Trew. London, 1926.
(2) *Sailing Ships. Their History and Development as illustrated by the Collection of Ship Models in the Science Museum.* London, 1932.

Colin, G.S. — *Technologie de la Batellerie du Nil.* B.I.F.A.O., XX, 45-87. Cairo, 1921.

Comparetti, D. and Vitelli., G. — *Papiri Greco-Egizii,* publ. dalla R. Accademia dei Lincei sotto la direz. di D. Comparetti e G. Vitelli, Milano, Ulbrico Hoepli. 3 Vols. 1905-15.

Conder, C.R. and Kitchener, R.E. — *The Survey of Western Palestine. Memoirs of the Topography, Orography, Hydrography and Archaeology.* 3 Vols. London, 1881-3.

Constantine Porphyrogenitos. — *De Administrando Imperio.* Ed. I. Bekker. Corpus Script. Hist. Byz., X. Bonn, 1840. Eng. Tr. by R.J.H. Jenkins.

Crum, W.E. — *Coptic Ostraca.* London, 1902.

Crum, W.E. and Bell, I.H. — *Wadi Sarga. Coptic and Greek Texts from the excavations undertaken by Byzantine Research Account.* Copenhagen, 1922.

Defrémery, C. —
(1) *Remarques sur l'Ouvrage Géographique d'Ibn Khordadhbeh et principalement sur le chapitre qui concerne l'Empire Byzantin.* J. As., VII, 1866, 239-277.

- (2) *Dictionnaire Etymologique des Mots de la Langue Française derivés de l'Arabe, du Persan ou du Turc, avec leurs Analogues Grecs, Latins, Espagnols, Portugaise et Italiens. Nouvelles et Mélanges.* August, 1867, 179-188.
- (3) *Nouvelles et Mélanges.* J. As., IX, April 1867, 6e Sér., 409-419.
- (4) *Glossaire des Mots Espagnols et Portugais par R. Dozy et Engelmann.* J. As., XIII, June 1869, 518-538.

Delaval, C. — *The Story of Umm Harám.* Ed. in the original Turkish and Tr. C. Delaval, J.R.A.S., 1897, 81-101.

Demombynes, G. — *Les Institutions Musulmanes.* Paris, 1913.

Denis, St. — *La Vitesse des Navires Anciens.* Revue Archéologique., 6e Sér., XVIII, 1941.

Devic, L.M. — *Dictionnaire Etymologique des Mots Français d'Origine Orientale.* Paris, 1876.

Dhahabî — *Tabaqât Al-Huffâz.* Ed. F. Wüstenfeld. Göttingen, 1833.

Diehl, C. —
- (1) *Histoire de la Domination Byzantine en Afrique.* Paris, 1896.
- (2) *Etudes Byzantines.* Paris, 1905.
- (3) *Byzance. Grandeur et Décadence.* Paris, 1919.

Dionysius I, Telmaharensis. — *Chronique de Denys de Tell Mahré.* Ed. and Tr. J.B. Chabot. Paris, 1895.

Dozy, R. —
- (1) *Supplément aux Dictionnaires Arabes.* 2 Vols. Leyden, 1881.
- (2) *Histoire des Musulmans d'Espagne.* 3 Vols. Leyden, 1932.

Dozy, R. et Engelmann. — *Glossaire des Mots Espagnols et Portugais derivés de l'Arabe.* Leyden, 1869.

Dussaud, R. — *Topographie Historique de la Syrie Antique et Médiévale.* Paris, 1927.

East, G.W. —
- (1) *An Historical Geography of Europe.* London, 1935.
- (2) *Mediterranean Problems.* London, 1940.

Ebersolt, J. — *Constantinople Byzantine et les Voyageurs du Levant.* Paris, 1918.

Edye, J. — *Description of the Various Classes of Vessels.* J.R.A.S., 1834, 1-14.

Elderidge, F.B. — *The Background of Eastern Sea Power.* Melbourne, 1944.

Elliot, H.M. — *The History of India as told by its own Historians. The Mohammadan Period.* Ed. from the posthumous papers of Sir H.M. Elliot by John Dowson. 8 Vols. London, 1867-77.

Eutychius, Saʻîd Ibn Al-Batrîq — *Al-Taʾrîkh Al-Majmûʻ ʻalâ Al-Tahqîq wa Al-Tasdîq.* Ed. Pococke. 2 Vols. in one. 1685. Ed. Cheikho. Corpus Script. Christ., VI, 1905, VII, 1909.

Fahmy, A.M. —
(1) *Muslim Sea-Power in the Eastern Mediterranean from the 7th. to the 10th. Century A.D. 1st Edition.* Cairo, 1966.
(2) *Muslim Naval Organisation from the 7th. to the 10th. Century A.D., 2nd. Edition.* Cairo, 1966.

Faulkner, R.D. — *Egyptian Sea-going Ships.* J.E.A., XXVI, 1940. 3-9.

Ferrand, C. —
(1) *Relations de Voyages et Textes Géographiques Arabes, Persans et Turks relatifs à l'Extrême-Orient du VIIIe au XVIIIe siècles.* 2 Vols. Paris, 1913-14.
(2) *Instruction nautiques et Routiers Arabes et Portugais des XVe et XVIe siècles.* 3 Vols. Paris, 1921-28.
(3) *Voyage du Marchand Arabe Sulaymân en l'Inde et en Chine. Silsilat Al-Tawârîkh.* Paris, 1922.
(4) *Introductions à l'Astronomie Nautique Arabe.* III. Paris, 1928.
(5) *L'Element Persan dans les Textes Nautiques Arabes des XVe et XVIe siècles.* J. As., April-June, 1924, 193-257.

Finlay, G. — *A History of Greece from the Conquest by the Romans to the Present Time. (146 B.C. — A.D. 1864).* 7 Vols. Oxford 1877.

Fîrûzâbâdî — *Al-Qâmûs Al-Muhît.* Ed. Nasr Al-Hurînî. 4 Vols. Bûlâq, 1301-3/1883-5.

Fleischer, H.L. — *Kleinere Schriften Studien über Dozy's Supplement aux Dictionnaires Arabes.* Leipzig, 1885.

Fleming, W.B. — *The History of Tyre.* Columbia University Press. 1915.

Foord, E. — *The Byzantine Empire.* London, 1911.

Fraenkel, S. — *Die Aramäischen Fredwörter im Arabischen.* Leyden, 1886.

Frisk, I.H. — *Bankakten aus dem Faijûm, nebst anderen Berliner Papyri.* Göteborgs K. Vetenskapsoch Vittershets Samhälles Handlunger. Ser. A, II, No. 2. Göteborg, 1931.

Gateau, A. — *Introduction à l'Etude du Vocabulaire Maritime en Tunisie. Technologie du Lûd.* Rev. Afr., Nos. 406-409, 1946, 140-183.

Gay, J. — *L'Italie Méridionale et l'Empire Byzantin depuis l'avènement de Basile I jusqu'à la prise de Bari par les Normands 867-1071.* Paris, 1904.

Gelzer, M. —
  (1) *Studien zur Byzantinischen Verwaltung Aegyptens.* Leipziger Historische Abhandlungen, XIII. Leipzig, 1909.
  (2) *Altes und Neues aus der Byzantinisch-Aegyptischen Verwaltungsmisere.* Archiv für Papyrusforschung, V. 1913.

Gfrörer, A.F. — *Byzantinische Geschichten.* Bd. II. Graz, 1874.

Gibb, H.A.R. —
  (1) *Ta'rîkh.* E.I., Supplement, 233 sq.
  (2) *Tûlûnids,* E.I., IV, 834-836.

Gibbon, E. — *The History of the Decline and Fall of the Roman Empire.* Ed. J.B. Bury. 7 Vols. London, 1911.

Giese, F. — *Crete.* E.I., I, 878-880.

Gildemeister, J. — *Ueber Arabisches Schiffswesen.* N.G.W. Gött., June 1882, 431-449.

Goeje, M.J. De —
  (1) *Mémoire sur la Conquête de la Syrie.* Leyden, 1900.
  (2) *Verslagen en Mededulingen.* Amsterdam, 1909.
  (3) *Die Istakhrî Balkhî Frage.* ZD.M.G., XXV, 1871, 42-58.
  (4) *Quelques Observations sur le Feu Grégeois.* Estudios de Erudicion Oriental. Saragossa, 1904.

Goldziher, I. —
  (1) *Muhammedanische Studien.* 2 Vols. Halle, 1888-90.
  (2) *Grammatik des Arabischen Vulgärdialectes von Aegypten.* Z.D.M.G., XXXV, 1881, 514-529.

(3) *Das Schiff des Wüste.* Z.D.M.G., XLIV, 1890, 165-167.

Gomme, A.W. — *Essays in Greek History and Literature.* Oxford, 1937.

Goodspeed, E.J. — *Greek Papyri from Cairo Museum, together with Papyri of Roman Egypt from American Collections.* Chicago, 1902.

Gordon, East. W. —
(1) *An Historical Geography of Europe.* London, 1935.
(2) *Mediterranean Problems.* London, 1940.

Gordon, T.C. — *Sicily. E.I., IV, 398-400.*

Grégoire, H. — *Etudes sur le Neuvième Siècle.* Byzantion, VIII, 1933, 515-550.

Grenfell, B.P. —
(1) *An Alexandrian Erotic Fragment and other Greek Papyri chiefly Ptolemaic.* Ed. B.P. Grenfell. I. Oxford, 1896.
(2) *New Classical Fragments and other Greek and Latin Papyri.* Ed. B.P. Grenfell and A.S. Hunt. II. Oxford, 1897.
(3) *The Oxyrhynchus Papyri.* Ed. with translations and notes by B.P. Grenfell, A.S. Hunt and I.H. Bell. London, 1898—.
(4) *The Amherst Papyri.* 2 Vols. Oxford University Press. London, 1900-1.

Grohmann, A. —
(1) *Arabic Papyri in the Egyptian Library.* The Egyptian Library Press. I, 1934 ; II, 1936 ; III, 1938.
(2) *Corpus Papyrorum Raineri Archiducis Austriae. III, Series Arabica.* Ed. A. Grohmann. Bd. I, Teil I. *Allgemeine Einführung in die arabischen Papyri, von Dr. Adolf Grohmann* (Wien, 1924). Bd. I, Teil 2-3. *Protokolle, bearb. und hrsg. von Dr. Adolf Grohmann* (Text und Tafeln ; Wien, 1924, 23).
(3) *Aperçu de Papyrologie Arabe.* Société Royale Egyptienne de Papyrologie. Etudes de Papyrologie, I, 1932.
(4) *Probleme der Arabischen Papyrusforschung.* Archiv Orientalni. V, 1933, 273 ; VI, 1933, 125 ; VI, 1934, 377.
(5) *Arabische Papyri.. im Oriental Institute zu Prag.* Archiv Orientalni. X, 1938, 149-162.

(6) *Stand und Aufgaben der Arabischen Papyruskunde im Rahmen der Arabistik.* Museon, LII, 325-336.

(7) *Arabische Papyri aus den Staatlichen Museen zu Berlin.* Der Islam, XXII, 1 sq.

Guest, R. —

(1) *A list of Writers, Books and other Authorities mentioned by El Maqrîzî in his Khitat.* J.R.A.S., 1902, 103-125.

(2) *The Foundations of Fustât and the Khittahs of that Town.* J.R.A.S., 1907, 49-85.

(3) *Al-Iskandarîya.* E.I. II, 535-539.

Guest, R. and Richmond, E.T. — *Misr in the Fifteenth Century.* J.R.A.S., 1903, 785-791.

Habîballah Bahâ'.— *Ikhtirâʿ Al-Bârûd.* Hilâl, XXI, 1912, 56-58.

Hâdî Hasan.— *A History of Persian Navigation.* London, 1928.

Haig, W. — *Comparative Tables of Muhammadan and Christian Dates.* London, 1932.

Hajjî Khalîfa. — *Kashf Al-Zunûn.* Arabic text with translation by G. Flügel. 7 Vols. Leipzig and London, 1835-58.

Hamdânî. — *Sifat Jazîrat Al-ʿArab. 2 Vols.* Ed. D.H. Müller. Leyden, 1884-91.

Hamîdullâh, M. — *Muslim Conduct of State.* Lahore, 1945.

Hamza of Isfahân — *Taʾrîkh Sinî Mulûk Al-Ard wa Al-Anbiyâ.* Ed. I.M. Gottwaldt. 2 Vols. in one. St. Petersburg, 1844-8.

Hartmann, M. —

(1) *Der Islamische Orient Berichte und Forschungen.* Bd. II. Leipzig, 1909.

(2) *China,* E.I., I, 839-854.

Hartmann, R. —

(1) *Cyprus.* E.I., I. 882-884.

(2) *Al-Djâr.* E.I., I, 1016.

Hautecœur, L. et Wiet, G. — *Les Mosquées du Caire.* 2 Vols. Paris, 1932.

Hell, J. — *The Arab Civilisation.* Eng. Tr. S. Khuda Bukhsh. Cambridge, 1926.

Herodotus — Literally translated from the Text of Baehr with a Geographical and General Index by H. Cary. London, 1847.

Heyd, W. — *Histoire du Commerce du Levant au Moyen Age.* Tr. F. Raynaud. 2 Vols. Leipzig, 1923.

Hill, G. — *A History of Cyprus to the Conquest by Richard Lion Heart.* I. Cambridge, 1940.

Hime, H.W.L. — *Cunpowder and Ammunition. Their Origin and Progress.* London, 1904.

Höfer, F. — *Histoire de la Chimie depuis les temps les plus reculés jusqu'à notre époque.* 2 Vols. Paris, 1842-3.

Hofmeir, K.W. — *Beiträge zur Arabischen Papyrforschung.* Der Islam, IV, 97-120.

Honigmann, E. —
  (1) *Al-Kulzum.* E.I., II, 1114-1115.
  (2) *Sûr.* E.I., IV, 557-559.
  (3) *Al-Thughûr.* E.I., IV, 738-739.

Hornell, J. —
  (1) *Water Transport. Origins and Early Evolution.* Cambridge, 1946.
  (2) *Origins of Plank-built Boats.* Antiquity, XIII, 1939, 35-44.
  (3) *A Tentative Classification of Arab Sea Craft.* Mariner's Mirror, XXVIII, No. 1, 1942.

Hournani, G.F. — *Direct Sailing between the Persian Gulf and China in Pre-Islamic Times.* J.R.A.S., 1947, 157-160.

Huart, Cl. — *A History of Arabic Literature.* London, 1903.

Husayn Fawzî — *Hadith Al-Sindbâd Al-Qadîm.* Cairo, 1943.

Hunt, A.S. —
  (1) *Catalogue of Greek Papyri in John Rylands Library.* Ed. A.S. Hunt, I, 1911. Ed. J. de M. Johnson, V. Martin and A.S. Hunt, 11. 1915 .
  (2) *Papyrology.* E.B., XVII, 1945, 243-246.

'Ibâda, 'Abd Al-Fattâh — *Sufun Al-Ustûl Al-Islâmî.* Hilâl, XXI, 1912, 360-366, 485-492; XXII, 1913, 34-42.

Ibn 'Abd Al-Hakam. — *Kitâb Futûh Misr wa Akhbâruhâ. The History of the Conquest of Egypt, North Africa and Spain.* Ed. C. Torrey. New Haven, 1922.

Ibn Abî Dînâr — *Kitâb Al-Mu'nis fî Akhbâr Ifrîqiyya wa Tûnis.* Tunis, 1286/1869.

Ibn Abî Zarʿ. —
- (1) *Rawd Al-Qirtâs.* Ed. C.J. Tornberg. Upsala, 1843-6.
- (2) *Roudh El-Kartas.* Histoire des Souverains du Maghreb. Fr. Tr. A. Beaumier. Paris, 1860.

Ibn Al-Athîr. —
- (1) *Kitâb Al-Kâmil fî Al-Ta'rîkh.* Ed. C.J. Tornberg. 14 Vols. Leyden, 1851-76.
- (3) *Usd Al-Ghâba fî Maʿrifat Akhbâr Al-Sahâba.* 5 Vols. Cairo, 1280/1863.

Ibn Al-Dâya.— *Al-Mukâfa'a.* Ed. Amîn 'Abd Al--'Azîz. Cairo, 1332/1914.

Ibn Al-Faqîh. — *Kitâb Al-Buldân.* Ed. De Goeje. B.G.A., V, 1885.

Ibn Al-Nadîm.— *Kitâb Al-Fihrist.* Ed. G. Flügel. 2 Vols. Leipzig, 1871-2.

Ibn Al-Tiqtaqâ. — *Kitâb Al-Fakhrî fî Al-'âdab Al-Sultâniyya wa Al-Duwal Al-Islâmiyya.* Cairo. 1317/1899.

Ibn Bassâm, Al-Tinnîsî.— *Al-Anîs Al-Jalîs fî Akhbâr Tinnîs.* MS. Egyptian Library, Adab No. 1852.

Ibn Battûta. —
- (1) *Voyages d'Ibn Batoutah.* Ed. and Tr. C. Defrémery and B.R. Sanguinetti. 5 Vols. Paris, 1893-1914.
- (2) *Travels in Asia and Africa,* 1325-54. Tr. and selected by H.A.S. Gibb. The Broadway Travellers. Ed. E. Denison Ross and E. Power. London, 1929.

Ibn Duqmâq. — *Al-Intisâr li-Wâsitat 'Iqd Al-Amsâr.* IV and V combined. Cairo, 1309-1891.

Ibn Hawqal. —
- (1) *Kitâb Al-Masâlik wa Al-Mamâlik.* Ed. De Goeje, B.G.A., II. Leyden, 1873.
- (2) *Kitâb Sûrat Al-Ard. Opus Geographicum.* Ed. J.H. Kramers. Lugundi Betavorum. Brill, 1938-39.

Ibn Hishâm.— *Kitâb Sîrat Rasûl Allâh.* Ed. F. Wüstenfeld, 2 Vols. Göttingen, 1858-60.

Ibn 'Idhârî. —
- (1) *Al-Bayân Al-Mughrib fî Akhbâr Al-Maghrib.* Ed. R. Dozy. 2 Vols. in one, Leyden, 1849.
- (2) *Histoire de l'Afrique et de l'Espagne.* Fr. Tr. E. Fagnan. 2 Vols. in one. Algiers, 1901.

Ibn Iyâs. — *Kitâb Ta'rîkh Misr. Badâ'i' Al-Zuhûr fî Waqâ'i' Al-Duhûr.* 2 Vols. in one. Bûlâq, 1311/1894.

Ibn Jubayr. — *The Travels of Ibn Jubayr,* Ed. W. Wright. Revised De Goeje. Gibb Memorial Series, V. Leyden, 1907.

Ibn Khaldûn. —
- (1) *Al-'Ibar wa Dîwân Al-Mubtadâ wa Al-Khabar.* 7 Vols. Cairo, 1284/1867.
- (2) *Muqaddima.* Ed. M. Quatremère. 3 Vols. Paris, 1858. Fr. Tr. M. De Slane. 4 Vols. Paris, 1843-71.
- (3) *L'Histoire de Berbères et des Dynasties Musulmanes de l'Afrique Septentrionale.* Ed. M. De Slane. 2 Vols. Algiers, 1847-51. Fr. Tr. 4 Vols. Algiers, 1852.

Ibn Khallikân. — *Wafayât Al-A'yân.* 2 Vols. Bûlâq, 1299/1882. Tr. De Slane. 4 Vols. Paris, 1842-71.

Ibn Khurdâdhbih — *Al-Masâlik wa Al-Mamâlik.* Ed. De Goeje. B.G.A., VI, Leyden, 1889.

Ibn Mamârî. — *Kitâb Qawânîn Al-Dawâwîn.* Ed. 'Azîz Suryâl 'Atiyya. Cairo, 1934.

Ibn Manzûr — *Lisân Al-'Arab.* 20 Vols. Bûlâq, 1300-7/1882-9.

Ibn Miskawayh. —
- (1) *Tajârib Al-Umam.* Ed. with Preface and Summary by L. Caetani. Gibb. Memorial Series, VII, VIII, IX. 3 Vols. Leyden, 1909-17.
- (2) *The Eclipse of the 'Abbâsid Caliphate.* Ed. H. F. Amedroz and D.S. Margoliouth. 7 Vols. Oxford, 1920,
- (3) Part VI. Ed. M.J. De Goeje. *Fragmenta Historicum Arabicorum.* II. Leyden, 1871.

Ibn Qutayba. — *Kitâb Al-Imâma wa Al-Siyâsa.* 2 Parts in one. Cairo, 1322/1904.

Ibn Rusta. — *Kitâb Al-A'lâq Al-Nafîsa.* Ed. De Coeje. B.G.A.. VII, 1891.

Ibn Sa'd. — *Tabaqât.* Ed. Sachau. 15 Vols. Leyden, 1905-28.

Ibn Sa'îd. —
- (1) *Al-Mughrib fî Hulâ Al-Maghrib.* Ed. K.L. Tallqvist. IV. Leyden 1899.

(2) *The Biography of Ibn Tûlûn after Ibn Al-Dâya. Fragmenta aus dem Mughrib.* Ed. K. Vollers. Weimar, 1895.

Ibn Shahriyâr Buzurg. — *'Ajâ'ib Al-Hind.* Ed. Van der lith with Fr. Tr. M. Devic. Leyden, 1883-86.

Ibn Sîda. — *Al-Mukhassas.* 17 Vols. Bûlâq, 1316-21/1898-1903.

Ibn Taghrî Birdî. — *Al-Nujûm Al-Zâhira fî Mulûk Misr wa Al-Qâhira.* Ed. Egyptian Library. Cairo, 1348/1929—.

Ibshîhî. — *Al-Mustatraf fî Kul Fan Mustazraf.* 2 Vols. Bûlâq, 1292/1875.

Idrîsî. —

(1) *Kitâb Nuzhat Al-Mushtâq.* Rome, 1952. Tr. Jaubert. Paris, 1836.

(2) *Description de l'Afrique et de l'Espagne.* Ed. Dozy-De Goeje. Leyden, 1866.

Isfahânî, Abû'l-Faraj.— *Kitâb Al-Aghânî.* 20 Vols. in 4. Cairo, 1285/1862.

Istakhrî. — *Kitâb Masâlik Al-Mamâlik.* Ed. De Goeje. B.G.A., I. Leyden, 1927.

Izeddin, M. — *Un Prisonier Arabe à Byzance au IXe Siècle. Hâroûn-ibn-Yahya.* Revue des Etudes Islamiques, 1947, 41-62.

Jâhiz. —

(1) *Kitâb Al-Hayawân.* 7 Parts in 2. Cairo, 1323-5/1905-7.

(2) *Al-Bayân wa Al-Tabyîn.* Ed. Muhibb Al-Dîn Al-Khatîb. 3 Parts in one. Cairo, 1332/1914.

Jal, A. -- *Glossaire Nautique.* Paris, 1948.

Jawâlîkî. — *Al-Mu'arrab min Al-Kalâm Al-A'jamî.* Ed. Sachau. Leipzig, 1867.

Jawharî. — *Al-Sihâh fî Al-Lugha.* A Lexicon of the Arabic language. Ed. with an Introduction by Nâsir Al-Hurînî. Bûlâq, 1282/1865.

Jenkins, C. — *Christian Pilgrimages. A.D. 500-800. Travel and Travellers of the Middle Ages.* Ed. A.P. Newton. London, 1926.

Jenkins, R.J.H. — *The «Flight» of Samonas.* Speculum, April 1948, 217-235.

Jernstedt, P. — *Die Kome-Aphrodito Papyri der Sammlung Lichaçov. Papyri Rossischer und Georgischer Sammlungen* (P. Ross.-Georg.) hrsg. von Gregor Zeretelli. IV. Tiflis, 1927.

Jones, W. — *The Moallakât or Seven Arabian Poems* — with a Translation and Arguments. London, 1783.

Kahle, P. — *Der Leuchtturm von Alexandria.* Stuttgart, 1930.

Kamal, Youssouf. — *Monumenta Geographica Africae et Aegypti.* III. *Epoque Arabe,* Fasc. I, 1930.

Kammerer, A. — *La Mer Rouge, l'Abyssinie et l'Arabie depuis l'Antiquité.* 2 Vols. Cairo, 1935.

Karabacek, J. Von — *Das Arabische Papier* [reprint, separately paged, from Vienna. Nationalbibliothek, Mittheilungen aus der Sammlung der Papyrus Erzherzog Rainer, II-III [(paged continuously) 87-178 (Wien, 1887)].

Kâzim Al-Dujaylî. —
(1) *Al-Sufun fî Al-'Irâq, Ashbâh Al-Sufun, Asmâ' Mâ fî Al-Safîna.* Lughat Al-'Arab, I-III. Baghdad, 1912.
(2) *Al-Dûr.* Lughat Al-'Arab, I, 1912, 470-479.

Kenyon, F.G. and Bell, I.H. — *Greek Papyri in the British Museum. Catalogue with Texts.* Ed. F.G. Kenyon and I.H. Bell, I, London, 1893 ; II, London, 1898; III, London, 1907.

Khafâjî, Shihâb Al-Dîn. — *Shifâ' Al-Ghalîl fîmâ fî Kalâm Al-'Arab min Al-Dakhîl.* Cairo, 1282/1865.

Kindermann, H. —
(1) *Schiff im Arabischen, Untersuchung über Vorkommen und Bedeutung der Termini.* Bonn, 1934.
(2) *Al-Safîna.* E.I., Supplement, 192-195.

Kindî. —
(1) *Kitâb Al-Wulâh wa Kitâb Al-Qudâh. The Governors and Judges of Egypt.* Ed. R. Guest, Gibb Memorial Series, XIX. London, 1912.
(2) *Fadâ'il Misr. Beskivelse Af Aegypten.* Ed. J. Ostrup. Copenhagen, 1896.

Kitâb Al-'Uyûn — *Fragmenta Historicum Arabicorum.* Ed. De Goeje. Leyden, 1871.

Kramers, J.H. —
- (1) *Geography and Commerce. Legacy of Islam.* Ed. T. Arnold and A. Guillaume. Oxford, 1931, 79-108.
- (2) *Djughrâfiyâ.* E.I., Supplement, 61-73.
- (3) *Kawsara.* E.I., II.

Kremer, A. Von. — *Culturgeschichte des Orients unter den Chalifen.* 2 Vols. Wien, 1875-7. Eng. Tr. S. Khuda Bukhsh. I, Calcutta, 1927; II, chs, II, IV, IX, X, *Studies : Indian and Islamic.* London, 1912.

Lalanne, M.L. — *Essai sur le Feu Grégeois.* Académie des Inscriptions et Belles-Lettres. Paris, 1843.

Lammens, H. —
- (1) *Remarques sur les Mots Français derivés de l'Arabe.* Beirut, 1890.
- (2) *Etudes sur le Régne du Calife Omaiyade Mo'âwiya 1er.* Beirut, 1908.
- (3) *La Mecque à la Veille de l'Hégire.* Mélanges de l'Université Saint-Joseph. IX, fase. IIII. Beirut, 1924.
- (4) *L'Arabie Occidentale avant l'Hégire.* Beirut, 1928.
- (5) *Un Gouverneur Omaiyade d'Egypte d'après les Papyrus Arabes.* Extrait du B.I. E., 5e Sér., II, 99-115. Alexandria, 1908.
- (6) *Abû'l-A'war.* E.I., I, 79.
- (7) *Busr ibn Abî Artât.* E.I., I, 804-805.

Lane, E.W. — *An Arabic-English Lexicon.* 8 Vols. London, 1863-93.

Lane-Poole, S. —
- (1) *The Barbary Corsairs.* London, 1890.
- (2) *Coins and Medals.* London, 1892.
- (3) *The Mohammadan Dynasties.* London, 1894.
- (4) *The Story of Cairo.* London, 1902.
- (5) *A History of Egypt in the Middle Ages.* London, 1925.

Leo VI. — *De Navali Praelio in Noumachika.* Ed. A.M. Dain Paris, 1943. Unpublished Eng. Tr. by R.H. Dolley.

Levi della Vida, G. — *Pre-Islamic Arabia. Arab Heritage.* Ed. Nabih Amin Faris, New Jersey, 1944.

Levi-Provençal, E. — *Histoire de l'Espagne Musulmane, de la Conquête à la Chute du Califat de Cordoue.* A.D. 710-1031. I. Cairo, 1944.

Levy, R. — *An Introduction to the Sociology of Islam.* 2 Vols. London, 1933.

Liudprand of Cremona. —
- (1) *Relatio de Legatione Constantinopolitana.* Eng. Tr. E. Henderson, in *Select Documents of the Middle Ages.* Bohn Library, 1896.
- (2) *Antopodosis.* Eng. Tr. F. Wright. London, 1930.

Lokotsch, K. — *Etymologisches Wörterbuch des Europäischen... Wörter Orientalischen Ursprungs.* Heidelberg, 1927.

Lopez, R.S. — *Mohammed and Charlemagne: A Revision.* Speculum, XVIII, No. I, January 1943, 14-38.

Lyall, C.J. — *The Pictorial Aspects of Ancient Arabian Poetry.* J.R.A.S., 1912, 131-152.

Maqrizî. —
- (1) *Kitâb Al-Mawâ'iz wa Al-I'tibâr fî Dhikr Al-Khitat wa Al-Athâr.* Ed. Muhammad Quttah Al-'Adawî. 2 Vols. Bûlâq, 1270/1853.
  Same, ed. G. Wiet. 5 *Vols.* in *M.I.F.A.O.*, XXX, XXXIII, XLVI, XLIX, LIII, Cairo, 1911-1927. Fr. Tr. U. Bouriant. I-II in Mémoires publiés par les membres de la Mission Archéologique Française au Caire, Paris. Tr. P. Casanova, III-IV in M.I.F.A.O., Cairo, 1906, 1920.
- (2) *Itti'âz Al-Hunafâ bi-Akhbâr Al-Khulafâ.* Jerusalem, 1908.
- (3) *Shudhûr Al-'Uqûd,* Ed. and Tr. L.A. Mayer. Alexandria, 1933.

Marcel, J.J. — *Dictionnaire Français-Arabe.* 2 Vols. Paris, 1869.

Marco Polo. — *The Book of Ser Marco Polo.* Ed. and Tr. with notes by H. Yule. 2 Vols. London, 1903.

Margoliouth, D.S. —
- (1) *Lectures on Arabic Historians.* Calcutta, 1930.
- (2) *Catalogue of Arabic Papyri in John Rylands Library.* Manchester, 1933.

Marzûqî, Al-Asfahânî — *Kitâb Al-Azmina wa Al-Amkina.* 2 Parts in one. Heyderabad, 1332/1914.

Maspero, J. —
  (1) *Histoire Ancienne des Peuples de l'Orient.* Paris, 1905.
  (2) *Etudes sur les Papyrus d'Aphrodité.* B.I.F.A.O., VI, 1908, 75-120; VII, 1910, 97-152.
  (3) *Papyrus Grecs d'époque Byzantine.* 3 Vols. I.F.A.O. Cairo, 1911-16.

Maspero, J. and Wiet, G. — *Matériaux pour servir à la Géographie de l'Egypte.* M.I.F.A.O., XXXVI. Cairo, 1919.

Mas'ûdî. —
  (1) *Murûj Al-Dhahab wa Ma'âdin Al-Jawar. Les Prairies d'Or.* Ed. and Tr. Barbier de Meynard et Pavet de Courteille. 9 Vols. Paris, 1861-77.
  (2) *Meadows of Gold and Mines of Gems.* Tr. A. Sprenger. I. London, 1841.
  (3) *Kitâb Al-Tanbîh wa Al-Ishrâf.* Ed. De Goeje. B.G.A., VIII. Leyden, 1893.

Madaynî. — *Sîrat Ibn Tûlûn.* Ed. Muhammad Kurd 'Alî. Damascus, 1385/1947.

Maydânî. — *Al-Sâmî fî Al-Asâmî.* Teheran ?, 1274/1857.

Meyendorff, A.F. — *Trade and Communication in Eastern Europe. A.D. 800-1200. Travel and Travellers.* Ed. A.P. Newton. London, 1926, 104-123.

Meyer-Lübke. — *Romanisches Etymologisches Wb.* Heidelberg, 1930-4.

Mez, A. — *The Renaissance of Islam.* Eng. Tr. Khuda Bukhsh and S.D. Margoliouth. London, 1937.

Michael the Syrian. —
  (1) *Chronicle.* Ed. and Tr. J.B. Chabot. 4 Vols. Paris, 1899-1924.
  (2) *Chronique de Michel le Grand.* Tr. V. Langlois. Venice, 1868.

Mieli, A. — *La Science Arabe et son Rôle dans l'Evolution Scientifique Mondiale.* Leyden, 1938.

Miller, K. Von. — *Mappae Arabicae.* Vols. I-IV. Stuttgart, 1926-9.

Milligan, G. — *Selections from the Greek Papyri.* Cambridge, 1927.

Millingen, Van. — *Byzantine Constantinople : The walls of the City.* London, 1899.

Minorsky, V. — *Mand.* E.I., III, 236-237.

Mookerji, R. — *A History of Indian Shipping and Maritime Activity from the earliest times.* London, 1912.

Moritz, B. —
  (1) *Arabic Palaeography.* Cairo, 1905.
  (2) *Ein Firman des Sultans Selim I für die Venetianer von Jahre 1517. Festchrift Eduard Sachau.* Berlin, 1915.

Muir, W. —
  (1) *The Caliphate: Its Rise, Decline and Fall.* Edinburgh, 1915.
  (2) *The Life of Mohammad.* 2 Vols. Edinburgh, 1923.

Muqaddasî. —
  (1) *Ahsan Al-Taqâsim fî ma'rifat Al-Aqâlîm.* B.G.A., III. Ed. De Goeje. Leyden, 1906.
  (2) Partial Eng. Tr. G.S.A. Ranking and R.F. Azoo. Bib. Ind., 4 Parts. Calcutta, 1897-1910.
  (3) The part concerned with Syria, Tr. G. Le Strange. *Description of Syria including Palestine by Mukaddasi (A.D. 985).* P.P.T.S., III. London, 1896.

Muslim, Ibn Al-Hajjâj. — *Al-Jâmi' Al-Sahîh.* 4 Vols. in 8 Parts. Cairo, 1329-32/1911-13.

Nadvi, Syed Sulaiman. —
  (1) *Early Relations between Arabia and India.* Is. Cult., 1937, 172 sq.
  (2) *Arab Navigation.* Is. Cult. :—
    XV, No. 4, October 1941, 435-449.
    XVI, No. 1, January 1942, 72-87.
    XVI, No. 2, April 1942, 182-199.
    XVI, No. 4, October 1942, 404-423.

Nâsirî, Khusrû. — *Safar Nâma. Relation du Voyage de Nasiri Khosrau en Syrie, en Palestine, en Egypte, en Arabie et en Perse.* Tr. C. Schefer. Paris, 1881. Ar. Tr. Yahyâ Al-Khashshâb. Cairo, 1364/1945.
A Diary of a Journey through Syria and Palestine. Eng. Tr. G. Le Strange. P.P.T.S., IV. London, 1897.

Neimans, R.F. — *Das Rothe Meer und die Küstenländer im Jahre 1857 in hadelspolitischer Beziehung.* Z.D.M.G. XII, 1858, 391-438.

Newbigin, M.I. —

(1) *The Mediterranean Lands. An Introductory Study in Human and Historical Geography.* London, 1928.
(2) *Southern Europe.* London, 1932.

Nicephorus. — *Brevarium.* Ed. Bekker, I. *Corpus Script. Hist. Byz.* Bonn, 1837. Ed. De Boor, C. Leipzig, 1880.

Nicole, J. — *Textes Grecs inédits de la collection Papyriologique de Genève.* Geneva, 1908.

Nicholson, R.A. — *A Literary History of the Arabs.* London, 1914.

Niebuhr, C. —

(1) *Reisebeschreibung nach Arabien und Andern Umliegenden Ländern.* 2 Vols. Copenhagen, 1774-8.
(2) *Voyage en Arabie et en d'autres pays circonvoisins.* Tr. F.L. Mourier. Amsterdam and Utrecht, 1776-80.

Nîfir, Muhammad Shadlî. — *Al-Ustûl fî Al-Lugha wa Al-Ta'rîkh. Al-Thurayya.* Rev. Tun., 1944-5.

Nöldeke, Th. —

(1) *Geschichte des Qor'âns.* 3 Vols. Leipzig, 1909-38.
(2) *Fünf Mo'allaqât.* Vienna, 1899.
(3) *Zur Geschichte der Araber im 1 Jahr. d, H. aus Syrichen Quellen.* Z.D.M.G. XXIX, 1876, 76-98.
(4) *Die Tradition über das Leben Muhammeds.* Der Islam, V, 1914, 160-170.

Nuwayrî. —

(1) *Nihâyat Al-Arab fî funûn Al-Adab.* Egyptian Library. 12 Vols. Cairo, 1923-35.
(2) *Historia de Musulmanes de España y Africa.* Pt. 5, Sec. 5, Vol. XXII of *Nihâyat Al-Arab.* Ed. and Tr. M.G. Remiro. Granada, 1917.

Oldfather, C.H. — *The Greek Literary Texts from Graeco-Roman Egypt.* Madison, 1923.

O'Leary, E. — *Arabia before Muhammad.* London, 1927.

Oman, C.W. — *A History of the Art of War in the Middle Ages.* A.D. 378-1278 I. London 1923.

Ormerod, H.A. — *Ancient Piracy in the Eastern Mediterranean.* Annals of Archaeology and Anthropology. University of Liverpool, VIII, 1921.

Parrain, C. — *La Mediterranée.* Paris, 1936.

Pears, E. — *The Destruction of the Greek Empire and the Story of the Capture of Constantinople by the Turks.* London, 1903.

« Periplus of the Erythrean Sea ». — *Travel and Trade in the Indian Ocean by a Merchant of the First Century.* Tr. from the Greek and annotated W.H. Schoff. London, 1912.

Pigeonneau, H. — *L'Annone Romaine et les Corps de Navicularii, particulièrement en Afrique.* Revue de l'Afrique Française, IV, 1886.

Pirenne, H. —
(1) *Mohammed and Charlemagne.* Eng. Tr. London, 1940.
(2) *Mediaeval Cities. Their Origin and the Revival of Trade.* Eng. Tr. F.D. Halsey. Princeton, 1925.
(3) *Economic and Social History of Mediaeval Europe.* Eng. Tr. I.E. Clegg. London, 1937.
(4) *A History of Europe from the Invasions to XVI Century.* Eng. Tr. B. Miall. London, 1936.

Pliny, S.C. — *Natural History.* With an Eng. Tr. H. Rackham. Loeb Classical Library. London and Cambridge, 1938.

Procopius. —
(1) *De Bello Persico.* Eng. Tr. H.B. Dewing. London and New York, 1914.
(2) *De Bello Gothico.* Eng. Tr. H.B. Dewing. London and New York, 1914.

Qalqashandî. —
(1) *Subh Al-A'shâ.* 14 Vols. Cairo, 1331-8/1913-8.
(2) Partial German Translation. F. Wüstenfeld. Göttingen, 1879.

Qazwînî. —
(1) *'Ajâ'ib Al-Makhlûqât wa Gharâ'ib Al-Mawjûdât.* Ed. F. Wüstenfeld. I. Göttingen, 1849.
(2) *Athâr Al-Bilâd wa Akhbâr Al-'Ibâd.* Ed. F. Wüstenfeld. II. Göttingen, 1848.

Quatremère, Et. —
- (1) *Histoire des Sultans Mamlouks de l'Egypte.* 2 Vols. Paris, 1837-45.
- (2) *Mémoires Géographiques et Historiques sur l'Egypte et sur quelques Contrées Voisines.* 2 Vols. Paris, 1811.

Qudâma. — *Nubadh min Kitâb Al-Kharâj.* Ed. with Fr. Tr. De Goeje. B.G.A., VI Leyden, 1889.

Qur'ân. — Eng. Tr. Maulvi Muhammad Ali. Islamic Review Office. Surrey, 1917.

Rambaud, A. — *L'Empire Grec au Dixième Siècle. Constantin Porphyrogénète.* Paris, 1870.

Ramsay, W.M. — *The Historical Geography of Asia Minor,* Royal Geographical Society. IV. London 1890.

Rawlinson, G. — *History of Phoenicia.* London and New York, 1889.

Reinaud, J.T. —
- (1) *Introduction Générale à la Géographie des Orientaux. La Géographie d'Aboul Féda.* 2 Vols. Paris, 1848.
- (2) *Fragments Arabes et Persans. Inédits relatifs à l'Inde antérieurement au XIe siècle de l'ère Chrétienne.* Paris, 1845.
- (3) *Relation des Voyages faits par les Arabes et les Persans dans l'Inde et à la Chine dans le IXe siècle de l'ère Chrétienne.* Paris, 1845.
  J.As., September 1848, 193-237.
- (4) *De l'Art Militaire chez les Arabes au Moyen Age.* J.As., September 1848, 193-237.

Reinaud et Favé, M.M. — *Du Feu Grégeois* XIII, October 1949, 257-327.

Richmond, H.W. — *Strategy in the Mediterranean.* The Listener, December, 1938.

Ritter, H. — *Arabische Flussfahrzeuge auf Euphrat und Tigris.* Der Islam, IX, 1919, 121-144.

Rodgers, W.L. — *Naval Warfare under Oars, 4th-16th Centuries. A. study of Strategy, Tactics and Ship Design.* U.S. Naval Institute, Annapolis. Maryland, 1939.

Rogers, E.T. — *Notice sur le Papyrus Postérieurs à l'Ere Chrétienne.* B.I.E., 2e Sér., No. 1, 1880.

Rose, H.J. — *The Mediterranean in the Ancient World.* Cambridge, 1933.

Rouillard, G. — *L'Administration Civile de l'Egypte Byzantine.* Paris, 1928.

Runciman, S. —
- (1) *The Emperor Romanus Lecapenus and his Reign. A Study of 10th Century Byzantium.* Cambridge, 1929.
- (2) *Byzantine Civilisation.* London, 1933.

Sacy, Silvestre De. — *Relation de l'Egypte* par Abd-Allatif. Tr. with historical notes. Paris, 1810.

Sarakhsî, Muhammad Ibn Ahmad. — *Sharh Al-Siyar Al-Kabîr.* 4 Vols. in 2 Heyderabad, 1335/1916.

Sarton, G. — *Introduction to the History of Science.* Carnegie Institution of Washington. 2 Vols. 1927-31.

Sauvaget, J. —
- (1) *Introduction à l'Histoire de l'Orient Musulman.* Paris, 1946.
- (2) *Historiens Arabes.* Paris, 1946.

Sauvaire, M.H. — *Matériaux pour servir à l'histoire de Numismatique et la Métrologie Musulmanes.* J.As., XIV, 1879, 7e Sér., 455-533. XV. 1880, 7e Sér., 228 sq. XIX, 1882, 7e Sér., 23-77, 97-163.

Savary, C. Et. — *Letters on Egypt.* 2 Vols. London, 1786.

Schaube, A. — *Handelsgeschichte der Romanischen Völker des Mittelmeersgebietes bis zum Ende der Kreuzzüge.* Munich, 1906.

Schiaparelli, C. — *Vocabulista in Arabico.* Ed. C. Schiaparelli. Florence, 1871.

Schlumberger, G. — *Un Empereur Byzantin au Dixième Siècle, Nicéphore Phocas.* Paris, 1923.

Sébillot, P. — *Legends, Croyances et Superstitions de la Mer.* Paris, 1886-7.

Semple, E.C. — *The Geography of the Mediterranean Region.* London, 1932.

Severus, Bishop of Al-Ashmûnayan —
- (1) *History of the Patriarchs of the Coptic Church of Alexandria.* Ed. and Tr. Evetts. Pat. Or., I, Fasc. II, IV; V. Fasc. I ; X, Fasc. V.
- (2) *History of the Patriarchs of the Egyptian Church, known as the History of the Holy Church.* II. Pt. I, 849-880. Ed. and Tr. Yassâ 'Abd Al-Masîh and O.H.E. Burmester. Cairo, 1943.

Seybold, C.F. — *Abû Hafs.* E.I., I, 87.

Simonsen, D. — *Les Marchands Juifs appelés « Radanites ».* Revue des Etudes Juives, IV, 1907, 141-142.

Sindbad the Sailor — v. Ferrand and Husayn Fawzî.

Sirhank, Ismâ'îl — *Haqâ'iq Al-Akhbâr 'an Duwal Al-Bihâr.* 2 Vols. Bûlâq, 1314/1896.

Slane, M. De — *Notice sur Codama et ses écrits.* J.As., XX, 5e Sér., 1862, 155-181.

Sprenger, A. — *The Compaign of Aelius Gallius in Arabia.* J.R.A.S., VI, 1873, 121-142.

Stace, E.V. — *English-Arabic Vocabulary.* London, 1893.

Stevens, W.O. and Wescott, A. — *A History of Sea Power.* New-York, 1942.

Strange, G. Le. —
- (1) *Palestine under the Moslems.* Boston, 1890.
- (2) *The Lands of the Eastern Caliphate.* Cambridge,
- (3) *A Greek Embassy to Baghdad in A.D. 917.* Tr. from Arabic Ms. of Al-Khatîb in British Museum. J.R.A.S., 1897, 35-45.

Streck, M. —
- (1) *Barka.* E.I., I, 660-661.
- (2) *Djûdî.* E.I., I, 1059-1060.
- (3) *Hît.* E.I., II, 322.
- (4) *Wâsit.* E.I., IV, 1128-1132.
- (5) *Kelek.* E.I., Supp., 114-116.

Suyûtî. —
- (1) *Husn Al-Muhâdara fî Akhbâr Misr wa Al-Qâhira.* 2 Vols. in one. Cairo, 1299/1882.

- (2) *Ta'rîkh Al-Khulafâ.* Cairo, 1305/1887. Eng. Tr. H.S. Jarrett. Calcutta, 1881.
- (3) *Kawkab Al-Rawda.* MS. British Museum, Or. 7978.

Tabarî. —
- (1) *Ta'rîkh Al-Rusul wa Al-Mulûk. Annales.* 15 Vols. Ed. De Goeje and others. Leyden, 1879-1901.
- (2) *Jâmi' Al-Bayân fî Tafsîr Al-Qur'ân. A Commentary on the Qur'ân.* 20 Vols. Cairo, 1325/1907.

Tanûkhî.— *Nishwâr Al-Nuhâdara.* Pt. I, Ed. and Tr. D.S. Margoliouth. London, 1921. Pt. VIII, Ed. with Introduction by D.S. Margoliouth. Revue de l'Académie Arabe. Damascus, 1930.

Tarn, W.W. — *Hellenistic Civilisation.* London, 1927.

Tha'âlibî. — *Latâ'if Al-Ma'ârif.* Ed P. Jong. Lugundi Betavorium, 1867.

Thompson, E.M. — *Papyrus.* E.B., XVII. New York, 1945, 246-248.

Thompson, J.W. — *The Commerce of France in the 9th Century.* Journal of Political Economy, XXIII, 1915.

Torr, C. — *Ancient Ships.* Cambridge, 1894.

Toussoun, Omar. —
- (1) *La Géographie de l'Egypte à l'Epoque Arabe.* I. Société Royale de Géographie d'Egypte. «*Mémoires*» *VII,* 1-3, Cairo, 1926-36.
- (2) *Mémoire sur l'histoire du Nil.* M.I.E., IX. Cairo, 1925.

Tritton, A.S. — *The Caliphs and their non-Muslim Subjects. A Critical Study of the Covenant of 'Umar.* Oxford, 1930.

Vansleb, J.M. — *Nouvelle Relation en forme de Journal d'un Voyage fait en Egypte.* Paris, 1677.

Vasiliev, A.A. —
- (1) *History of the Byzantine Empire.* Madison. 2 Vols. 1928-9.
- (2) *Byzance et les Arabes. La Dynastie d'Amorium. A.D. 820-67.* Tr. H. Grégoire, M. Canard, etc. I. Brussels. 1935.

(3) *Harun-ibn-Yahya and his Description of Constantinople.* Seminarium, Kondakovianum. V, 1932 149-163.

Vincent, W. — *Commerce and Navigation of the Ancients in the Indian Ocean.* London, 1807.

Vienna. — *Papyrus Erzherzog Rainer. Führer durch die Ausstellung.* Nationalbibliothek. Vienna, 1894.

Vinogradoff. — *Social and Economic Conditions of the Roman Empire in the Fourth Century.* C.M.H. I, 542-566.

Vollers, K. — *Beiträge zur Kenntniss der Lebenden Arabischen Sprache in Aegypten.* Z.D.M.G., L, 1896, 607-657; LI, 1897, 291-328.

Vonderheyden, M. — *La Berbérie Orientale sous la Dynastie de Benou-L-Arlab.* Paris, 1927.

Vullers, J.A. — *Lexicon Persico-Latinum.* Bonn, 1855.

Wâqidî. — *Kitâb Al-Maghâzî.* Ed. A. Kremer. Calcutta, 1856.

Warmington, E.H. — *The Commerce between the Roman Empire and India.* Cambridge, 1928.

Watt, D.G. — *On the Causes of Oriental Words existing in European Languages.* J.R.A.S. April 1834, 1-12.

Weil, G. — *Geschichte der Chalifen.* 5 Vols. Manheim (later Stuttgart), 1846-62.

Wellhausen, J. —
   (1) *Das Arabische Reich und Sein Sturz.* Berlin 1902. Eng. Tr. M.G. Weir. *The Arab Kingdom and Its Fall.* Calcutta, 1927.

   (2) *Die Kämpfe der Araber mit den Römaern.* N.G.W. Gött., 1901, 414-447.

Wensinck, A.J. —
   (1) *A Handbook of Early Muhammadan Tradition, Alphabetically arranged.* Leyden, 1927.

   (2) *Concordance et Indices de la Tradition Musulmane.* 17 Parts, Leyden, 1936-46.

   (3) *Mecca.* E.I., I, 437-448.

Wessely, C. — *Griechische Papyruskunden Kleineren Formates... Studien zur Palaeographie und Papyruskunde,* hrg. v. Dr. Wessely. III, and VIII. Leipzig, 1904-8.

Wiet, G. —
- (1) *Précis de l'Histoire d'Egypte.* II. Cairo, 1932.
- (2) *Les Communications en Egypte au Moyen Age, dans Egypte Contemporaine.* Revue de la Société Royale d'Economie Politique, de Statistique et de Legislation, XXIV, Cairo.
- (3) *L'Historien Abul-Mahâsin.* B.I.E., XII, 1929, 89-105.
- (4) *Matériaux pour un Corpus Inscriptinum Arabicarum* M.I.F.A.O., LII, Cairo, 1930.

Willibard, Saint. — *The Hodoeporicon of Saint Willibard.* Tr. Rev. Canon Brownlow. P.P.T.S., III. London, 1895.

Wright, W. — *The Paleographical Society, Facsimiles of Manuscripts and Inscriptions.* Ed. W. Wright. London, 1875, 1883.

Wroth, W. — *Catalogue of the Imperial Byzantine Coins in the British Museum.* 2 Vols. London, 1908.

Wüstenfeld, F. —
- (1) *Die Namen der Schiffe im Arabischen. Report of Meeting of Royal Society of University of Göttingen.* N.G.W. Gött., 1880.
- (2) *Die Geschichtschreiber der Araber und ihre Werke.* Göttingen, 1882.

Yahyâ Ibn Sa'îd.— *Al-Ta'rîkh Al-Majmû' 'alâ Al-Tahqîq. Continuation of Eutychius.* 2 Vols. Ed. Cheikho. Beirut, 1909. Ed. and Tr. I. Kratchkhovsky and A. Vasiliev, in Pat. Or., XVIII.

Ya'qûbî. —
- (1) *Ta'rîkh. Historiae.* 2 Vols. Ed. Th. Houtsma. Leyden, 1883.
- (2) *Kitâb Al-Buldân.* Ed. De Goeje. B.G.A., VII. Leyden, 1892.

Yâqût. —
- (1) *Mu'jam Al-Buldân. Geographisches Wörterbuch.* Ed. F. Wüstenfeld. 6 Vols. Leipzig, 1866-73. Sachindex, Von Oscar Rescher. Stuttgart, 1928.
- (2) *Irshâd Al-Labîb Ilâ Ma'rifat Al-'Adîb.* Ed. D.S. Margoliouth. Gibb Memorial Series, VI. 7 Vols. Cairo, 1907-11.
- (3) *Al-Mushtarak.* Ed. F. Wüstenfeld. Göttingen, 1846.

(4) *Marâsid Al-Ittilâ' 'alâ Asmâ' Al-Amkina wa Al-Biqâ'*. An Abridgement of Yâqût's work by Ibr 'Abd Al-Haqq. Ed. T.G.J. Junboll. 4 Vols. Leyden, 1853.

Yâsîn Al-Hamawî. — *Ta'rîkh Al-Ustûl Al-'Arabî*. Damascus 1364/1945.

Yule, H. — *Cathay and the Way Thither*. London, 1916.

Yule-Burnell. — *Hobson-Jobson*. London, 1903.

Zabîdî, Muhammad Al-Murtadâ. — *Tâj Al-'Arûs. Dictionary*. 10 Vols. Cairo, 1306/1888.

Zâhirî, Khalîl Al- — *Zubdat Kashf Al-Mamâlik*. Ed. P. Ravaisse in Publ. Sc. L. Or., Sér. 3e, 16e. Paris. 1894.

Zakî Mohamed Hassan. — *Les Tulunides. Etude de l'Egypte Musulmane à la fin du IXe siècle*, 868-905. Paris, 1933.

Zakî Mubârak. — *La Prose Arabe au IVe siècle de l'Hégire*. Paris, 1931.

Zaydân, Jûrjî. — *Ta'rîkh Al-Tamadun Al-Islâmî*. 5 Vols. Cairo, 1902-6.

Zayyât, Habîb Al- — *Al-Sufun wa Al-Marâkib fî Baghdâd*. Lughat Al-'Arab, V, 1927, 461-465.

Zûzanî. — *Sharh Al-Mu'Allaqât Al-Sab'*. Cairo, 1325/1907.

ABBREVIATIONS

A.P.E.L.	*Arabic Papyri in Egyptian Library.* Ed. A. Grohmann. 3 Vols. Cairo, 1934-8.
Ar. Pal.	Moritz, B. *Arabic Palaeography.* Cairo, 1905.
B.A.S.	*Bibliotheca Arabo-Sicula.* Leipzig, 1857.
B.G.A.	*Bibliotheca Geographorum Arabicorum.* Ed. M.J. De Goeje. Leyden, 1879-1927.
B.I.E.	*Bulletin de l'Institut d'Egypte.*
B.I.F.A.O.	*Bulletin de l'Institut Français d'Archéologie Orientale.* Cairo, 1901.
Bib. Ind.	*Bibliotheca Indica.*
Byz. Zeit.	*Byzantinische Zeitschrift.*
C.M.H.	*Cambridge Mediaeval History.* Cambridge, 1936
C.P.R.	v. Bibliography under Grohmann. *Corpus Papyrorum Raineri Archiducis Austriae. III.*
E.B.	*Encyclopaedia Britannica.*
E.H.R.	*English Historical Review.*
E.I.	*Encylopaedia of Islam.* Leyden 1913—.
E.I. Supp.	*Encyclopaedia of Islam. Supplement* . Leyden, 1938.
Is. Cult.	*Islamic Culture.* Heyderabad, 1927—.
J. As.	*Journal Asiatique.*
J.E.A.	*Journal of Egyptian Archaeology.* London, *1914*—.
J.H.S.	*Journal of Hellenic Studies.* London, 1880—.
J.R.A.S.	*Journal of Royal Asiatic Society.*
Leo, D.P.N.	*V. Bibliography under* Leo VI.
M.I.E.	*Mémoires présentés de l'Institut d'Egypte.*
M.I.F.A.O.	*Mémoires publiés par les Membres de l'Institut Français d'Archéologie Orientate,* Le Caire.
N.G.W. Gött.	*Nachrichten der Königlischen Gesellschaft der Wissenschaften zu Göttingen. Philosophische - Historische Klasse.*
P.A.F.	Becker, C.H. *Arabische Papyri des Aphroditofundes.* Z.A., XX.

P. Amherst.	Grenfell, B.P. and Hunt, A.S. *The Amherst Papyri*. 2 Vols, London, 1900-1.
P. Cairo Maspero.	Maspero, J. *Papyrus Grecs d'époque Byzantine*. 3 Vols. Cairo, 1911-16.
P.E.R.F.	v. Bibliography under Vienna.
P. Flor.	v. Bibliography under Comparetti, D. and Vitelli, G.
P. Grenfell. I-II	Grenfell, B.P. *An Alexandrian Erotic Fragment and other Greek Papyri*. Oxford, 1896. Grenfell, B.P. and Hunt, A.S. *New Classical Fragments and other Greek and Latin Papyri*. Oxford, 1897.
P. Lond. II	Kenyon, F.G. and Bell, I.H. *Greek Papyri in British Museum*. London, 1893.
P. Lond. IV	Bell, I.H. *Greek Papyri in British Museum. The Aphrodito Papyri IV, with an Appendix of Coptic Papyri*, Ed. E. Crum. London, 1910.
P. Oxy.	Grenfell, B.P., Hunt, A.S. and Bell, I.H. *The Oxyrhynchus Papyri*. London, 1898.
P.P.T.S.	*Palestine Pilgrims' Text Society*.
P. Ross.— Georg. IV.	v. Bibliography under Jernstedt, P.
P.S.R.	Becker, CH. *Papyri Schott-Reinhardt*. Heidelberg, 1906.
Pat. Or.	*Patrologia Orientalis*.
R.H.C.	*Recueil des Historiens des Croisades*. Paris, 1899—.
Rev. Afr.	*Revue Africaine*.
Rev. Tun.	*Revue Tunisienne. Al-Thurayya*, 1944—.
Z.K.F.	v. Bibliography under Wessely.
Z.A.	*Zeitschrift für Assyriologie und Verwandte Gebiete*. Leipzig, 1886—.
Z.D.M.G.	*Zeitschrift der Deutschen Morgenländischen Gesellschaft*. Leipzig.

ABBREVIATIONS

A.P.E.L.	*Arabic Papyri in Egyptian Library.* Ed. A. Grohmann. 3 Vols. Cairo, 1934-8.
Ar. Pal.	Moritz, B. *Arabic Palaeography.* Cairo, 1905.
B.A.S.	*Bibliotheca Arabo-Sicula.* Leipzig, 1857.
B.G.A.	*Bibliotheca Geographorum Arabicorum.* Ed. M.J. De Goeje. Leyden, 1879-1927.
B.I.E.	*Bulletin de l'Institut d'Egypte.*
B.I.F.A.O.	*Bulletin de l'Institut Français d'Archéologie Orientale.* Cairo, 1901.
Bib. Ind.	*Bibliotheca Indica.*
Byz. Zeit.	*Byzantinische Zeitschrift.*
C.M.H.	*Cambridge Mediaeval History.* Cambridge, 1936
C.P.R.	v. Bibliography under Grohmann. *Corpus Papyrorum Raineri Archiducis Austriae. III.*
E.B.	*Encyclopaedia Britannica.*
E.H.R.	*English Historical Review.*
E.I.	*Encylopaedia of Islam.* Leyden 1913—.
E.I. Supp.	*Encyclopaedia of Islam. Supplement .* Leyden, 1938.
Is. Cult.	*Islamic Culture.* Heyderabad, 1927—.
J. As.	*Journal Asiatique.*
J.E.A.	*Journal of Egyptian Archaeology.* London, *1914*—.
J.H.S.	*Journal of Hellenic Studies.* London, 1880—.
J.R.A.S.	*Journal of Royal Asiatic Society.*
Leo, D.P.N.	*V. Bibliography under* Leo VI.
M.I.E.	*Mémoires présentés de l'Institut d'Egypte.*
M.I.F.A.O.	*Mémoires publiés par les Membres de l'Institut Français d'Archéologie Orientate,* Le Caire.
N.G.W. Gött.	*Nachrichten der Königlischen Gesellschaft der Wissenschaften zu Göttingen. Philosophische - Historische Klasse.*
P.A.F.	Becker, C.H. *Arabische Papyri des Aphroditofundes.* Z.A., XX.

P. Amherst.	Grenfell, B.P. and Hunt, A.S. *The Amherst Papyri*. 2 Vols, London, 1900-1.
P. Cairo Maspero.	Maspero, J. *Papyrus Grecs d'époque Byzantine*. 3 Vols. Cairo, 1911-16.
P.E.R.F.	v. Bibliography under Vienna.
P. Flor.	v. Bibliography under Comparetti, D. and Vitelli, G.
P. Grenfell. I-II	Grenfell, B.P. *An Alexandrian Erotic Fragment and other Greek Papyri*. Oxford, 1896. Grenfell, B.P. and Hunt, A.S. *New Classical Fragments and other Greek and Latin Papyri*. Oxford, 1897.
P. Lond. II	Kenyon, F.G. and Bell, I.H. *Greek Papyri in British Museum*. London, 1893.
P. Lond. IV	Bell, I.H. *Greek Papyri in British Museum. The Aphrodito Papyri IV, with an Appendix of Coptic Papyri*, Ed. E. Crum. London, 1910.
P. Oxy.	Grenfell, B.P., Hunt, A.S. and Bell, I.H. *The Oxyrhynchus Papyri*. London, 1898.
P.P.T.S.	*Palestine Pilgrims' Text Society*.
P. Ross.— Georg. IV.	v. Bibliography under Jernstedt, P.
P.S.R.	Becker, CH. *Papyri Schott-Reinhardt*. Heidelberg, 1906.
Pat. Or.	*Patrologia Orientalis*.
R.H.C.	*Recueil des Historiens des Croisades*. Paris, 1899—.
Rev. Afr.	*Revue Africaine*.
Rev. Tun.	*Revue Tunisienne. Al-Thurayya*, 1944—.
Z.K.F.	v. Bibliography under Wessely.
Z.A.	*Zeitschrift für Assyriologie und Verwandte Gebiete*. Leipzig, 1886—.
Z.D.M.G.	*Zeitschrift der Deutschen Morgenländischen Gesellschaft*. Leipzig.

INDEX (1)

A

'Abbâsid(s), 36, 41, 45, 54, 61, 63, 71, 98, 107, 109, 127, 140, 150.
'Abd al-A'lâ ibn Abî Hakîm, 37, 77, 78, 81.
'Abd al-'Azîz ibn Marwân, 66, 70.
'Abd-Allâh ibn Mûsâ ibn Nusayr, 64.
'Abd al-Latîf al-Baghdâdî, 13, 14, 76-79, 143, 146, 147, 151.
'Abd al-Malik ibn Marwân, 53, 69, 70.
Abû 'Amr al-Qurtubî, 21.
Abû Hafs, 72.
Abû Hanîfa al-Dînawarî, 76.
Abû Ja'far al-Mansûr, 107.
Abû Kâmil Shujâ' ibn Aslam, 43.
Abû'l-Fidâ, 18, 59.
Abû Sâlih, the Armenian, 13, 77, 78.
Abû Shâma, 132.
Abû Zayd al-Sirafî, 22.
Acatia, 53, 64, 106, 125, 126.
Acatenaria, 37, 78, 81, 91, 126.
Adaeratio, 101, 102, 107, 108.
Adana, 92.
Aegean Sea, 61, 92; — islands, 73.
al-Afdal ibn Badr al-Jamâlî, 39, 49.
Africa, 10, 19, 45, 46, 50, 63, 64-71, 83, 87, 88, 91, 92, 104, 138, 139, 153.
Ahmad ibn Dînâr, 127.
Ajdâbiya, 65.
Ajiya, 65.
'Akkâ (Acre), 17, 52-55, 106, 130.
Alexandria, 15, 19, 23, 27, 28, 29, 30, 38, 45, 46, 65, 72, 91, 95, 107, 123, 130, 143.
al-Amîn (Caliph), 134, 135.
Amîr Abû'l-Hârith, 82, 83.
'Amr ibn al-'As, 11, 40
'Anbassa ibn Ishâq, 36.
Ansina (Antinoopolis), 64, 76.
Antioch, 19, 52.
Aphrodito (Kûm Ashqûh), 5, 6, 7, 24, 26, 37, 53, 81, 99, 102, 110.
'Aqaba, 136.
Arculf, 14, 29.
al-'Arîsh, 114.
Arsenal(s), 7, 10-16, 19, 21, 23, 24, 26, 27, 29, 35, 36 37-39, 41-43, 45-53, 64, 69-71, 77, 81, 106, 107, 128.
Arsuf, 56.
Ascalon, 56, 79, 130.
Ashtiyâm, 139, 157.
'Atâ' ibn Râfi', 19, 65, 66, 69.
Ayyûbid, 13, 131.

B

Babylon, 21, 24-26, 35, 37, 38, 40, 42, 77, 78, 81, 85, 91, 96, 102, 106, 107, 110, 126.
Bahnasâ (Oxyrhynchus), 3, 125.
Bakrí, 19, 65, 69, 70, 71.
Balâdhurî, 14, 32, 52, 53, 105. 156.
Balkhî, 16, 33, 57, 67, 93.
Banâniya, 138.
Barallus, 35.
Barges, 24, 26, 153, 156.
Barka, 155.
Barnîq, 65.
Barqa, 46, 64, 65, 91.
Bâsilyûs (Pagarch of Ashqûh),

---

(1) The index refers only to the text.

199

5, 6, 7, 24, 25, 29, 30, 65, 81, 99, 100, 102, 108.
Beirut, 56, 82.
Benjamin of Tudela, 18, 30.
Bernard the Wise, 15, 113.
Bîrja, 156.
Bubastis, 24.
Buhturî, 21, 127.
Bur'ânî, 157.
Burâkiyya, 157.
Burma, 155.

C

Caesarea, 53, 123.
Cairo, 5, 6, 10, 11, 21, 40, 50, 98, 121, 130, 134, 145, 146.
Cameniates 62, 123.
Candia, 72.
Carabus, 132; *Carabi,* 25, 26, 37, 64, 81, 84, 85, 100, 126.
Carthage, 69, 71, 123.
Clysma (al-Qulzum), 23-27, 83, 88, 91.
Constantine Porphyrogenitos, 85, 129, 133.
Constantinople, 3, 6, 52, 61, 62, 92, 97, 126, 130, 153.
Corvée, 97.
Crete, 31, 51, 72-74, 80, 95.
Crews, 21, 63, 103, 104, 138, 152 156.
Cumbarii, 73, 129.
Cursus, 87, 103.
Cyclades, 72.
Cyprus, 52, 63, 73, 74, 83, 105.

D

Damascus, 15, 56.
Damietta, 20, 30, 31, 32, 35, 36, 62, 96, 119, 130.
Damyâna, 60, 62, 63.
Dâr al-Sinâ'a. v. Arsenal.
Dawnîj, 157, 158.
Dhât al-Sawârî, 104, 105, 125.
Dînawarî, 77.
Dîwân al-'Amâ'ir, 49.
Droman, 116, 126; *Dromonaria,* 37, 53, 100, 106, 125.

E

Egypt, 1-3, 5-7, 10-12, 14, 16-19, 24, 27-29, 35, 36, 38, 39, 41-43, 45-49, 51-53, 63-66, 69, 70, 84, 87, 88, 91, 95, 96, 99, 100, 104-107, 113, 114, 116, 119-121, 125, 126, 132, 134, 137, 151, 153; trees in —, 76-79; forests in —, 143-147.
Emessa (Hims), 151, 152.
Eutychius, 13, 63.

F

Fâkhita, 105.
Faramâ, 27, 36.
Fâtimids, 5, 13, 39, 45, 49, 50, 63, 119, 130, 132, 151.
Fayyûm, 3, 45, 46, 145.
Fighting men, 8, 28, 29, 88, 104, 119, 120, 131, 132, 160.
Fleet(s), 8, 9, 12, 13, 19, 21, 23, 26-31, 35, 36, 42, 43, 45, 46, 49, 51, 52, 53-55, 61-66, 69, 72, 73, 79, 87, 88, 91, 92, 95, 96, 99, 100, 103-108, 119, 120, 124-126, 128-130, 132, 134, 137-140, 149, 150, 153, 154, 161, 163.
Fustât, 11, 17 27, 36, 38, 39, 41, 45, 48, 49, 63, 65, 78, 95, 96, 104, 106, 145, 146, 150.

G

Galeae, 130.
Galley(s), 73, 77, 85, 97, 116, 121, 125, 126, 127, 128, 129, 131, 132, 134.
Gaza, 56.
Ghulâm Zurâfa. v. Leo of Tripolis.
Ghurâb, 126, 132, 133, 157.

H

Hamâma, 149, 150, 155 157.
Harbî, 129; *harbiyya,* 149; *harâbî,* 131; *harbiyyât,* 49.
Harrâqa, 134-135, 136, 151.
Hassân ibn al-Nu'mân, 69, 70.
Hayfa, 79.

Hayyân ibn Shurayh, 75, 100.
Humûl, 150.

I

Ibn 'Abd al-Hakam, 10, 11, 39, 66, 75, 105, 125.
Ibn Abî al-Sarh, 11, 51, 105.
Ibn Abî Habîba, Muhammad, 24, 27.
Ibn Abî Zar', 133.
Ibn 'Abs, al-Hârith, 29.
Ibn al-'Amîd, 21.
Ibn al-Athîr, 20, 62, 63, 129, 130.
Ibn Battûta, 32, 153, 154, 160.
Ibn al-Dâya, 12, 72, 113.
Ibn Dînâr, 128.
Ibn Duqmâq, 11, 39, 40, 50, 128.
Ibn al-Faqîh, 16, 38, 59, 76, 84.
Ibn Hawqal, 16, 17, 18, 35, 39, 40, 41, 56, 60, 71, 73, 84, 130, 131, 166.
Ibn 'Idhârî, 19, 132.
Ibn al-Ikhshîd, Abû'l-Hassan 'Alî, 13.
Ibn Iyâs, 32, 35, 147.
Ibn Jubayr, 18, 80, 159.
Ibn Khaldûn, 19, 62, 70, 75, 88, 106, 119, 120, 128, 129, 133, 138, 139.
Ibn Khallikân, 20, 136.
Ibn Khurdâdhbih, 15, 27, 59, 73, 95.
Ibn Mâjid, 22.
Ibn Mamâtî, 13, 128, 131, 132, 133, 134, 137, 144, 150.
Ibn Miskawayh, 21.
Ibn Qutayba, 19.
Ibn Rusta, 16.
Ibn Sa'd, 'Arîb of Cordova, 20, 163.
Ibn Sa'îd, 12, 13, 46.
Ibn Sa'îd, Yahyâ, 13, 47.
Ibn Shahriyâr, Buzurg, 22, 153, 157.
Ibn Sharîk, Qurra, 5, 6, 9, 24, 25, 28, 29, 37, 64, 65, 81, 87, 91, 99, 100, 101, 102, 108, 109.

Ibn Sîna, 143.
Ibn Taghrî Birdî, 164.
Ibn Tûlûn, 12, 13, 17, 40, 42, 43, 44, 46, 48, 54, 62, 114, 149, 150, 153, 164.
Ibn Zûlâq, 13, 46.
Idrîsî, 17, 39, 40, 129, 131, 150.
al-Ikhshîd, Muhammad ibn Tughj, 13, 45, 46, 47, 48, 50.
Ikhshîdids, 12, 45, 49.
'Imâra, 128.
India, 27, 157.
Indian Ocean, 22, 80, 81, 124, 138, 139, 156, 158.
'Irdâs, 155.
Istakhrî, 16, 17, 39, 40, 59, 60, 65, 67, 73, 89, 119, 155, 166.

J

Jaffa, 56.
Jalba, 159.
al-Jâhiz, 76.
al-Jâr, 27.
Jawharî, 138, 165.
Jayhânî, 33, 57, 67, 93.
al-Jazîra, 41, 43, v. al-Rawda.
Jazîrat al-Sinâ'a. v. Arsenal.
Jerusalem, 14, 15, 17, 54.
Jidda, 27.
Jîza, 11, 40, 41, 44, 146.

K

Kâfûr al-Ikhshîd, 47.
Karawân, 159.
Katinae, 126, 153.
Khafâjî, 127.
Khalîj Amîr al-Mu'minîn, 23, 24, 27.
Khaytiyya, 159.
Khumârawayh, 12, 45.
Kindî, 11, 12, 13, 31, 45, 48, 62, 76, 125, 150.
Kûm Ashqûh. v. Aphrodito.

L

al-Lâmis, 59, 60.
Laodicea, 53, 91.
Lateen sail, 123, 124.
Leo VI, 124, 126, 127.

Leo of Tripolis, 21, 61, 62, 63, 123, 138.
Liturgy, 96, 97, 112; liturgical system, 3, 97.

M

Madaynî, 12, 42, 43, 45, 62, 149, 153, 154, 163.
Maghrib, 12, 13, 16, 32, 60, 88, 129, 133.
al-Mahdî, 56, 59, 65.
Mahdiyya, 19, 128, 131.
Makkiyya, 160.
al-Malik al-Nâsir ibn Qalâwûn, 40.
Malqûta, 155.
al-Ma'mûn, 41, 72.
al-Mansûr, 156.
Maqrîzî, 11, 12, 24, 29, 31, 36, 40, 44, 49, 62, 70, 77, 78, 119, 120, 127, 128, 129, 130, 131, 133, 136, 146, 149, 150, 151, 153, 154.
Markib, 125, 129, 150, 155, 165; *marâkib,* 131, 149, 158, 159.
Maritime civil service, 3, 7, 98, 101, 102, 105; secret service, 141, 158.
Marwân 11, 36.
Maslama ibn Mukhallad, 35.
Mas'ûdî, 20, 21, 22, 29, 41, 59, 60, 61, 62, 63, 80, 127, 128, 129, 138, 139, 156, 158, 163.
Mawâlî, 103, 105, 106.
Mediterranean, 3, 10, 18, 20, 22, 23, 27, 30, 32, 36, 59, 60, 62, 63, 65, 71, 75, 80, 92, 114, 116, 119, 120, 123, 124, 131, 133, 136, 137, 138, 139, 152, 156, 156, 158, 166.
Me'êbir, 160.
Memphis, 38.
Mi'bar, 159.
Michael the Syrian, 52.
Mu'allim, 138.
Mu'âwiya, 28, 51, 52, 92, 104, 105.
al-Mu'izz, 13, 130.
Muhâjirûn, 30, 38, 103-106.

Muhammad ibn al-Khalîj, 63.
Muhammad ibn Sulaymân, 62.
Muqaddasî, 15, 16, 17, 20, 27, 32, 33, 39, 48, 53, 54, 55, 57, 59, 60, 73, 79, 82, 84, 127, 130, 131, 139, 150, 155, 156, 158, 159, 160, 161, 162, 163, 165.
al-Muqtadir, 150.
Musabbahiyya, 160.
Mûsâ ibn Bughâ, 42, 43, 44.
Mûsâ ibn Nusayr, 66, 69, 87.
Musattah, 130, 131.
al-Mustakfî, 163.
al-Mu'tadid, 60.
al-Mu'tasim, 35.
al-Mutawakkil, 31, 32, 53, 54, 55, 65.
Muthallatha, 160.
al-Muttaqî, 165.
al-Muwaffaq, 42, 43, 161.

N

al-Nâbulsî, 145, 146.
Nâsirî Khusrû, 17, 30, 35, 55, 56, 79.
Naval centre(s), 14, 16, 20, 23, 27, 28, 30, 33, 51, 53, 56, 61, 63, 64, 65, 71, 72, 73, 74, 84, 91, 93, 106.
Navy, 7, 8, 12, 51, 91, 106, 119, 124, 137.
Nicephorus, 63, 79.
Nile, 2, 24, 30, 32, 36, 32, 40, 41, 48, 49, 91, 97, 110, 120, 125, 134, 143, 151.
Nûtî, 138.
Nuwayrî, 21, 129, 132.

O

Oriens, 30, 53, 87, 88, 91, 106, 125.
Oxyrhynchus. v. Bahnasâ.

P

Papyrology, 1, 4.
Papyrus(i), 1-5, 7-9, 19, 23, 24, 53, 64, 76, 84, 87, 90, 95, 97,

98, 104, 107, 113, 120;
Aphrodito papyri, 4-7, 24, 26, 28, 30, 37, 38, 64-66, 77, 83-85, 91, 98-112, 120, 125, 126; Arabic —, 2, 4-6, 64; Coptic —, 2, 4, 26, 101.
Pentapolis. v. Barqa.
Phoenix, 79.
Piracy, 115, 134.
Pirates, 135, 156.

Q

al-Qâdir, 164.
Qalqashandî, 11, 39, 41, 128.
Qarâqîr, 166.
Qârib, 125, 126, 133, 154, 155, 158, 165; qawârib al-khidma, 149.
al-Qâsim ibn Ka'b, 37, 88.
Qasr al-Sham', 38.
Qayrawân, 69, 70, 71, 104.
Qazwînî, 18, 32, 55.
Qit'a, 129.
Qudâ'î, 11.
Qudâma, 22, 53, 61, 65, 140.
al-Qulzum. v. Clysma.
Qur'ân, 125.
Qurra. v. Ibn Sharîk.

R

al-Râdhâniyya, 27.
al-Ramla, 56.
Raqqa, 42, 44.
Raqqiyya, 161.
al-Rashîd, 59.
Rashîq al-Wardâmî. v. Leo of Tripolis.
al-Rawda, Island of, 11, 35, 39, 40-42, 44, 46, 48, 49, 75.
Red Sea, 80, 91, 124, 154, 159.
Rosetta, 30, 32, 63, 150.
Rubbânî, 139.
Ra'îs, 139.

S

Safîna, 125, 155, 165, sufun, 162.
Sailors, 22, 24-26, 28-30, 37, 38, 53, 66-69, 85, 91, 103, 104, 106, 108, 120, 138, 139, 152, 153; recruitment of —, 3, 8, 9, 64, 65, 98-101, 106, 112, 140; provisions for —, 96, 99, 107, 110; wages of —, 8, 91, 109; security for —, 102.
Samos, 92.
Sandal 149, 152, 153, 154.
Sardinia, 66, 69.
Saturae, 73, 129, 133.
Sea power, 3, 9, 11, 18, 28, 92, 116, 119.
Severus (Bishop of Ushmûnayn), 10, 36, 106, 110, 113.
Shabbâra, 136, 151.
Shabûq, 161.
Shadhâ, 161, 162; shadhawât; 160, 165; shadhâ'ât, 163.
Shalandî, 126, 130, 131, 155; shalandiyyât, 49, 130.
Shamût, 155.
Shankûliyya, 162.
Shînî, 131, 132, 133, 137, 155, 156; Shawânî, 49, 119, 130, 131, 132, 134, 156.
Shipbuilding, 19, 24, 27, 36, 37, 38, 43, 49, 51, 53, 54, 69, 80, 81, 96, 107, 119, 123, 124, 128, 130, 141, 151, 164; materials for —, 7, 13, 75-86, 144, 145; Instructions for —, 12.
Ship(s), 30, 37, 120, 126, 138, 139; merchant ships, 22, 116, 117, 128, 132, 134, 139, 150, 158; transport —, 125, 129, 131, 134, 137, 150, 160, 166; pirate —, 28, 132, 134, 156; warships, 10, 20, 22, 28, 37, 42, 45, 47, 49, 62, 63, 69, 88, 114, 116, 117, 119, 120, 124-132, 134, 140, 149, 156, 16.
Sicily, 64, 66, 83, 84, 92, 130.
Sindbâd the Sailor, 22, 165.
Sinâ'at al-'imâra. v. Arsenal.
Spain, 19, 72, 82, 83, 88, 138, 139.
Squaresail, 115, 116, 123.
Sulaymân al-Khâdim, 63.

203

Sulaymân ibn 'Abd al-Malik, 107.
Sulaymân the Merchant, 22.
Sumayriyyât, 160, 161, 162, 165.
Sunbûk, 153, 154.
Sûqiyya, 162.
Sûr. v. Tyre.
Surt, 65.
al-Suways, (Suez), 27. v. Clysma.
Suyûtî, 11.
Syracuse, 130.
Syria, 10, 14-18, 32, 45, 51-54, 59, 61, 73, 79, 88, 91, 114, 131, 158, 163, Syrian(s), 51, 52, 61, 138, Syrian shipwrights, 120; — coast, 14, 16, 52, 53, 55, 59, 106; — ports, 14, 15, 130.

T

Tabarî, 14, 20, 21, 31, 35, 60, 61, 103, 104, 105, 130, 135, 156, 160, 161, 162, 166.
Talawway, 162.
Tanûkhî, 21, 163.
Tarrîda, 126, 133, 136, 137.
Tarsus, 20, 56, 59, 60, 60-63, 92.
Tayra, 163.
Tayyâr, 163, 164, 165.
Taxes, 7, 8, 87, 96, 99, 107, 145, 146; taxation, 98, 113; taxcollectors, 102; taxpayers, 28, 30, 98, 106, 108, 109.
Thamil al-Khâdim, 63.
Theodore, The Augustal, 28, 106.
Theophanes, 52, 79, 126, 153.
Thessalonica, 62, 123.
Thughûr, 59.
Timâ, 5.
Tinnîs, 30, 35, lake —, 32, 35, 62, 71.
Trajan Canal, 24, 25, 29.
Tripolis, 52, 56, 134.
Trireme, 116.
Tulmaytha, 65.

Tûlûnid(s), 12, 42-45, 62, 113.
Tûnis, 19, 69-71, 91, 131, 132.
Tyre, 14-16, 52-54, 56, 106, 130.

U

'Ubâda ibn al-Sâmit, 105.
'Ubaydallah ibn al-Habhâb, 70.
'Ulâbiyyât, 149.
'Umar (Caliph), 51, 105.
'Umar ibn 'Abd al-'Azîz, 75.
Umayyads(s), 6, 9, 52, 54, 80, 98.
Umm Harrâm, 105.
Urdun, 52, 53.
'Uthmân (Caliph), 51, 53, 105.
Usâma ibn zayd al-Tanûkhî, 39.
'Ushâriyyât, 47, 49, 149, 150, 151, 152.
Ustûl, 123, 127, 128.

V

Venice, 79.

W

al-Walîd I, 29, 40.
Walajiyya, 164.
Wâqidî, 14, 52, 53, 56.
Wâsitiyya, 164.
St. Willibard, 15, 73.
Workmen, 24, 26, 37, 106; skilled —, 9, 14, 28, 29, 85, 106; recruitment of —, 3, 9, 28, 102, 106, 140; provisions for —, 96, 108, 110; wages of —, 8, 109.

Y

Ya'qûbî, 16, 30, 32, 38, 52, 53, 56, 65, 71, 82, 159.
Yâqût, 18, 32, 39, 55, 56, 59, 63, 65, 135, 158.
Yazîd ibn 'Abdallah, 32 .
Yazîd ibn Abî Yazîd, 88.
Yazîd ibn Mu'âwiya, 95, 107.
Yazmân al-Khâdim, 61.

Z

Zabarbâdhiyya, 164, 165.
Zabzab, 161, 165; *zabâzib,* 163, 165.
Zawraq, 155, 165, 166.

National Publication & Printing House,
Cairo, U.A.R.

Price : £ 1/10/ - (P.T. 150)

V
45
F3
1966